# From Human Dignity
# to Natural Law

# From Human Dignity to Natural Law

## AN INTRODUCTION

Richard Berquist

Foreword by Steven J. Jensen

The Catholic University of America Press
Washington, D.C.

Copyright © 2019
The Catholic University of America Press
All rights reserved
The paper used in this publication meets the minimum requirements of American
National Standards for Information Science—Permanence of Paper for Printed
Library Materials, ANSI Z39.48-1984.

∞

To Dolores,
my beloved wife

*Mulier timens Dominum,*
*ipsa laudabitur*

# Contents

## 4. Virtue · 48

## 5. The Natural Law · 66

## 6. The Life Issues: Part 1 · 95

## 7. The Life Issues: Part 2 · 113

## 8. Sex, Marriage, and Family:
### Part 1 • 132

## 9. Sex, Marriage, and Family:
### Part 2 • 151

## 10. The Contemplative Life
### and Life in Society • 166

## 11. Natural Rights • 185

# Foreword

Steven J. Jensen

We live in dark times. We have all heard of the Nazi atrocities against the Jews and Slavs of the 1930s and 1940s, including the gassing and incineration of millions of human beings. Less well-known cruelties opened the troubled twentieth century. Beginning in 1915, the Turkish government massacred Armenian males and sent women and children on death marches, killing one and a half million Armenians. In the 1930s, communist Russia starved to death seven million Ukrainians. In the 1970s, Pol Pot's Khmer Rouge communist regime killed two million Cambodians through forced labor and killing fields. In 1994 the Rwandan Hutu militia clubbed and hacked to death 800,000 members of the Tutsi tribe. In the latter part of the twentieth century—and continuing to our own day—we have witnessed a holocaust of babies killed in abortion. Each year throughout the world over thirty million babies are killed.

As we overlook the bloodshed around us, we imagine ourselves as a kind and tolerant age. We are, rather, the age of man's inhumanity to man. Throughout their history, human beings have been mostly brutish to one another, but something seems to have gone profoundly wrong in our own age. We have lost sight of a fundamental principle. We have lost sight, it seems, of the value of human beings.

This loss of the sense of human worth, according to Richard Berquist, is no accident. It follows inexorably from our denial of purpose in the world around us. Most profoundly, it follows from our denial of purpose in human life. If there is no purpose to life, then there is no true good in life. And if there is no good in human life, then neither is there any good in human beings.

Without purpose, we can hope, at best, to satisfy our selfish desires. Without worth or dignity in others, we have no reason to unite with others in pursuit of a shared good. We have reason only to band together with others to achieve our own personal goals. Other human beings become tools or instruments for our own selfish ends. The world is filled with things that are meant to be instruments—chemicals, trees, crops, fish, dogs, and many more. Human beings are different. We are not meant to be instruments. One person is not made to be used merely as a means for another; rather, all are made to share in the one human good together. We have a purpose beyond mere utility. We are made to share the good with others. This sharing in the good, possessing the good with others, is precisely what it means to have dignity.

In order to defend human dignity, then, we must defend human purpose. And in order to defend human purpose, Berquist shows, we must resist the lure of a mechanistic conception of living things. We must acknowledge that the world is more than atoms bumping into one another. We must acknowledge that human beings are not simply cosmic accidents. We can be more than instruments only if we are made to attain the good ourselves. But a cosmic accident, like any accident, just happens; it is made for no purpose.

We are no accidents. We are made for a definite purpose. In finding this purpose, we find our true human fulfillment; we find the source of our true happiness. As Berquist examines this purpose, he discovers that we are not made for merely material goods. We are spiritual beings with spiritual goods. Our life is fulfilled not by having things or by collecting pleasures. We are fulfilled through a proper order in our human actions.

Berquist draws a link between human dignity and the natural law. Sometimes the term "natural law" is used to refer simply to objective morality. Berquist certainly acknowledges objective morality. By "natural law," however, he means something more.

He refers to the norms of behavior that arise from the purpose we find within our nature. These norms, he argues convincingly, can all be perceived in the unfolding of human dignity. When that dignity is denied, so also will objective morality be denied. And where objective morality is denied, human passion—all too often, brutal human passion—will have its way.

Dignity engenders love, and love in its turn demands a firm commitment to the shared good. Berquist defends the absolute prohibitions against suicide, killing the innocent, euthanasia, and abortion. If we allow exceptions in difficult situations, we subject human dignity to the needs of the moment.

Berquist looks beyond these strict demands of human dignity, however, to recognize some cases where human life may be taken. On the one hand, it might be taken indirectly, in what is sometimes called "double-effect reasoning." In that case, a person does not choose to subject human worth to the momentary circumstances. Rather, the pursuit of some human good brings with it unfortunate consequences. At other times, however, human life may be taken directly, as with capital punishment and just war. If we exclude these possibilities, we are left impotent in the face of evil. These cases do not oppose human dignity because that dignity rests upon the shared good. The criminal has chosen to place himself above the shared good, thereby rejecting it.

Berquist, in his application of dignity and love to the concrete situations of our lives, examines sexual ethics in this book. Once again, he defends the traditional natural law: sexual activity is reserved for marriage between a man and a woman. Sex is not—as we so often suppose today—merely a private matter. To the contrary, by its nature it is ordered to the shared good— namely, the coming to be and raising of children. Our dignity demands, then, that we seek sexual relations within the context of the shared good. This shared good generates love and affection, a most intimate friendship, between the man and the woman. Sex is not made for pleasure. It is made for love of others, for love of our children and for love between the spouses.

Our confusion in sexual matters is part of a greater confusion over the importance of spiritual goods. We focus too much upon material happiness. We suppose that we will be happy by possessing more and more things. We fail to recognize the true value of our lives, which is found in spiritual realities. In particular, our lives take on true meaning through the pursuit of truth and through our human relations. But today the truth, now ridiculed as an unattainable fantasy, no longer seems worth pursuing, and our human relations take second place to things; we relate more to our computers and phones than to one another. We must regain our sense of the spiritual and thereby regain our sense of dignity.

As Berquist informs us, in the modern age people do not wish to be subject to the order revealed by nature. Instead, we want to invent our own way of life. To satisfy our desire we go so far as to deny nature itself. Through this very denial, however, we are left with nothing. We have no goods, and we ourselves have no worth. Richard Berquist goes far in showing us what has been lost and in revealing the road we must take to restore it. He provides both the bigger picture and the concrete details. He provides a broad introduction for the beginner while providing needed connections and arguments for the scholar. Let us enter into his argument and rediscover our true worth.

# Acknowledgments

It is a pleasure to acknowledge with gratitude the many people who have read all or portions of this book during the many stages of its development: Gary Atkinson, Dolores Berquist, Duane Berquist, John Boyle, John Goyette, Steve Heaney, Steve Jensen, Warren Murray, Chris Toner, and John van Ingen. Their criticisms and suggestions have greatly improved it. Also very helpful were the comments of the two scholars who reviewed the book for the Catholic University of America Press; my thanks to them as well. I am, of course, entirely responsible for the final result. I am especially grateful to Steve Jensen for his thoughtful and inspiring foreword. Finally, my thanks to John Martino and the staff at CUA Press, who have patiently shepherded me through the publication process, and to Kachergis Book Design, who designed the cover.

# A Note on Abbreviations and Citations

The following abbreviations have been used in the footnotes:

CDF   The Vatican *Congregation for the Doctrine of the Faith*
NE    The *Nicomachian Ethics* of Aristotle
SCG   The *Summa Contra Gentiles* of St. Thomas Aquinas
ST     The *Summa Theologiae* of St. Thomas Aquinas

References to the *Summa Theologiae* are given according to its parts: I, I-II, II-II, III, and Suppl. This is followed by the question number, the article number, and a specific reference either to the main body of the article, to an objection, or to an answer to an objection. Thus: I-II, q. 94, a. 2, obj. 1 refers to the first objection in article 2 of question 94 in the first part of the second part of the *Summa*. The expression "ad 1" would refer to the answer to that objection, and "c" would refer to the main body of the article (the "corpus"). References to the *Summa Contra Gentiles* are by book, chapter, and paragraph, as given in the English translation listed in the bibliography. Thus *SCG* III, cap. 122, n. 5 refers to Book III, chapter 122, paragraph 5. The same for the Latin text, except that the paragraphs are not numbered.

English translations of papal encyclicals, CDF documents, and documents from Vatican Council II can be found on the Vatican website as well as in various publications.

# From Human Dignity
# to Natural Law

# Introduction

There is nothing fundamentally new in this book. Yet, in a way, there *is* something new, or at least a little different. The principles and many of the arguments in this book are derived primarily, though not exclusively, from Aristotle and Thomas Aquinas. They include not only general principles, like the definition of the natural law and its relation to human law, but also specific principles concerned with human life, with sexual morality, and with natural rights. On none of these topics do I have anything fundamentally new to offer.

What then is new? Briefly, I propose to sketch or outline a way to the natural law from human dignity. The value of this will be clear to anyone who has attempted to teach the natural law, particularly its implications for controversial moral issues. One is immediately faced with questions about whether there is a natural law and whether it can be known by reason alone or must be accepted on faith. When the starting point is in question, it is impossible to move forward. Human dignity, on the other hand, is readily accepted; most people believe that human beings have some sort of value or status that deserves respect. Not that this intuitive sense of human dignity takes us very far; we need to know more precisely what it is before we can investigate its moral implications. But it is enough to get us started.

A sign that it is possible to proceed from human dignity to the natural law can be taken from Kant's first and second formulations of the categorical imperative.[1] For the first formulation,

---

1. Immanuel Kant, *Foundations of the Metaphysics of Morals*, trans. Lewis White Beck (Upper Saddle River, N.J.: Prentice-Hall, 1900), sect. 2.

1

that we should act only on maxims that can be simultaneously willed as universal laws, is a legal formulation, and the second, that we should treat humanity in ourselves and others as an end and not as a means only, is a human dignity formulation. Kant applies these to his four paradigmatic examples: suicide, the lying promise, developing one's talents, and helping those in need. The results are the same for both formulations, and they are all traditional natural law precepts. The same thing appears in the emphasis on human dignity in contemporary Catholic Church documents concerned with moral and social issues, an approach that also leads to natural law precepts.

Our first task will be to define human dignity and to show that it is something real in the nature of things. I will attempt to do this a posteriori by proposing a case of murder that I believe we would all condemn and by arguing that our condemnation can be justified only if human beings exist by nature for their own good. This, roughly speaking, is human dignity, and the first chapter will be devoted to showing its importance and to defining it more precisely. But there is a serious objection to human dignity, since, as we shall see, it implies finality in nature, and contemporary natural science rejects the idea that anything in nature takes place or exists for the sake of an end. In chapter 2, we will consider this objection.

In chapters 3 and 4, following Aristotle's *Nicomachean Ethics*, we will consider the natural end or good for which we exist—that is, happiness. This will complete the definition of human dignity. Then, in chapter 5, we will consider the natural law itself, understanding it as the law that directs us to happiness. In this connection, we will have to consider whether our approach to the natural law commits the fallacy of attempting to derive statements of moral obligation from statements of fact, the "is/ought" or naturalistic fallacy. In chapters 6 through 11, we will consider fundamental precepts of the natural law: those concerned with human life in chapters 6 and 7; those concerned with sexual morality and marriage in chapters 8 and 9; those concerned with the obligation to seek truth and with the political order and natural rights in chapters 10 and 11. In chapter 12, we will consider the natural law in relation to some other approaches to normative ethics.

To derive the natural law from human dignity, we shall have to consider a number of difficult questions. First among these is whether there is finality in nature. Again, assuming that human beings exist for their own good, is this primarily the individual good or the common good? And what is the common good? Is the natural law truly a law, and, if so, must there not be a lawgiver? Finally, in the chapters concerned with particular natural law precepts, we shall have to consider many controversial questions.

This is an essay in moral philosophy, not moral theology, if we understand theology as a discipline based on principles divinely revealed and accepted on faith. Of course, a number of my sources are documents of the Catholic Church, as was inevitable, given the importance of the natural law in the Catholic tradition. But although I have sometimes touched upon theological matters, I have not argued from theological premises, but only from premises accessible to natural reason.

One may object that my project is too ambitious for a work of this size. Indeed, I think so myself. To keep things within bounds, therefore, I have emphasized the starting points, especially human dignity and happiness, while discussing particular natural law precepts more briefly, with an eye on the main theme, the connection of these precepts with happiness. For the same reason, I have avoided polemics. Not that I am averse to controversy; for much of my teaching career, I was concerned with controversial questions of biomedical and sexual ethics. But to engage other authors responsibly would be impossible in a work of this size and, moreover, would distract the reader from the main goal, which is to show how human dignity leads to the natural law.

Nevertheless, for readers not familiar with current discussions of natural law, I should note that the approach explored in this book belongs to the neo-Scholastic or neo-Thomistic tradition as distinguished from a contemporary approach commonly referred to as the "new natural law."[2] This latter approach begins with a listing of the goods that are desirable for themselves, the basic goods, and proposes ethical principles (modes of responsibility) for choosing these goods coherently and responsibly, never acting intentionally against any of them, all with a view to achieving what is called "integral human fulfillment" or "integral communal fulfillment." As noted above, my approach begins from human dignity and derives natural law principles from man's ultimate end—that is, from a proper understanding of human happiness.[3] It would be interesting and useful to compare these two approaches to the natural law, but this is beyond the scope of the present work.

Let me conclude by noting that this book is intended not only for academics specializing in ethics and legal philosophy, but also for professionals in other disciplines, for students, and for anyone interested in the foundations of law and its relationship to human happiness. This is why I have tried to develop the argument as simply and straightforwardly as possible, not presupposing extensive background knowledge or introducing complex scholarly debates. My hope is that even those not convinced by the arguments advanced in this book will at least come to a better understanding of the natural law as a coherent whole, with significant implications for all areas of human life.

---

2. Germain Grisez, Joseph Boyle, John Finnis, and others have developed the new natural law theory through numerous publications beginning in the 1960s and continuing today. For a clear and concise introduction to this theory, see Christopher Tollefsen, "The New Natural Law Theory," *Lyceum* 10, no. 1 (2009): 1–17.

3. For a brief statement of the approach to the natural law through man's ultimate end, happiness, see Ralph McInerny, "Thomistic Natural Law and Aristotelian Philosophy," in *St. Thomas Aquinas and the Natural Law Tradition: Contemporary Perspectives*, ed. John Goyette, Mark S. Latkovic, and Richard S. Myers (Washington D.C.: The Catholic University of America Press, 2004), 25–39. See also McInerny, *Ethica Thomistica: The Moral Philosophy of Thomas Aquinas*, rev. ed. (Washington, D.C.: The Catholic University of America Press, 1997), esp. chapters 2 and 3, and McInerny, *Aquinas on Human Action: A Theory of Practice* (Washington D.C.: The Catholic University of America Press, 1992), 103–32. These books discuss topics on human action that are useful as background for the study of the natural law.

CHAPTER 1

# Human Dignity

## A Case of Murder

To understand what human dignity is and why it is necessary, it is helpful to begin by proposing a case of murder with a view to investigating why it is wrong. After exploring a series of plausible but not fully satisfactory responses to this question, we shall be able to find a definitive answer in the principle of human dignity. As we shall see, human dignity, properly understood, not only justifies our condemnation of heinous crimes like murder, but also establishes a secure foundation for the whole of moral philosophy.

Speaking very generally, we may say that murder is the wrongful killing of a human being. But we must distinguish between murder understood as an act that is regarded as wrong by a particular culture or declared to be wrong by the criminal law of a particular state and murder understood as an act that is absolutely wrong, wrong in itself, and not wrong just from some "point of view." We shall be concerned in this chapter with a murder that is wrong in this unqualified sense, a murder so obviously wrong that I think we will all be willing to condemn it categorically.

Consider the case of a man who kills his uncle to gain an inheritance, or a man who kills a woman he has raped to prevent her from testifying against him, or a man who assassinates the leader of a minority race to prevent his people's social advancement. Is there anyone who would not condemn killings like these?

But perhaps there were unusual circumstances. Take the first

5

case.[1] Let us suppose that the uncle is a greedy, vicious landowner in a poverty-stricken country ruled by a tyrant, and that his nephew is appalled by the misery around him and wishes to use the inheritance to help people in need. Given enough circumstances of this sort, we might become less emphatic in our condemnation of the killing. Some of us might even feel that, all things considered, the murder is justifiable, that it is not *really* wrongful killing, even though it is illegal. The beast must die!

The very fact that we look for extenuating circumstances is a sign that we regard the killing of another human being as at least *prima facie* wrong. So let us pursue the example further by supposing that there are no extenuating circumstances. The uncle is neither better nor worse than most people, and the nephew would not be likely to use the money any differently than his uncle would use it. The murder, let us suppose, is of no advantage to the community or to any individual other than the murderer. How, then, could it be justified?

While agreeing that the murder is wrong, someone might nevertheless maintain that it is not wrong without qualification. For if it were wrong without qualification, would it not be wrong at all times and in all cultures? But in some cultures, at some times, actions that we find abhorrent have been tolerated and even justified. So perhaps our rejection of the murder does not show that it is evil in itself. Rather, it reflects a cultural bias. We should note, however, that this objection abstracts from the life experiences that moved us spontaneously to condemn the murder. It relies instead on a deduction from ethical relativism, a thesis according to which the murder we are considering cannot be wrong in itself, however much we abhor it, because no action is wrong in itself. Let us, therefore, briefly consider ethical relativism.

---

1. I have chosen the first of these three cases for our investigation not because it is more evil—the second and third cases are much worse—but because it is less emotionally charged. I want to focus on the evil of murder per se, setting aside the aggravating circumstances that make some murders uglier and more socially harmful than others.

## Ethical Relativism

I shall be concerned here with a view of ethical relativism that goes something like this. Our moral judgments are relative to the values of our culture. Because these values are public rather than private, we tend to believe that judgments based on them are objectively true. But an increased awareness of other ways of life in other cultures undermines this certitude. We begin to think critically, and, being enlightened, we come to realize that the customs and traditional values of our society have conditioned our moral judgments. Even the most certain of them may then seem open to question.

With respect to homicide, for example, we read of practices in other cultures that we find intolerable: the killing of captives or slaves in religious sacrifices or cannibalistic ceremonies, the killing of elderly parents or of couples who elope,[2] the practice called *suttee* (once practiced in India) where a wife is burned to death on the funeral pyre of her husband, and similar evils. Worse than these, in our own times, are the mass killings of innocent people resulting from racial or communist ideologies or from fanaticism. If practices like these have sometimes been found acceptable, at least to some people, then perhaps the murder just described is not really evil in itself, but merely seems so to us because of our traditions.

Nevertheless, although it may cause us to question our traditional values, the study of other cultures cannot establish the truth of ethical relativism. We can indeed document significant differences in the moral and legal judgments of different cultures or even of the same culture at different times. And it is certainly true that cultural values influence our individual moral judgments. But these facts cannot establish that moral values are purely relative. Are some beliefs and practices morally right and

---

2. These and other practices are described by Ruth Benedict in *Patterns of Culture* (New York: New American Library, 1959).

others wrong? Do some reflect an awareness of moral truth, while others reflect mainly ignorance, vice, or superstition? Or are all moral beliefs purely subjective, none being objectively better or worse than any other? To answer such questions, we must either have true principles for evaluating moral beliefs and customs or we must be able to prove that such principles do not exist. Neither of these alternatives is established by factual studies of different cultures.

Moreover, with respect specifically to homicide, we ought to take account not only of the kinds of killing that various cultures accept, but also of those that they reject. In the murder example we are considering, I deliberately eliminated extenuating circumstances in order to remove any plausible justification. We must approach judgments in other cultures in the same way. Perhaps a culture allows captives in war to be enslaved and used as victims in religious sacrifices. But not free persons. Perhaps it allows a widow to be burned on her husband's funeral pyre. But not a widower. The value of human life may be recognized more extensively in some cultures than others. Outsiders and slaves and even women and children may be seen as having a lesser value. Killing them may be allowed in certain circumstances and for certain purposes where the killing of persons of higher status would not be tolerated.

We should note also that cultural diversity affects our judgments about sexuality, marriage, and the family more than it affects our judgments about homicide. Life is the most obvious and fundamental human good, necessary for the enjoyment of any further good. Hence, unless we are making deductions from a general principle of ethical relativism, we are not inclined to doubt the moral validity of laws against murder. But different sexual practices and different marriage and family arrangements, when life and physical harm do not seem threatened, have a greater tendency to make us question the objective truth of traditional beliefs. This is why I began with a case of murder.

None of this is meant to question the value of studying other cultures. Besides promoting mutual understanding among peoples, it can be a principle of renewal for our own culture. For if we judge that certain practices in other cultures are morally wrong or at least inferior to ours, we are forced to ask why they are wrong or why they are inferior and so to clarify the foundations of morality. This, in turn, will help us to reflect critically on our own practices, making us aware of the ways in which we are deficient and inspiring us to seek cultural renewal.[3]

In summary, it is impossible to prove ethical relativism, the thesis that no ethical principles are absolutely true, from the diversity of attitudes and behavior in different cultures. Hence, the data gathered by researchers in this area need not weaken our confidence in the objective evil of the murder we are considering. If we are satisfied, on the basis of our life experiences, that this murder is really or unqualifiedly wrong, we must go on to investigate *why* it is wrong.

*[handwritten: Self-interest as the foundation for morality. | disinterested and selfless concern for other's well-being.]*

## Egoism vs. Altruism

In this section, we shall consider the nephew's murder of his uncle in the light of the distinction between egoism and altruism and the related concept of the "moral point of view." This will not be enough to show us precisely why the murder is wrong, but it will help prepare the way for a better answer.

Let us begin with the nephew's motivation. It is simple enough. He wants the inheritance, and he wants it immediately, and the only way he can get it is by murder. Of course, there are dangers involved. To remove these, we shall assume that the murder can be done secretly and that it will look like an accident. Therefore, the nephew need not fear either that his action will lead to pun-

3. For a discussion of natural law in relation to the lived values of particular communities, see Joseph Boyle, "Natural Law and the Ethics of Traditions," in *Natural Law Theory: Contemporary Essays*, ed. Robert P. George (Oxford: Clarendon Press, 1992), 3–30.

ishment or that it will encourage others to commit murder. For he does not want to live in a lawless society. Given these assumptions, why should he hesitate?

Our first reply is that the nephew is egoistic, focused exclusively on getting what he wants for himself, unconcerned with what happens to anyone else. This, we believe, is immoral. But the nephew may concede this. He realizes that others will call his action egoistic and immoral. In fact, he would probably use the same language himself, if someone else were to commit murder. But he will refuse to admit that the murder is either irrational or wrong *from his point of view*. Why should he prefer the viewpoint of others to his own?

Can we persuade him to change his point of view by trying to arouse in him a feeling of compassion toward his uncle, who has always been kind to him and has never done him any harm? But why should he allow feelings to stand in his way? Maybe he should feel sorry for himself, deprived of an inheritance at the age in which he could most enjoy it. In any event, a feeling is no substitute for an argument.

But has he not conceived his self-interest too narrowly? Is it not more human and ultimately more satisfying to live honorably and to respect one's fellow man? Money, after all, is not the main thing in life; it is no more than a means to an end. Our chief concern must be with the way we live. A life characterized by courage, generosity, justice, and the other virtues is the happiest life. Blinded by egoism, the nephew acts in a way that is not really in his self-interest, properly understood.

This is a good argument, confirmed by the testimony of those who have chosen to live virtuously. Still, the nephew is not without a reply. What does it mean to live honorably? To conform one's life to what others approve? What others approve in my actions is what is useful to them. This is why murder is publicly condemned. Everyone thinks that the condemnation of murder and the establishment of a law enforcement system will protect him from harm. But when he wishes to gain an advantage by harming others, law enforcement is simply an obstacle to be gotten around. As for living virtuously, does this mean living rationally? If not, then it must be rejected as unenlightened sentiment. If so, then only what is contrary to reason will be contrary to virtue. The question, then, is this: Is the murder contrary to reason and, if so, why?

What shall we say then? That even if the nephew can justify his action from an egoistic point of view, he certainly cannot justify it from a moral point of view? For the moral point of view would seem to be defined primarily by its opposition to egoism— that is, by altruism or concern for others. His action can therefore be shown to be immoral by a simple deduction. But the nephew will certainly not be satisfied with this, for it leaves unanswered the question *Why be moral?*

Actually, there is something rather paradoxical about the question *Why be moral?* For morality requires that we do what we ought to do and that we not do what we ought not to do. But then it seems odd to ask, *Why be moral?* For even the egoist will admit that he should do what he ought to do and should not do what he ought not to do, although he will not agree with us about *what it is* that he ought or ought not to do. When defining moral obligation, therefore, it seems preferable to begin not by specifying a particular moral ideal like altruism, but by distinguishing, as Kant does, between conditional obligations and unconditional or categorical obligations. Conditional obligations: "If you want to win the lottery, you must buy a ticket" or "If you want to get to New York from here, this is the road you must take." Categorical obligations: "You must pay your debts" or "You must take care of your children." Before determining moral ideals, we must first consider the kind of obligations morality imposes—that is, categorical obligations. We can then avoid the awkward question *Why be moral?* and phrase our question as follows: *Why is the nephew unconditionally obligated to respect his uncle's life?*

## The Common Good

Let us try another approach, arguing that the murder is immoral because it is irrational and that it is irrational because it is opposed to the common good. It is true that the uncle's death will seem to be an accident and so will not encourage a breakdown of law and order. Nevertheless, the murder is inconsistent with the most basic advantage of living in community, the security of personal life and property. The nephew himself desires this security and realizes that it can only be obtained through a legal system that prohibits murder. It seems, then, that, on the one hand, he wills that life and property should be secure for everyone (since he supports the public institutions established for this purpose) and that, on the other hand, he wills that the life of his uncle should *not* be secure, at least not from him. Is this not inconsistent and hence irrational?

It seems to be irrational because it is opposed to the principle of universalizability. Kant tells us that we must never act on a maxim that we cannot at the same time will as a universal law.[4] There must be a consistency between what I will as a member of the community—or, more generally, what I will from the point of view of a universal rational order—and what I choose as an individual. If I violate the law against murder, a law upon which the common security depends, I implicitly authorize everyone else to violate it. But this destroys the law itself and hence the foundation of my own security that, as a rational being, I necessarily will.

Nevertheless, the nephew may argue that there is no inconsistency *from his point of view*. My personal security does not depend on whether or not I will the security of life and property as a common good—although it does seem to depend on whether *others* so will it. Why is it irrational for me to will that others act on principles different from my own? If I am miserly, for example,

4. Immanuel Kant, *Foundations of the Metaphysics of Morals*, trans. Lewis White Beck (Upper Saddle River, N.J.: Prentice-Hall, 1900), sect. 2.

it is not irrational for me to desire that others should be generous. Nor is it irrational for me to publicly profess principles that I do not myself act upon, since this puts people off their guard and allows me to gain my real ends more effectively.

## Human Dignity

The nephew's case depends on the rationality of egoism. For he is willing to admit that the murder of his uncle cannot be rationally justified from the point of view of the community. He does not deny that it would be rational for the community to punish him if the crime were discovered. But he insists that the murder can be rationally justified from his point of view. To refute him decisively, therefore, we must show that the murder is contrary to reason *by its very nature*. For then the murder will be wrong absolutely and without qualification.

Let us begin our refutation of the nephew by asking what value we are to assign to his uncle. By this I do not mean what value he has in the eyes of his nephew or in the eyes of the community or even in his own eyes, but what value he has objectively and by nature. Now the nephew clearly regards his uncle as valuable ultimately in relation to him. If this is his uncle's true value, then the nephew is justified in killing him for an inheritance, just as one might kill an animal for food. In order to condemn the murder unconditionally, therefore, we must assume that the uncle has a value that is not exhausted by or defined by his usefulness to his nephew. Moreover, this value must be an objective value, belonging to the uncle by his very nature. Otherwise, it will be a value created by human beings, and the nephew will be free to evaluate his uncle as he pleases.

What does it mean to have a value that is not defined by one's usefulness to others? The answer becomes clear if we consider that to exist as an object of utility is to exist for the good of something else. Therefore, to have a value that transcends utility, a thing must exist for its own good. This value or status in human beings defines *human dignity* as I shall understand it in this book. As we shall see, human beings must possess this dignity if the nephew's act is to be condemned without qualification.

Let us define human dignity as *the value of a human being as existing by nature for his own good as an ultimate end*. To understand this properly, we must clearly distinguish the way in which human beings exist for their own good from the way in which this is true also of animals. For since animals naturally seek their own good, they also can be said to exist for their own good. But this does not define their ultimate value. For animals that are higher on the food chain naturally prey on animals that are lower down, and man makes use in various ways of all the animals. Ultimately, then, prey animals exist for the good of their predators and all the animals for the good of man. Man, however, is not ordered to the good of something else, but rather to his own good as an ultimate end. Furthermore, if human beings exist for their own good as an ultimate end *by nature*, then human dignity is real, not a human creation, and this implies that it belongs equally to all human beings, without regard to race, sex, age, physical or mental condition, or to differences of culture or religion.

Human dignity does not mean that we cannot be useful to each other, for we can and do help each other and collaborate for mutual advantage. Our own good includes not only our individual good but also the common good. For the common good is the good of all those who participate in a common endeavor, although not the good of any one participant exclusively. Existing for our own good excludes existing for an alien good, a good in which we have no share, but it does not exclude existing for a common good. This will become clearer in later discussions.

Our definition of human dignity is closely related to Kant's second formula for his categorical imperative: *Act so as to respect humanity in your own person and in others as an end in itself and not as a means only.*[5] For if it is wrong to use ourselves or others mere-

5. Ibid.

ly as means to an end, then our value as human beings must transcend our usefulness—that is, we must exist for our own good. Kant's formula is therefore, in substance, a consequence of the value or status of the human person as expressed in our definition of human dignity.

If we grant the principle of human dignity, we can refute the egoistic justification of the nephew's murder. For if the uncle exists by nature for his own good, then it will clearly be irrational to treat him as though his ultimate value consisted in his usefulness to his nephew. But this is just how the nephew treats him. From this it follows that the nephew's action is irrational by its very nature and therefore wrong without qualification.

Or should we question even this—I mean the obligation of acting rationally? But such a question would be absurd. For every "why" question must be answered by giving reasons. Therefore, if we ask why we should act rationally, we are seeking guidance from the very faculty whose right to guide us is being questioned. Of course, the nephew may decide to commit the murder whether it can be rationally justified or not. All we can do is to show that his action is objectively irrational, since it uses his uncle in a way that is inconsistent with his uncle's true value. But this may not prevent him from doing it.

Furthermore, none of this implies that the nephew's murder of his uncle is totally unreasonable. For an action can be rationally justified conditionally, as useful in relation to a particular end, even when it cannot be justified unconditionally or categorically. The nephew's action, as we have described it, is certainly rational in relation to his end, which was to gain an inheritance without being punished or disturbing the social order. But it is not rational without qualification, and this is what is decisive for moral evaluation.

Let us now summarize the foregoing argument. First of all, it is a posteriori—that is, it relies on the strength of our condemnation of the murder. If the fact that the murder is wrong is clear to us and more obvious than any explanation of *why* it is wrong, then it is possible to argue to the principle of human dignity in the way I have attempted. For human dignity is the principle that shows precisely why the murder is wrong in itself and not just from some point of view. Thus, our certainty that human beings exist by nature for their own good depends, so far as the present argument is concerned, on our certainty that the nephew's murder is absolutely wrong.

It is possible, however, to go beyond this. For human dignity is plausible in its own right, apart from the argument we have been pursuing. We have a kind of connatural awareness of it. For when our dignity is challenged, when we realize that someone is using us as a means to an end without regard for our good, we feel not only that we are being harmed, but also that we are being insulted. It is not difficult to see why. As rational beings, we are capable of understanding our own good as an ultimate end and of directing ourselves toward it precisely under this formality. We cannot endure the idea of being ultimately no more than a means to an alien good. In this respect we differ from the animals, which pursue their natural good instinctively, quite unconcerned with their ultimate value. If you treat an animal well, it is content, even if it is no more than your pet. It has no understanding of status and cannot react to the fact that you value it ultimately not for its good but for yours. Not so a human being. We resent the status of being a slave even more than we resent ill treatment.

### The Cause of Human Dignity

If human beings exist by nature for their own good, then it seems that there must be a cause of this in nature. But how can nature cause anything to exist for a purpose? When Vesuvius erupted and destroyed Pompeii, was this why it erupted? If chance and Darwinian evolution produce an organism that functions well, would we say that these causes were aiming at this organism and its functioning as an end? Causes like this do not act for a purpose. There may be the appearance of purpose, but not the reality.

If a thing exists for an end or purpose, therefore, it must have a cause of a different sort, a cause capable of ordering things to an end. But only intelligence can establish order. For a thing is ordered to an end by an agent who understands the end and is able to determine what is necessary to achieve it. Thus, it is because we are rational that we are able to understand the purpose of a machine we propose to build and to design it so as to achieve that purpose. Similarly, if human beings really exist for a purpose, there must exist an intelligence who has established human nature with this purpose in view. The cause of human dignity, therefore, must be the Author of nature, whom we call God.

This argument is based on Aquinas's fifth way of proving the existence of God, a proof that proceeds from the premise that natural things and natural processes exist or take place for the sake of an end that they do not know. From this premise, Aquinas concludes that there must exist an intelligent being directing them to their ends, as the archer directs the arrow to the target.[6] It can reasonably be objected that I should have discussed Aquinas's proof in more detail, in particular the fundamental premise on which it is based: that nature acts for an end. However, I have not been concerned with this general thesis, but only with a special case: that human beings exist by nature for their own good. If this is true, then I think it is possible to prove, as Aquinas does, that there must exist an intelligent being who has established this order.

But what about this fundamental premise: that man exists for his own good? I argued for it a posteriori, as the principle that allows us to condemn the nephew's murder as wrong in itself, not simply from some point of view. Indeed, if human beings did not exist by nature for their own good, how could we condemn any crime against anyone as being absolutely wrong? For whenever we commit a crime against someone, we use him as though he exist-

6. *ST* I, q. 2, a. 3.

ed ultimately not for his own good, but as a means to our good, or perhaps to some other alien good. If these consequences seem utterly inhuman, fundamentally opposed to our self-understanding and life experiences, then it seems we must admit human dignity as a natural reality.

Nevertheless, if our argument for finality in nature is to be completely satisfactory, we also need a proof based on natural principles, independent of the proof from moral experience. This is especially important in view of the fact that contemporary science rejects finality in its explanations of the natural world. The task of chapter 2 will be to develop such a proof.

## Conclusion

Our concept of human dignity is still very vague. We have the general idea that human beings exist by nature for their own good. But what is this good? We seek life, health, pleasure, friendship, knowledge, virtue, and many other good things. But it does not seem that any one of these, by itself alone, could be the good that defines human dignity. For this purpose, we need a more inclusive, more ultimate good. But what is it? Happiness is clearly the name for it, since we believe that when we have achieved happiness, we will have fully achieved the human good. What more could we ask for? But what is happiness? An answer to this question will clarify our concept of human dignity and provide the starting point for our investigation of the natural law. For, as I stated in the introduction, the natural law is directed to the achievement of happiness. Therefore, after considering the scientific objection to finality in nature in the next chapter, we will turn, in chapter 3, to the definition of happiness.

# CHAPTER 2

# Finality in Nature

If we exist by nature for our own good, then there must be finality in nature. But contemporary science rejects the idea that natural processes take place for the sake of an end or that natural things exist for the sake of an end. We must therefore consider this objection to our thesis.

We may begin by noting that there are three possible ways of stating the scientific objection to finality in nature. For science has shown either (a) that there is no finality in nature, or (b) that, if there is, this cannot be proved rationally, or (c) that, at any rate, it cannot be shown by the scientific method. Of these, only the third is a properly scientific objection; the others raise questions that go beyond the domain of science. For if finality cannot be shown by the scientific method, it is not thereby disproved; perhaps it can be shown in some other way. And it is clearly impossible to prove by the scientific method that nothing can be proved rationally except by the scientific method. To understand and evaluate the scientific rejection of finality, therefore, we shall have to consider the scientific method and what may be its limitations.

We shall not be concerned here with finality in general, but with the more limited question of finality in living things. Specifically, I want to ask whether a living thing exists for the sake of achieving the way of life proper to it. The answer to this question will depend on the answer to a more fundamental question: does the process of organic development take place for the sake of an end—that is, for the sake of the mature organism that results

19

from the process? If so, then the answer to the first question will also be affirmative; the living thing will exist to achieve the way of life proper to it. For it will have been formed precisely for this way of life. On the other hand, if the developmental process is *not* for the sake of the resulting organism, then the organism will not exist for the sake of its proper way of life. It will function in a characteristic way because it happens to be structured so as to function in this way, but not because it was formed for this purpose.

We will proceed as follows. First, I will briefly sketch Aristotle's main argument for finality in Book II of the *Physics* and show how contemporary science can respond to it with a mechanistic conception of living things. Second, I will endeavor to show that the scientific rejection of finality in living things results from the limitations of the scientific method. Third, I will argue that a mechanistic conception of living things is mistaken; living things are *not* machines. But if living things are not machines, then, as we shall see, the process of organic development must be for the sake of the new organism that results from it. This will allow us to draw the main conclusion: that a living thing exists for the way of life proper to it.

## (1) Finality in Aristotle and Contemporary Science

We observe that the process of organic development leads to the existence and ultimately to the maturity of a living organism. Because of this, we naturally suppose that the process is directed toward the mature organism as an end, just as happens in the creation of works of art. This commonsense impression is confirmed by reasoning. Aristotle argued that a natural process either takes place for the sake of an end or arrives at an end by chance. But natural processes do not arrive at their ends by chance, since they arrive there regularly or for the most part, whereas chance events happen rarely. It follows that natural processes take place for the sake of an end.[1] Furthermore, according to Aristotle, a natural process involves a sequence of steps or stages, each of which is related to the preceding and succeeding stages in such a way as to arrive at the end. But what regularly follows an orderly sequence of stages leading to a determinate result is naturally disposed or adapted to attain that result. Hence, the process is naturally directed to the end.[2]

A contemporary scientist can agree with Aristotle that the process of organic development does not reach its end by chance. But this does not mean that it takes place *for the sake of the end*. For there seems to be a third alternative: that the process arrives at the end by mechanical necessity. In this conception, every organism will be a kind of machine—a self-constructing machine, in Jacques Monod's useful formula.[3] If organisms are self-constructing machines, both their functioning and their coming-to-be will take place by mechanical necessity, not for the sake of an end.

In man-made machines, of course, we see both mechanical necessity and finality. For the functioning of a man-made machine is both the necessary result of the working together of its parts and the end intended by the engineer who designed and built it. But if a living thing is a self-constructing machine, it will not only function mechanically, but also build itself mechanically. Its coming-to-be will be the necessary result of the way in which the composing materials are ordered by the genetic program. The developmental process will not take place for the sake of the resulting organism; it will arrive at this result because it is so structured mechanically that it must arrive there, unless it is impeded. Of course, questions still remain. How did the first machine-organisms come to be, before there were genetic programs to direct their development? How have they evolved into the organisms we see today? Here we may introduce chance, hypothesizing that the first primitive living

1. Aristotle, *Physics* II.8.198b35–99a8.
2. Ibid., 199a9–15.
3. Jacques Monod, *Chance and Necessity* (New York: Alfred A. Knopf, 1971), 10–12, 46.

entities were formed by chance from certain nonliving materials, and that more complex organisms evolved from these through chance mutations. Because some of these mutations were advantageous and others not, some organisms survived and prospered, while others perished. By such reasoning, finality seems to be entirely excluded from nature.

## The Limitations of the Scientific Method

To understand why organisms and the processes by which they come to be are viewed in this way, we must investigate the nature of the scientific method. I will begin by distinguishing the four causes posited by Aristotle in his discussion of the principles of natural science: the material cause, the formal cause, the efficient cause, and the final cause.[4] They are clearly illustrated in the coming-to-be of a work of human art, like a house. The builder needs first of all materials, the sort of materials out of which a house can be built: bricks, cement, stone, timber, etc. In addition, he needs an architectural design specifying the form of the house, since many different houses might be built from the same materials. This is the formal cause, that by which one house differs from another. Again, the builder, the efficient cause, must actually set about building the house. However, he cannot build coherently without having in mind the form of the house as specified by the architectural design; this shows him why he should assemble the materials in one way rather than another. The form of the house, insofar as it causes the builder to build in a certain way, is the final cause, that for the sake of which the builder acts.

Insofar as they apply to works of human art, these four causes are not controversial. But the matter becomes more difficult when we apply them to the natural world. The first difficulty concerns the formal cause. In works of art, the forms are superficial; they

4. Aristotle, *Physics* II.3, esp. 195a15–26.

cause no fundamental change in the nature of things. Different houses, for example, are no more than different arrangements of the same materials, like the different things children make from a set of Lego blocks. Forms like these are traditionally called "accidental forms." In the natural world, however, the differences are more fundamental; human beings differ from horses and cabbages not superficially, but essentially, by their very nature. The forms by which natural things are distinguished essentially from each other are therefore called "substantial forms." But since these forms are not perceptible—only their effects are—their existence is less obvious than the existence of the forms of artificial things. A second and similar difficulty concerns the final cause, whose existence is less obvious in natural processes than it is in the coming-to-be of works of art. For while we see clearly that the building process is for the sake of an end, since we know what the builder is trying to build, we may question whether or not a natural process is taking place for the sake of an end.

As usually understood, the scientific method recognizes only material and efficient causes. By this I mean (a) that science considers the materials out of which things are made, together with their motions and interactions, and (b) that it posits efficient causes—for example, forces like gravity and electromagnetism—that are inherent in the material world. It recognizes accidental forms, which are visible, but not substantial forms, because these are not visible. Nor does it recognize the final cause, that for the sake of which each thing comes to be or acts. This is not because there are scientific reasons for rejecting final causes, but simply because a consideration of such causes is outside the scope of the scientific method.

When formal and final causes are systematically excluded, the inevitable result is a mechanistic explanation of living things. For without substantial forms, it is impossible to explain essential differences. Hence, a living thing does not appear as essentially different from the materials out of which it is made. This means that an organism will not be a substance in its own right, but rather a complex of materials so interconnected as to form a functioning whole. But a whole of this kind is a machine. Furthermore, without final causes, organic development must result from material elements and natural forces acting in such a way as to bring about this result mechanically. In the case of the first living organisms, as we have seen, the coming together of the appropriate elements in a suitable way must have been by chance, or, if not by chance, then by a process naturally ordered to this result. But that would introduce finality. Similarly, the mutations through which more complex forms of life evolved must also have occurred by chance.

We find something like this in the theory of Empedocles, an early Greek natural philosopher. Like the other natural philosophers of those times, he searched for the primary matter out of which things come to be and into which they return, for this seemed to be the first cause. In his theory, the primary matter was fourfold: earth, water, air, and fire. But he also posited two other first principles: Love, a cosmic unifying force that causes mixed bodies to exist by bringing the elements together, and Strife, a cosmic disunifying force, which destroys mixed bodies by separating the elements. However, Love does not bring the elements together according to any determinate plan, but at random. Empedocles therefore faced the same problem that contemporary biologists face: how to explain the fact that living things turn out to be well organized, as though intelligently designed. Since he did not recognize final causes, his answer was a form of natural selection: the organisms that happened to be well formed survived, while the others perished.

It might be objected that I have defined the scientific method too narrowly, arbitrarily excluding the formal and final causes that Aristotle included among the principles of natural science. Moreover, the exclusion of final causes, in particular, would seem to reflect more the method of physics and chemistry than that of biology, which explains many structures and processes in terms of their purpose. However, biologists typically reduce explanations by final causes to explanations by material and efficient causes.[5] It has also been argued that science should be open to the best or most reasonable explanations of particular phenomena, even if these explanations go beyond material and efficient causes—for example, that certain natural structures are irreducibly complex and could not have come to be through Darwinian natural selection, but only through the action of an intelligent agent.[6] Indeed, an intelligent agent would seem to be the best explanation of the existence of the universe as a whole and of its order and intelligibility.

In reply, I want to emphasize that I am not maintaining that the scientific method *should* be limited in the way I have defined it, or even that its limitations are always rigorously observed in actual scientific practice. Explanations through formal and final causes and arguments for an intelligent cause, if necessary for an adequate understanding of the natural world, can reasonably be called "scientific." But the narrower concept of the scientific method is more common, and it is this concept that gives rise to a mechanistic conception of living things and to the rejection of finality. Hence, my concern with it here.

## Are Living Things Machines?

Are living things really machines? This question is decisive because, as I shall argue, if a living thing is not a machine, it cannot come to be by a mechanical process. We will then be left with the two alternatives that Aristotle posited: finality and chance. But if these are the only alternatives, and if processes that arrive at their end always or for the most part cannot arrive there by

5. Konrad Lorenz, *The Foundations of Ethology* (New York: Springer-Verlag New York, 1981), chap. 1; Monod, *Chance and Necessity*, chaps. 1, 2, and 9.
6. Michael J. Behe, "Evidence for Design at the Foundation of Life," in *Science and Evidence for Design in the Universe* (San Francisco: Ignatius Press, 2000), 113–29.

chance, then the process of organic development must be for the sake of the organism that results from it. To establish my thesis, therefore, I must first show that living things are not machines.

What, then, is a living thing? Obviously, it depends on what life is. To understand what life is, we must first ask how we became aware of it. Was it by external observation? This might seem to be sufficient. For we see that a living thing sustains itself, heals itself, grows and reproduces itself by its own activities. It is self-moving. But a machine is not self-moving; its movements are entirely the result of the movement of its parts. It seems, therefore, that we can distinguish living things from machines simply by external observation.

But maybe not. Consider, for example, the external movements of an animal. Clearly, these movements are distinguishable from the movements of the crude machines we make ourselves. But could they not be the workings of incredibly complicated machines? Could not the individual movements and sequences of movements observed in animals result from intricate mechanisms not yet fully discovered and explained by science? So perhaps living things really are machines, even though life seems to be something more than mechanical functioning.

To solve this puzzle, we need to ask again how we first became aware of life. Clearly it was from internal experience, our experience of being alive. Because of this experience, we are able to recognize signs of life in plants and animals, signs of a reality in them that is like the reality we find in ourselves. Therefore, while it is true that we recognize that plants and animals are alive by external observation, we do not recognize this by external observation alone, but only in conjunction with our understanding of what life is, as revealed by our personal experience of it.

What does the internal experience of life show us? The most important thing is that living activities are *our* activities, carried out through faculties and organs that are parts of ourselves. This means that we are substances in our own right, essentially different from the materials out of which we were made. But a machine, as we have seen, is not itself a substance; it is rather a complex of materials, organized so as to function in a characteristic way. Its activities are primarily the activities of its parts, producing the functioning of the whole as an effect. But the activities of a living thing are primarily the activities of the whole, exercised through its parts as instruments. The functioning of a living thing, therefore, is just the opposite of the functioning of a machine. From this it is clear that a living thing is a substance in its own right and not a machine.

The fact that our concept of life results from internal experience might suggest that life is only conscious experience. But this is not true. To live is not only to sense, to feel emotions, to understand, and to will, but also to nourish oneself and to grow and to reproduce. These vegetative activities are known to us through their results. We are aware, for example, that we have grown, although growing itself is not a conscious experience. And the same is true for nourishing ourselves and reproducing.

If living things are substances in their own right, not merely complex organizations of nonliving substances, they are essentially different from nonliving things. To understand them, therefore, we must consider not only what they were made from, but also what kind of things they are. For this purpose, we require another kind of cause, the cause by which a thing is what it is essentially, the kind of formal cause that we call a "substantial form." For if we ask whether living things are essentially different from nonliving things, or whether human beings are essentially different from animals, or whether various species of animals and plants, all or some of them, are essentially different from each other, a scientific inquiry using the machine model has no way to give us an answer. For the scientific method does not make use of substantial forms in its explanations.

## Nature Acts for an End

We are now at the heart of our question. If a living thing is not a machine, then it will not construct itself mechanically; for a mechanical process cannot construct anything more than a machine. But if the coming-to-be of a living thing is not a mechanical process, in which the earlier stages explain the later stages, it must be a goal-directed process in which the later stages explain the earlier stages and the final result explains the process as a whole. The only other alternative would be to suppose that the result takes place simply by accident—that is, by chance, and this, as Aristotle proved, is impossible. Therefore, the process of organic development is for the sake of the organism that results from it.

Again, if the living thing that comes to be through a process of organic development is a new substance, essentially different from the materials out of which it was made, it is necessary to posit a substantial form to account for this difference. The process of organic development may therefore be described as a movement toward an essentially new substantial form and toward the full maturity of the organism constituted by that form. A process that leads to such a form—a substantial form that in living things is called a soul—is not a process that mechanically reconfigures materials that remain essentially the same, but rather a process that transforms these materials into a new substance. But a process cannot transform materials into a new substance unless it is oriented toward that new substance as an end.

If the process of organic development is actually for the sake of an end, not forced to an end by mechanical necessity, then there really is order in nature. But, as we saw in chapter 1, order implies intelligence. For a process cannot be ordered to an end unless by an agent who understands the end and can order the process so as to attain the end. Thus, by an argument like the one advanced in chapter 1, we can conclude the existence of an intelligence, the Author of nature, who orders natural processes to their ends.

To grasp the end-directedness of natural processes more concretely, it is helpful to compare the natural production of a living thing with the human production of a machine. In both, we find a certain ordering, in which the earlier stages of the process are ordered to the later stages, all for the sake of the final result. In the production of a machine, however, the ordering is external, imposed by human art, whereas in nature, the ordering is internal, within the process itself. Thus, commenting on an analogy of Aristotle's, Aquinas stated that nature is a principle of the divine art inherent in things, similar to what would be the case if a human artist were able, by his art, so to endow timbers that they would of themselves be formed into a ship.[7]

We may now draw our final conclusion: that living things exist in order to live the life proper to them. For they were formed by the natural process of organic development in such a way as to be precisely suited to this way of life, and an intelligent agent would not form an organism for a particular way of life without intending that way of life. From this, in turn, we can deduce the conclusion that is immediately relevant to our investigation of human dignity and its consequences—namely, that human beings are by nature ordained to the way of life that is proper to them. What is man's proper way of life? We shall be considering this in chapter 3. All that I wish to insist upon at this point is that human beings are ordained to their proper way of life by their very nature.

## Two Objections

To anyone who might object that I am attacking or denigrating science, I want to state clearly that the argument of this chapter is not meant to deny the accomplishments of modern science, which are enormous, or to suggest that science has not discov-

7. Thomas Aquinas, *Commentary on Aristotle's "Physics,"* Book II, Lectio 14, n. 519, trans. C. I. Litzinger (1964; repr. Notre Dame, Ind.: Dumb Ox, 1993). Aquinas is commenting on lines 199b26–32 of Aristotle's text.

ered important truths about nature. To maintain that there is something more to nature than can be revealed by the scientific method is not to diminish the importance of what that method can reveal and has revealed. Without the patient work of generations of scientists, our knowledge of the natural world would be meager and unreliable.

An objection might also be raised about deriving a concept of life from internal experience. This would seem to be useless for scientific purposes. For internal experience is subjective, and the natural sciences have made great progress by focusing on what is externally observable and rigorously testable. It seems, therefore, that the derivation of a concept of life from internal experience and the introduction of formal and final causes as a consequence of this contributes nothing to the advance of science.

The point of this chapter, however, was not to advance science, but to respond to an objection to the principle of human dignity. For this purpose, I have sought to enrich our understanding of living things beyond what is possible through the scientific method. This is not because I think that human dignity is uncertain until finality in nature has been conclusively proved; rather, I think the opposite—that is, that our moral judgments and our self-understanding make us certain that human dignity is real. Nevertheless, as I noted at the end of chapter 1, a completely satisfactory argument for finality in nature requires a proof based on natural principles, independent of the argument from moral experience. This is the proof I have attempted here.

Furthermore, the internal experience on which my argument relies is not subjective in the sense of being uncertain or idiosyncratic. It is no more than our ordinary experience of being alive. Nor does it in any way diminish the value of scientific research. For whether we think of a living thing as a substantial whole or as a machine, the processes through which it develops and functions can be usefully investigated. Just as the functioning of a machine is analogous to the activities of a living organism, so a process of mechanical self-construction is analogous to natural organic development. In both cases, the later steps follow in sequence from the earlier ones, leading to the end. Hence, the data acquired scientifically under a mechanistic model can easily be interpreted to apply to living things understood as substantial wholes.

Though inadequate for a complete understanding of living things, the mechanistic model is undeniably attractive. For however complicated and intricate a machine may be, the mechanistic model itself is easy to understand. We make machines ourselves, and a reduction of living things to machines brings them down, so to speak, to our level. This accounts in some measure for the machine model's popularity. But if living things are substantial wholes rather than machines, we will have to understand them as proceeding from an art that surpasses the mechanical arts with which we are familiar. In any event, even if a living thing is not *really* a machine, the model can be useful as a kind of simplification. The scientific data that result from research under this model can then be applied to living things understood as substances.

It should be noted, however, that although the mechanistic model is not without value for research that seeks to explore the instrumentalities through which an organism develops and acts, it is not well suited for research that focuses on the organism as a whole. I am thinking of research that investigates the life cycles and characteristic activities of different kinds of living things and their interactions with each other and with the environment. For this purpose, it is better to understand living things as they really are, as substances that exist for the sake of their natural way of life. It will then be meaningful to speak of what is advantageous or harmful for them, the former being what promotes the achievement of their natural ends, the latter what hinders this. For nothing is really advantageous or harmful for a machine, since machines are not themselves entities, but only organized collections of the materials from which they were made. That these materials be assembled into a machine is of no advantage to them, and if the machine is disassembled, they suffer no harm.

## Conclusion

Let me conclude this chapter by summarizing what we have seen thus far and what remains to be considered. In chapter 1, we saw that human beings exist by nature to achieve their own good as an ultimate end. This value or status is human dignity. Without it, we could not unqualifiedly condemn even a heinous crime like murder. But human dignity thus defined implies finality in nature, and, since contemporary science rejects finality, it was necessary to respond to this objection to our thesis.

But what is "our own good," the good to which we are ordained by nature? As stated in chapter 1, happiness would seem to be the name for it, since we believe that if we were perfectly happy, we would not wish for anything more. In this chapter, we learned that a living thing exists by nature for the way of life proper to it according to its species. From this, it follows that we exist by nature for the life proper to us. It seems, then, that happiness must lie in the life proper to human beings as such. If so, what sort of life will this be? To answer this question, we must define happiness and show how it is related to other human goods. This will be the task of chapters 3 and 4. We will then be prepared to study the natural law and its precepts.

CHAPTER 3

# Happiness

What is the good to which we are ordained by nature? Without an answer to this question, we cannot come to a clear understanding of human dignity. Nor can we investigate the precepts of the natural law, which are meant to guide us in attaining our natural good. In this and the following chapter, we will attempt, following Aristotle, to define and clarify this good.

The natural good we are seeking must have the character of an ultimate end; for if everything we desire were desired for the sake of something further, then, as Aristotle argued, our desires would be vain and empty, never arriving at anything desirable simply for itself.[1] It is reasonable to call the ultimate end "happiness," since we think of happiness as that for the sake of which we desire everything else. However, not everyone has the same idea of it, so that the word seems to designate something vague and subjective, as if happiness were whatever happens to bring pleasure to an individual or whatever "works for me." But we are seeking to define it objectively, as the ultimate end to which we are ordained by nature. For this purpose, we will examine the definition of happiness proposed by Aristotle in Book I of the *Nicomachean Ethics*.[2] Since virtue appears in this definition, we shall also consider Aristotle's definition of virtue and summarize his discussion of some particular virtues in chapter 4.

1. *NE* I.2.1094a19–23.
2. For a helpful explanation of Book I of the *Nicomachean Ethics*, see Thomas Aquinas, *Commentary on Aristotle's "Nicomachean Ethics."* For Aquinas's own teaching, see *ST* I-II, q. 1–5, and *SCG* III, caps. 25–40.

33

Aristotle's investigation of the essence of happiness can be clarified sufficiently for our purposes under four headings. He begins by stating and criticizing various opinions about happiness. He then establishes its definition. Following this, he returns to the opinions he had considered earlier and shows how various human goods are related to happiness. Finally, he considers the question of whether happiness is possible in the present life. We will consider each of these topics, basically following Aristotle, but with some elaboration.

## Opinions about Happiness

What is happiness? It is often described as "doing well" or "the good life" or "flourishing." However, these descriptions connote different things to different people, depending on their sense of what is most important in life. Is it pleasure? Is it money? Is it perhaps something more noble, like honor? Each of these has plausibility. Pleasure and honor have the character of something ultimate, since desire comes to rest in pleasure, and our efforts on behalf of noble causes are rewarded with honors. Even money is plausible in a way; for although it is only a means to an end, it seems to be a kind of universal means, a way to whatever we want. According to Aristotle, these three are the most common opinions about what happiness is. However, people also name other goods when they have a special need for them: health, for example, when they are sick or companionship when they are lonely.

While all of these are important for happiness, there are obvious difficulties in supposing that any one of them is happiness itself. Take pleasure, first of all. Since there are many different kinds of pleasure, arising from many different kinds of activities, what kind of pleasure is happiness? The pleasures we know best are the sense pleasures. Is happiness found in these? If so, how do we differ from the beasts? Shall we say that happiness is play and that we work in order to play? For work seems to be onerous and unpleasant and a means to an end, whereas play seems to be pleasant and desirable for itself. On the other hand, fun and "having a good time" are recreation, and it seems frivolous to think that recreation is the purpose of life. Perhaps happiness is to be found in higher pleasures, pleasures that we do not share with the beasts. In any event, it seems clear that a happy life must be a pleasant life, and so perhaps happiness will be pleasure or some kind of pleasure or a mix of pleasures.

Money is no more than a means to an end, and therefore cannot be happiness itself. Nor does it always lead to happiness; everything depends on how it is used. Furthermore, no one thinks that money is the key to happiness when suffering physically from incurable illness or emotionally from unrequited love. There are things that money can't buy. Even so, happiness does not seem to be possible without money, enough at least for the necessities of life.

Honor might seem to be happiness more than pleasure, since we honor those who put duty above pleasure, believing that they have chosen the greater good. But honor consists essentially in the way we are regarded by others, while happiness must be something we possess within ourselves. Furthermore, we honor people because of their virtues—their courage, their honesty, their public-spiritedness, etc.—and so virtue is better than honor. But virtue does not seem to be the ultimate end, either. For since virtues are qualities of character, it is possible to possess them when asleep or in a coma or when being tortured. But how could anyone be happy when he is altogether unaware of it or suffering excruciating pain?

## The Definition of Happiness

### Part 1

So much for the difficulties inherent in the common opinions about happiness. Let us turn now to Aristotle's definition. He begins by showing that happiness must be an ultimate, perfect, and self-sufficient good. These characteristics do not actually define happiness; rather, they state certain requirements that a satisfactory definition must satisfy. After considering these, he turns to the definition itself.

That happiness is unqualifiedly ultimate can be seen by comparing it with ends that are ultimate in particular domains, like medicine and military science. In medicine, the ultimate end is health, and every particular medical intervention is justified by its contribution to health. Similarly, the ultimate end in military science is victory, and all military strategy and tactics are ordered to this. Happiness, however, is the ultimate end of all human activity, not the end in some particular domain.

Happiness is a perfect good—that is, we desire it only for its own sake and not for the sake of anything further. Other goods are less perfect. Some things we desire *only* for the sake of something further; we desire a surgical procedure, for example, only because it will lead to health. Goods of this kind are most imperfect. Better than these, but still imperfect, are goods that we desire both for themselves *and* for the sake of something further. Thus, we desire such things as health, intelligence, honor, and virtue both for themselves and for the contribution that they make to happiness. Happiness, however, we desire only for itself. Thus, it makes sense to say that we want to be healthy in order to be happy, but not that we want to be happy in order to be healthy.

Finally, happiness must be a self-sufficient good—that is, a good from which nothing essential is lacking. For we think that if we were truly happy, we would be satisfied and would not desire anything more. But this is not true of other goods. We would not be completely happy possessing intelligence and virtue, for example, if we lacked health and pleasure.

## Part 2

The derivation of Aristotle's definition of happiness can be shown in five steps. The first step is the principle from which the derivation begins. It is this: *Whatever has an activity proper to itself finds its end or good in that activity.* Thus, if the proper activity of a violinist is to play the violin, then it is precisely in this activity that the violinist *as such* will achieve his good. Similarly, in nature. An apple tree has an activity or way of life proper to it—that is, a life of nourishing itself, growing, and bearing the apples that contain the seeds for its reproduction, and it is precisely in this life that the apple tree attains its good. Similarly, a beaver achieves its good in the life proper to a beaver. It would not find fulfillment in the sort of life that is proper, say, to a hippopotamus.

This principle assumes that living things are substances, not machines. For if a living thing is a substance, then, as we saw in chapter 2, it will be naturally oriented toward the way of life proper to it according to the kind of thing that it is. This will be its natural good. But a machine is not oriented toward its characteristic function by nature; it functions as it does by mechanical necessity. If we speak of the end or purpose of a machine, as we do with man-made machines, we are thinking of the purpose of the designer. It is not as if the machine were itself acting for an end, as a living substance does.

The second step applies the principle just discussed to human beings. If everything that has an activity proper to itself finds its good in that activity, and if there is an activity proper to human beings as such, then the human good will be found in that activity.

Do we have a proper activity? Aristotle replies that if we have activities proper to us insofar as we are carpenters and shoemakers, it would be strange if we had no activity proper to us precisely as human beings. Moreover, if our eyes, ears, hands, feet, etc., all have proper activities for which they are naturally adapted, surely we ourselves, as whole organisms, must have a proper activity for which we are naturally adapted. Otherwise, a human being would be a kind of functionless collection of functioning parts. It seems then that there must be an activity or way of life that is proper to us precisely as human beings.

The third step considers what this activity must be. It cannot be nutrition, growth, and reproduction, because these activities are common to all living things. Nor can it be found in external or internal sense perception and emotion, since we share these with the animals. There remains only rational activity, which we alone possess—that is, if we understand reason in its proper sense as the capacity to understand universal concepts, to derive their logical consequences, and to express all this in speech. For such acts are essentially superior to what is called "reasoning" in animals. It follows that the human good is found in the life of reason. This does not mean just abstract thinking, but includes our emotional life and external actions as well, insofar as these are ordered by reason, as we shall see in chapter 4.

If the life of reason is our natural end, it must be a life where reason is in control, ruling our desires, not ruled by them. I say this because reason can be at the service of desires that do not themselves have rational justification, as when lust moves reason to plan a seduction or greed to plan a robbery. Actions based on such plans may be very rational, considered in relation to the desires that motivated them, but they are not rational without qualification. Similarly, pride or ruthless ambition could move reason to pursue a plan of life inconsistent with a pure or unbiased desire to live in accord with reason. Or a desire to be free of any superior law or authority could lead reason to embrace a way of thinking and acting that rejects any restraint that is not self-imposed. A life in which reason is fully in control must be a life free from all subversive motivations.

Furthermore, the life of reason, as understood here, is not an activity of technical reason—that is, reason ordered to the perfection of a product, like a building or a painting, or to the perfection of a performance, as in playing a musical instrument, acting in a play, or making a speech. Rather, it lies in the actions by which a human being is perfected precisely insofar as he is a human being. Only in this way can the life of reason be man's natural end. Actions that are rationally appropriate in this sense are actions that are suited, in general, to man's nature as a rational animal and, in particular, to his talents and vocation and to the circumstances of his life. Thus understood, the life of reason is the essence of human happiness.

One might wonder whether human happiness lies essentially in one way of life or whether it can be found in many different ways of life. If human nature is one, it might seem that all human beings will find happiness in the same way, just as we see for each species of animal. There is a definite way of life proper to the beaver, a life in which all beavers find their natural fulfillment, and the same is true for the hippopotamus and for all other species. But, in fact, human beings find fulfillment in many different ways of life. The lives of farmers and politicians and scholars, for example, though not without common elements, are very different. Indeed, we should expect this diversity, since human beings are guided by reason, not by animal instinct. But if human happiness is found in many different ways of life, how can it have a single definition?

The answer to this puzzle is not difficult, if we consider that happiness lies essentially in rationally appropriate actions. The mother feeding her child, the laborer working or taking his rest, the scientist devising an experiment—they are doing many different things, and yet, in a way, they are all doing the same thing. For let us assume that each of them is doing what he or she should be doing at that time. Each of them, therefore, is acting in the way that is rationally appropriate. But rationally appropriate actions are the actions proper to human beings as such. Consequently, though their occupations are many, the ultimate end they are seeking is one. A sign of this is the fact that each of them will approve what the others are doing. Each one can say: that is what I would do if I were in his or her situation.

This does not mean that happiness is to be found equally in all ways of life, for some ways of life are objectively better than others. The life of a conscientious statesman, focused immediately on the common good of the political community, is superior to the life of a common citizen, even one who faithfully carries out all of his civic duties. Aristotle thought that the happiness to be found in the contemplative life exceeds the happiness to be found in the active life, the life of practical action. This is a question we will consider later. For the present, it suffices to note that a way of life that is better absolutely speaking may not be better for every person, at least not at a particular time, since not everyone has the same talents and responsibilities.

The fourth step. If the rational life is the life proper to a human being as such, what will be the life proper to a *good* human being? For the rational life can be lived well or badly, and happiness will surely consist in living the life proper to a human being well. To clarify this, let us return to the violinist. If the work proper to a violinist is to play the violin, the work proper to a good violinist will be to play it well, and the work proper to a bad violinist will be to play it badly. To play the violin well, the violinist must acquire the excellence or perfection that is proper to a violinist as such, the art of playing the violin. Therefore, a violinist can achieve his end only when perfected by this art.

The same reasoning must be applied to the activity proper to a human being. If we are to live the rational life well, we must acquire the qualities that constitute human excellence, the qualities by which we become good precisely as human beings. These are the virtues. For it is through qualities like courage and temperance and justice that we become good human beings who live the life of reason well. On the other hand, through vices like cowardice, intemperance, and injustice, we become bad human beings who live the life of reason badly. We may conclude, then, that happiness is found in a life of reason perfected by virtue.

As a fifth step, Aristotle adds that the life of virtue must endure for a complete lifetime. For happiness would be imperfect if it were not lasting. Just as a few days of good weather are not enough for a good summer, so a brief period of living virtuously is not enough for a good life. We must persevere in virtuous activity until the end of life.

Happiness, therefore, consists essentially in *the life of reason, perfected by virtue, and enduring for a complete lifetime.*

Note that this definition is in accord with how happiness is commonly described, as "the good life" or "doing well" or "flourishing." But it clarifies such expressions by specifying what living a good life or flourishing means for a human being, as distinguished from what it would mean for a beaver or a hippopotamus.

## Happiness and Other Human Goods

Does Aristotle's definition capture the essence of happiness? If so, it should be able to explain why such goods as virtue, pleasure, health, honor, and money are thought to be necessary for happiness and how each of them is important and valuable.

That the virtues are necessary for happiness is clear from the definition. It is also clear that happiness does not lie in the possession of the virtues but in the use of them. Aristotle clarified this with an analogy. In the Olympic Games, the crown of victory goes not to the strongest or best-looking athletes, but to those who win in the competition. In the same way, happiness, the crown of life, goes not to those who possess excellent qualities but to those who make excellent use of them.

Is the life of virtue a pleasant life? This is a question of the greatest importance, since we all think that a happy life must not only be enjoyable, but most enjoyable, more than any other way of life. Experience, of course, is the best proof of the pleasure to be found in the virtuous life. We must, as it were, *taste* the virtuous life to fully appreciate its goodness. Nevertheless, we can be convinced of its attractiveness by observing the behavior of virtuous people. For we see that those whose virtue is deeply rooted refuse to abandon their noble way of life even under the severest trials. Nothing would pain them more than to act dishonorably.

Why is the virtuous life enjoyable? Part of the answer lies in the nature of virtue as an acquired habit. By repeatedly acting as a virtuous person would act, we gradually habituate ourselves to acting this way. We become virtuous persons and enjoy living virtuously. For we enjoy activities that are natural to us, and habit is a kind of second nature. This shows again why virtues are necessary for happiness. For it is through the virtues that the actions that are best and most desirable in themselves become connatural and pleasing to us.

However, this line of argument applies also in some measure to the life of vice. For those who acquire bad habits find wicked actions congenial and, in a way, connatural. Unjust people, for example, enjoy taking advantage of others, and intemperate people enjoy illicit pleasures. Nevertheless, the pleasure of virtuous actions is greater, since such actions are pleasant in themselves as well as by habit. For they are rationally appropriate and therefore suited to our nature as rational beings. Wicked actions, on the other hand, are contrary to reason, and therefore cannot *of themselves* please a rational being. The life of vice, therefore, is not pleasant by nature, but only by habit.

A sign that virtuous actions are natural to us is the fact that they are in harmony with each other. Courageous actions, for example, are not opposed to just or generous or temperate actions, because all of these actions aim fundamentally at one and the same thing: to do what is rationally appropriate in every situation. Wicked actions, on the other hand, are not in harmony, but are often opposed to each other. Thus, cowardly actions are opposed to foolhardy ones, and stingy actions to prodigal ones. For wicked actions spring from irrational motivations and judgments that lack any unifying principle. We may conclude that the life of virtue is pleasant by nature as well as by habit and therefore that it is more enjoyable than the life of vice.

One might object that virtuous actions are not always in harmony with each other. For example, if lying is contrary to the virtue of truthfulness, and if lying to avoid giving pain to someone can sometimes be an act of the virtue of mercy, then it seems that mercy is sometimes opposed to truthfulness. However, if lying is *always* opposed to the virtue of truthfulness, it cannot be an act of any virtue, since no virtue does what is evil in order to bring about a good result. On the other hand, if lying is *not always* opposed to the virtue of truthfulness, then perhaps lying to avoid giving pain could sometimes be an act of the virtue of mercy. I shall not attempt to respond to the question of whether lying is always wrong, since this would require a detailed discussion of truthfulness and the vices opposed to it.[3] What I want to emphasize here is that virtuous actions are always in accord with reason because this is what makes them virtuous. Reason determines what is virtuous; virtue does not determine what is reasonable. This is why the acts of different virtues are necessarily in harmony.

If, therefore, we believe that a more enjoyable life is a happier life, and that the most enjoyable life is the happiest of all, then happiness will clearly be found in the life of virtue. But should we say that happiness is the virtuous life itself or the pleasure of the virtuous life? It might seem to be pleasure, since pleasure brings a kind of fulfillment or completeness to virtuous actions. But since pleasure is the satisfaction we take in a good possessed, the pleasure we experience in virtuous actions will be an effect of the goodness of these actions. Therefore, the essence of happiness will lie in the virtuous life itself, not in the pleasure that naturally results from it.

The value of the other goods we seek in life can be fully understood only through their relationship to the life of virtue. Thus, bodily goods, like life, health, strength, and energy, are necessary instrumentally for carrying out virtuous activities. This does not mean that those who suffer from ill health or who lack strength and energy cannot act virtuously; on the contrary, virtue is of-

3. Aquinas teaches that lying is intrinsically wrong; see especially *ST* II-II, q. 110, a. 3. However, he does allow the use of ambushes in war, since this is not lying to the enemy but concealing what one intends to do; see *ST* II-II, q. 40, a. 3.

ten revealed with special clarity in the way such persons make the best use of sickness and handicaps. Nevertheless, virtuous persons desire to possess these bodily goods, not only because of their intrinsic worth, but also and above all because without them many good actions would be very difficult or even impossible to perform. Furthermore, just as good health and great energy enable good people to do excellent things, so they enable wicked people to do terrible things. They make the life of the good better and the life of the wicked worse. Bodily goods find their ultimate value, therefore, as instruments of the life of virtue.

What is true of bodily goods is true also of external goods like wealth and power. These are valuable as instruments of virtuous actions, but harmful as instruments of wicked ones. They enable good people to do great good and wicked people to do great evil. Although the value of these goods can be assessed abstractly according as they are more or less well adapted to possible uses, their value in any particular situation depends on how they are *actually* going to be used, whether for good or for evil. External goods like friends and honor are not instruments of virtuous actions, but are nevertheless related essentially to the virtuous life. For honor is the reward of virtuous actions, and true friendships, as we shall see, are based on virtue.

Finally, we might note that bodily and external goods are appropriate concomitants of the virtuous life. Aristotle mentions good birth, good children, good friends, personal beauty, and, more generally, external prosperity and good fortune.[4] For these make a person's life more agreeable and more beautiful in the eyes of others. These and similar goods are clearly related to the life of virtue. For we think it fitting that virtuous persons should be good-looking and prosperous, their personal beauty and the beauty of their external circumstances reflecting the interior beauty of their character, whereas it seems utterly unfitting that wicked persons, who are inwardly ugly, should appear outwardly as other

4. *NE* I.8.1099b1–8.

than what they are. Of course, often this does not happen, and so we think that beauty is deceptive and that success and prosperity are often undeserved.

## The Possibility of Happiness in the Present Life

Aristotle's definition seems to meet the three conditions that a satisfactory definition of happiness must satisfy: that it be an ultimate, perfect, and self-sufficient good. For in virtuous activities we achieve the human good itself, which is more ultimate than the goods that are ultimate in particular domains, like health in medicine or victory in military science. Furthermore, as we saw in the preceding discussion, only the life of virtue is desirable without qualification for its own sake. For the other goods of human life, even those that are desirable in themselves, find their ultimate value in relation to the life of virtue. Finally, by adding the phrase "for a complete lifetime," Aristotle satisfies to some extent the third condition, that happiness should be self-sufficient. For a happiness that lasts for a complete lifetime suffices at least for this life.

Nevertheless, the happiness possible in the present life does not seem to fully satisfy the requirement of self-sufficiency. Solon, one of the seven sages of ancient Greece, observed that a man may be prosperous and happy during most of his life, and then suffer severe misfortunes and die in misery. Such, for example, was the fate of Priam, the king of the Trojans. From examples like this, he concluded that no man should be called happy until he is dead. For only then will we be able to judge whether or not his happiness endured for a complete lifetime.

Aristotle considered Solon's objection and in effect conceded that it would be reasonable if happiness were to be judged primarily on the basis of bodily and external goods. For these goods are easily affected by good and bad fortune. But if happiness consists essentially in virtuous actions, then Solon's conclusion is too extreme. This is because the goods of the soul, goods like the arts and sciences and virtues, are not easily affected by external causes. Furthermore, among the goods of the soul, virtues are the most enduring. For we always have occasion to practice the virtues, so that they are not lost by disuse, whereas we do not always have occasion to make use of particular arts and sciences.

Nevertheless, since bodily and external goods are required instrumentally for virtuous actions and since the loss of them can cause pain and suffering, happiness will be affected by changes of fortune. How much it is affected will depend on whether the misfortunes are great or small, many or few. Many misfortunes, if they are small, or even great misfortunes, if they are few, can be tolerated by a person of strong virtue, but many great misfortunes, one after another, as in the case of Job, will certainly diminish happiness significantly. Nevertheless, even here, it will not be altogether lost, since the virtuous person knows how to make the best use of the circumstances, favorable or unfavorable, in which he finds himself, just as a good shoemaker makes the best use of whatever materials are available and a good general makes the best use of whatever forces are at his disposal.

The virtuous person will lose his happiness altogether only if he begins to act dishonorably. But this is not likely to happen if he has been living virtuously for a long time, so that his virtue is deeply rooted. We may therefore call such a person happy, even before we see how his life will end. For we can be reasonably confident, though not absolutely certain, that the virtuous person will continue to live as he has been living, that he will be able to withstand even serious reverses should they occur, and that he will die honorably.

Although Aristotle's reply is perhaps sufficient as an answer to Solon's objection, it is nevertheless clear that the happiness possible in the present life is far from perfect. It is always in danger of being diminished by misfortunes, and even the best life must finally come to an end in death. And since the virtuous person is keen to do his duty, his life can be filled with toil and hardship, much of it due to the folly of others and to evils in society beyond his power to remedy. No doubt these difficulties can be met virtuously, and there will be satisfaction in that, but to be endlessly involved in them is onerous and often disappointing. The happiness of the contemplative life, which Aristotle thought superior to that of the active life, is free from many of these evils. But even the contemplative life, at least so far as it is possible in the present life, falls far short of what we desire, as we shall see in chapter 10. Furthermore, happiness is meant not just for the few but for everyone. Yet how many grow up without enough of the basic necessities of life and without the discipline and moral formation that could help them achieve the life of virtue!

It is clear that Aristotle recognized the imperfection of human happiness in the present life. For in concluding his discussion of Solon's objection, he stated that those who are happy are happy *as human beings*—that is, in the measure possible for human beings.[5] We will return to the question of perfect happiness in chapter 10, when discussing the contemplative life, and again, briefly, in a concluding comment in chapter 12.

5. *NE* I.10.1101a18–22.

# CHAPTER 4

# Virtue

If happiness consists in the life of reason perfected by virtue, we shall be able to gain a clearer understanding of it by investigating what virtue is and by briefly considering some important virtues. This will complete our reflections on happiness, the end to which the natural law is ordained. In chapter 5, we will begin our consideration of the natural law itself.

In this chapter, we will first examine Aristotle's definition of virtue in Book II of the *Nicomachean Ethics*. Then, after distinguishing between the moral and intellectual virtues, I will summarize his discussion of some fundamental moral virtues. This will be followed by a consideration of his theory of friendship. In conclusion, I will offer some thoughts on the relationship between virtue ethics and natural law ethics.

## What Is Virtue?

From the definition of happiness, we know that virtue is a praiseworthy quality or excellence that makes us good persons and enables us to live the life of reason well. But what is the essence of virtue? Aristotle's answer to this question may be stated succinctly as follows: *Virtue is a habit of making choices according to a mean in relation to us as determined by right reason.*[1]

---

1. *NE* II.6.1107a1–5. Aristotle states that the mean of virtue is to be determined as a man of practical wisdom would determine it. Here, I use "right reason" to express this element of the definition.

Since we cannot be good persons until the tendency to act rationally is deeply rooted and lasting, virtue must be a habit. For a habit is a firmly established disposition to act in a certain way. Experience shows that we acquire good habits by repeatedly acting as we should, until good actions become second nature and enjoyable. It is the mark of a good person that he enjoys living virtuously.

Furthermore, virtue must be a habit "of making choices"—that is, a habit of actually choosing to act appropriately in every situation. We are good persons not because we know how we should act, but because we act as we should. In this, virtue differs from art. For someone might be a great artist, having acquired the skill to create great works of art, and yet refuse to use this skill at a time when he should use it. But a virtuous person always acts when he should.

Since vices are also habits of making choices, we must determine what distinguishes virtue from vice. The difference becomes evident when we consider that in any situation there are many ways to go wrong, either by going too far or by not going far enough. The right way, therefore, will be found in a mean between opposite extremes. Courage and temperance illustrate this clearly. If we run away from every danger we become cowardly, and if we rush indiscriminately into danger we become rash or foolhardy. We become courageous, therefore, by facing the dangers that we ought to face and by facing them at the right time, in the right way, etc., and by avoiding the dangers that we ought to avoid. Similarly, by yielding to every sensual temptation we become self-indulgent or intemperate, and by going to the opposite extreme we become, as it were, insensitive to pleasure. We become temperate, therefore, by seeking appropriate sensual pleasures under appropriate circumstances.

Aristotle describes the mean of virtue as a mean *in relation to us* because what is neither too much nor too little is not the same for everyone. It is like shoe size: the correct size is what is neither too large nor too small in relation to one's foot. Thus, an action that might be courageous for someone who is strong and agile would be rash for someone who is handicapped or weak, and a generous gift from a poor person would be a stingy gift from a rich one. Similarly, an action that would be appropriate for one person, given his particular responsibilities, would not be appropriate for another person whose responsibilities were different.

We tend to think of the mean of virtue as a quantitative mean —that is, as an amount lying between too much and none at all. Thus, we think that we should not eat too much food or drink too much wine, but rather a moderate amount. But sometimes even a moderate amount may be too much. Consider, for example, total abstinence from alcoholic beverages. One might think that this is going too far, and that the "golden mean" would be a certain amount of such beverages, varying according to the capacity of different persons, but something more than none at all, which seems to be an extreme. But it would not be an extreme for a recovering alcoholic; for him, total abstinence is neither too much nor too little. Similarly, total and permanent abstinence from sexual activity is neither too much nor too little for someone who wishes to be free from the obligations of marriage and family in order to dedicate his life more fully to a higher good, as in the case of clerical celibacy. The mean of virtue, therefore, is essentially a *mean of reason*, not a quantitative mean.

Can there be a virtuous mean for every action and every feeling? According to Aristotle, there are some actions and feelings that are evil by their very nature, and for these there is no virtuous mean. Murder, adultery, and theft are actions of this sort. It is impossible, for example, to murder the right person, at the right time, in the right way, for the right reason etc., since murder is always wrong. The same is true with respect to feelings like envy, shamelessness, and spite.[2] This raises, of course, the much-discussed question of what actions, if any, are intrinsically evil—that is, evil at all times and under all circumstances. Responses to this question will emerge later in our discussion of the precepts of the natural law.

Finally, the mean of virtue must be *determined by right reason*.

2. *NE* II.6.1107a9–25.

This is obvious, if virtue is to perfect us in living the life of reason well. But how is right reason determined? Aristotle tells us that it must be determined in the way that a person of practical wisdom, a prudent person, would determine it. For prudence is the virtue that applies the appropriate moral principles to each particular situation, taking account of all the relevant circumstances. As appears from our previous reflections, and as we shall see more clearly in the following chapters, the first principles of prudential reasoning are the precepts of the natural law.

## Moral and Intellectual Virtues

The moral virtues are habits like courage, temperance, and justice; the intellectual virtues are habits like prudence, art, science, and wisdom. Both kinds of virtues are properly human perfections, but they differ in that they perfect different faculties. The intellectual virtues perfect reason itself, while the moral virtues perfect the emotional powers and the will. Moreover, they perfect us in different ways, because by the moral virtues we become good in an unqualified sense, we become good persons, whereas by the intellectual virtues we become good only in certain qualified ways— that is, we become good artists or good scientists or good philosophers. Prudence, although it is essentially an intellectual virtue, is numbered also among the moral virtues, because it guides the acts of these virtues, as we shall see.

From this it is clear that Aristotle's definition of virtue refers to the moral virtues, not the intellectual virtues. For the idea of virtue is realized most perfectly in the virtues by which we become good persons, and these are the moral virtues. They perfect us in our practical activities, in what is called the "active life." The contemplative life, however, is perfected not by the moral virtues but by the intellectual virtues of science and philosophical wisdom, as we shall see in chapter 10. Until then, we shall be concerned only with the active life and the moral virtues.

## The Moral Virtues Discussed by Aristotle

Following Aristotle, we shall first consider the moral virtues concerned with the emotions, since these are best known to us and illustrate the mean of virtue most clearly. These are the virtues of self-control, the virtues by which we gain control of our emotions, and the social virtues, the virtues by which we behave well in our encounters with others. After these virtues we will consider justice, which is not in the emotional powers but in the will, and finally prudence, the intellectual virtue that guides the acts of the moral virtues.[3]

Our consideration of the moral virtues will be very brief, a kind of sketch of those that Aristotle discussed in detail in the *Nicomachean Ethics* and that Aquinas discussed, in even greater detail, together with many other virtues, in the *Summa Theologiae*.[4] Our concern here is to clarify the nature of moral virtue through some examples to complete our understanding of the definition of happiness. This is sufficient for the purpose of this book, which is not concerned with the virtues per se.

## The Virtues of Self-Control

The most fundamental virtues of self-control are courage and temperance—above all, courage, since it requires the greatest self-control to stand firm in the face of terrible dangers. Courage seeks a mean between the utter fearlessness and overconfidence that lead to rash acts and the excessive fearfulness and lack of confidence that lead to cowardly ones. Temperance, through its various species, seeks the mean in relation to the sensual desires for food, drink, and sex. Thus, courage and temperance concern the emotions that are most intimately connected with life and therefore

---

3. In *ST* I-II, q. 60, a. 5, Aquinas explains how the moral virtues discussed by Aristotle differ essentially from each other.

4. *NE* III–V. Aquinas discusses the virtues in detail in *ST* II-II.

most difficult to control: courage with what endangers life and temperance with what preserves it for the individual and for the species. This is why courage and temperance are included among the four cardinal virtues, together with justice and prudence.

After courage and temperance, Aristotle discusses two virtues concerned with money and things of monetary value. The first of these, liberality or generosity, is a mean between prodigality, which wastes money, and stinginess, which clings to it excessively, almost as if it were life itself. The second virtue is magnificence, which concerns the special difficulty involved in spending very large sums of money for a suitable purpose in an appropriate way. Obviously, one who hopes to create a magnificent effect can fail either by not spending enough, producing a shabby result, or by spending too much, making a vulgar display of his wealth.

In a somewhat parallel way, there are two virtues concerned with honor: one concerned with great honors and the other with ordinary honors. The first may be called "magnanimity"; the second lacks a special name. The magnanimous person has the talents and opportunity to do great things and exerts himself to do them. He thus achieves a mean between the presumptuousness or vanity of the person who seeks great honors of which he is unworthy and the small-mindedness of the person who might have done great things, but holds back, thinking himself unworthy. The other virtue, concerned with ordinary honors, can be practiced by anyone who aspires to excellence within his particular vocation, however humble.

Finally, there is gentleness, the virtue of good-tempered or even-tempered people who manage anger well. There are many names for those who exceed the mean, since bad temper, like stinginess, is a common vice and takes many forms. Some bad-tempered people are irascible, others hot-tempered or quick-tempered, others sullen or bitter, yet others vengeful or wrathful. At the other extreme are those whom we think of as spineless or spiritless, since they feel little or no anger even when they should.

## The Social Virtues

The virtues considered thus far enable us to get control of ourselves, so that our emotions are no longer a hindrance but rather a help to acting rationally. But there are also moral virtues by which we are perfected in our relations with others. Under this heading, Aristotle first discusses three social virtues that, like the virtues of self-control, are concerned primarily with our feelings, but that also have something in common with justice, inasmuch as they dispose us to render to others what is due to them in social encounters. These social virtues are concerned with what is *morally* due to others, whereas justice, as we shall see, is concerned with what is *legally* due.

The three social virtues are friendliness, truthfulness, and wittiness. The friendly person seeks to make social encounters pleasant—but not at any price. He aims at a mean between obsequiousness and flattery, on the one hand, and cantankerousness and grouchiness, on the other. The truthful person is straightforward, representing himself and his thoughts as they are. Of course, he does not reveal all of himself or all of his thoughts—only what is appropriate to the situation. But what he does reveal is true. The excess is boastfulness and exaggeration, which go beyond the truth, and the deficiency is self-deprecation and understatement. The witty person observes good taste in joking and laughter, while the buffoon doesn't seem to know what is appropriate or when to stop, and the boor takes offense even at good-natured kidding. As already noted, these three virtues concern what is morally due to others, the kind of social behavior that our fellow human beings can reasonably expect of us. But such behavior is not legally due. We cannot be prosecuted for exaggerating our accomplishments, for example, unless someone is harmed by relying on what we said.

## Justice

Justice is the virtue by which we render to others what is due to them by law—by human law or by natural law or by divine law. What is legally due is called a "right." It follows that our actions are called just not because they demonstrate our emotional self-control or our social graces, but because they correspond appropriately to what others have a right to demand of us. Justice, therefore, perfects the will, not the emotional faculties. The mean of justice is said to be an objective mean because it is measured by a definite external standard. We see this in the payment of a monetary debt, where what is neither too much nor too little for the debtor to pay is precisely the amount owed. In this respect the mean of justice differs, for example, from the mean of generosity, where the appropriate amount to give depends on the personal circumstances of the giver. But the amount the debtor should repay is not affected by personal circumstances; it depends only on the size of the debt.

A question might be raised here about Aristotle's definition of moral virtue. According to that definition, the mean of virtue is a mean in relation to us. But this would seem to exclude justice, which, as we have just seen, observes an objective mean, not determined by personal circumstances. Yet justice is clearly a moral virtue. Aristotle's definition of virtue must therefore be modified so as to extend beyond the virtues concerned with the emotions. We should say then that all the moral virtues are concerned with a mean between excess and deficiency, a mean of reason, not a quantitative mean. But the mean of reason is not always determined in the same way. In justice, the mean is determined objectively by the rights of others, whereas in the other moral virtues, it can vary subjectively, according to personal circumstances.[5]

Although there are forms of justice proper to the relationships within the family, justice primarily regards relationships in the po-

5. For a further discussion of this point, see *ST* I-II, q. 60, a. 2 and q. 64, a. 2.

litical community. According to Aristotle, the ordering of such a community requires three kinds of justice.[6] The first is general or legal justice, the virtue by which public authority directs the acts of the citizens to the common good and by which the citizens, in their turn, serve the common good by respecting the law and contributing the goods and services that the authorities require of them. The other two are forms of particular justice, which seeks equality in what is rendered to private citizens and associations. The first of these, called "distributive justice," seeks proportional equality in the distribution of the benefits and burdens of community life—taxes, military service, public offices and honors, expenditures for public welfare, etc.—so that each citizen or association receives its appropriate share. Thus, we think that wealthy people should pay more taxes than people of moderate income and that the highest military honors should go to the soldiers who performed best in combat. The other form of particular justice, called "commutative justice," seeks simple equality in exchanges between private citizens and associations, as in buying and selling.

How are these three forms of justice related to what today is called "social justice"? Rather than as a new form of justice, I think social justice is best understood as a new emphasis on the common good and on a full recognition of the natural rights and obligations that follow from it. As John XXIII described it, the common good comprises *all those conditions of social living whereby individuals are enabled to achieve their perfection.*[7] As we shall see in chapter 11, this gives rise to an understanding of human rights that goes well beyond an emphasis on the protection of individual persons and property and the enforcement of private contracts. Social justice, therefore, should be thought of as a development and clarification of our understanding of justice and as a corrective to excessive individualism.

6. *NE* V.1–4.

7. John XXIII, *Pacem in Terris*, Encyclical Letter (April 11, 1963), no. 58. The same definition is found in his *Mater et Magistra*, Encyclical Letter (May 15, 1961), no. 65, and in Vatican Council II, *Gaudium et Spes* (December 7, 1965), no. 26.

To conclude this brief note on justice, I would like to emphasize its importance for revealing the dignity of the human person. We are most aware of our dignity when it is violated, and it is violated most obviously by injustice. For when I suffer injustice, I am treated as if I were without rights, as if I existed simply to be used by others for their advantage. But this is intolerable. That is why, when deriving the principle of human dignity in chapter 1, I used as an example an obvious and fundamental violation of justice, a case of murder.

## Prudence

We turn finally to the virtue of prudence, which I shall understand here as true practical wisdom, not simply as cleverness in getting what we want and avoiding unpleasant consequences. For true practical wisdom must be directed to true happiness. Prudence, therefore, is concerned with how to achieve the good of virtue in all of our actions. There are many forms of prudence, since it is one thing to be prudent in one's personal affairs and another thing to be prudent in managing the affairs of a family or of a political community. But we will be concerned here only with the relationship between prudence and the moral virtues in general.

The nature of prudence can be grasped most clearly if we contrast it with art, since art is also concerned with practical action. An art enables us to produce a good product or to put on a good performance, but it does not guarantee that we will choose to do this. A skilled carpenter, for example, might deliberately do shoddy work or refuse to work at all. But prudence always commands us to act appropriately and at the right time. This is because it is rooted in the moral virtues, the virtues through which we are habitually inclined toward the true human good.

Without prudence, the moral virtues would be blind. For although they orient us toward the true human good *as an end*, they show us nothing about the *means* to the end. These means must be determined in each situation through rational deliberation, followed by a judgment about what to do and the actual doing of it. This is the function of prudence, understood here as including good deliberation and good judgment. Prudence does not determine the means to the human good in general—this is the task of moral philosophy—but rather the means to the human good as we hope to achieve it by action in these circumstances here and now. This shows even more clearly why prudence is impossible without the moral virtues. For in concrete situations we deliberate about how to obtain what we actually want, and it is through the moral virtues that we are habituated to want what is right. Because of their mutual dependence, prudence and the moral virtues must develop together.

Since it determines the means to happiness, the ultimate end, prudence is a kind of wisdom. People who give us good advice about particular human goods, like how to succeed in business or politics, may be shrewd and helpful, but only those who know the way to happiness are thought to be truly wise. Nevertheless, prudence is not wisdom in an unqualified sense, for it is not, absolutely speaking, the highest form of knowledge attainable by natural reason. This honor belongs to philosophical wisdom, through which we come to know what reason can discover about the first cause or causes of all reality. This is the wisdom of the contemplative life. Prudence, therefore, is wisdom only in a qualified sense; it is *practical* wisdom.

## Friendship

After discussing the moral virtues, Aristotle considered friendship, which, he said, is either a virtue or involves virtue.[8] It is clear that he regarded it as of the greatest importance, since he devoted two books of the *Nicomachean Ethics* to it and treated many as-

8. *NE* VIII.1.1155a1–3.

pects of it in detail. Inasmuch as acting virtuously toward one's friends out of love surpasses all other motivations, friendship seems to be a kind of fulfillment of the virtuous life. Moreover, it seems to be more important for the community even than justice. For when we are united with our fellow citizens in friendship, we are disposed to help them and not to injure them, but the opposite is the case when we hate and distrust them.[9]

Aristotle distinguished three kinds of friendship, based, respectively, on utility, on pleasure, and on virtue. Friendships of utility are many, since people can be useful to each other in many ways. Employees, for example, are useful to employers by the work they do, and employers are useful to employees by the wages they pay. Similarly, physicians, lawyers, mechanics, and others who provide services are useful to their clients or customers and vice versa. So long as the utility is mutual, these friendships endure, but not beyond this, for we love this kind of friend for what he can do for us. Friendships based on pleasure, the friendships of people who enjoy each other's wit and conversation or who like the same activities and entertainments or who find each other sexually attractive, are not enduring either. For as our tastes and interests change, so the things that please us change, and, as a consequence, friendships based only on pleasure also change. Thus, neither utility nor pleasure can give rise to friendships that are true and lasting.

To be true and lasting, a friendship must be rooted in virtue. For it is through the virtues that someone becomes a good person and therefore lovable for what he is, and not for superficial reasons. Moreover, such friendships are also useful and pleasant, and preeminently so. For virtuous persons are always helpful to each other, in good times and bad, and they always enjoy each other's company, since they take pleasure in the same excellent and praiseworthy activities. Virtuous friendships are therefore both true and lasting: true, because virtuous friends genuinely

9. *NE* VIII.1.1155a23–28.

love each other as persons, and lasting, because virtues are lasting.[10] This is why Aristotle discussed friendship only after he had discussed happiness and virtue.

Can we be a true friend of a person who is not virtuous? Apart from what usefulness or pleasure such a person might bring, it would seem that there is nothing to love in him or even that there is something to hate, since vices are hateful. Yet it seems inhumane not to love our fellow human beings, who, like ourselves, exist to achieve the true human good as their ultimate end. We should therefore wish what is truly good for all human beings and wish it *for their sake*, since this is to love them as human beings should be loved.[11] It also means that if we see someone who lacks the bodily or external goods necessary for human life or who seems to have lost the way to true happiness, we ought to express our love in appropriate practical action. Even if we are not united with someone in a friendship based on virtue, we can still act toward him as a true friend would act. As Aristotle notes, true friends neither go wrong themselves nor let their friends go wrong.[12]

These reflections bring us close to the second of the two great love commandments: that we should love our neighbor as ourselves. Of course, there are practical limits to what we can do for others, and we are certainly more obligated to help our close friends and relatives than to help strangers. But we should love every human being just because he is a human being meant for happiness, even if there is little else to love in him. This is why we praise those who are merciful, for they are moved to action precisely by a concern for the good things their fellow human beings are lacking. Furthermore, as Aristotle explains, we naturally love ourselves most of all,[13] and so the way we love others will reflect the way we love ourselves. Hence, if we love ourselves

10. *NE* VIII.3.
11. *NE* VIII.2.1155b31 and 7.1159a9–10.
12. *NE* VIII.8.1159b5–7.
13. *NE* IX.4.

rightly, seeking true happiness, we will also love others rightly. This would seem to capture the spirit of the commandment to love our neighbor as ourselves.

What about the first love commandment: that we should love God above all things? Aristotle does not consider this commandment per se, since his main concern in the *Nicomachean Ethics* is with friendship among human beings sharing a common life, especially in the political community. But he does say some things that are relevant. When discussing friendships between persons of unequal status, he remarks that we do not expect to be friends with the gods because of their exceeding superiority in all good things, just as ordinary people do not expect to be friends with kings or with those who are far wiser and better than they are. This might seem to exclude the possibility of friendship with God.[14]

In another place, however, Aristotle does admit a kind of friendship with the gods. For friendship, he says, does not always demand an equal return for the benefits we have received, but only what is possible. Therefore, since it is impossible for us to repay our parents or the gods for the great benefits we have received from them, friendship with them does not require this, but only that we do what we can, and especially that we give them due honor.[15] Furthermore, if we look beyond the gods (the spiritual substances we call "angels") to the supreme God, the first cause of all that is good, it becomes clear that we ought to love God most of all. For we ought to love our benefactors in proportion to what they have given us.[16] However, this would be a distant sort of relationship with God, not an intimate friendship. A truly intimate friendship with God is beyond our natural powers and is possible only through God's invitation and supernatural grace. But even on the natural level, a kind of friendship or at least a loving relationship with God would seem to be possible.

14. *NE* VIII.7.1158b33–59a3.
15. *NE* 12.1162a4–5, and 14.1163b13–18.
16. *NE* 7.1158b24–29.

I will say something further about the love commandments in chapter 5, following Aquinas's explanation of the primacy of these commandments in his discussion of the Ten Commandments.

## Beyond the Nicomachean Ethics

Let me conclude these notes on the virtues with a comment on the *Nicomachean Ethics* as a whole. Important as this work is for our understanding of happiness, it is far from complete. Many virtues are not discussed, including, in particular, the virtues by which man is related to God. This is explained, at least in part, by Aristotle's special focus. He was writing a kind of introduction to his *Politics* and chose to emphasize the virtues by which individuals are well disposed to live together in a political community. But if Aristotle does not take us as far as we would like to go, he has the great merit of showing us where to begin and of putting us on the right track. This, I believe, is the reason for the enduring relevance of the *Nicomachean Ethics*.

Theologians speak of supernatural virtues, virtues that cannot be acquired by repeated actions, like the natural virtues, but must be infused in us by God. These are the theological virtues of faith, hope, and charity and the infused moral virtues. A discussion of them would take us beyond the scope of the present work, which is philosophical rather than theological. But we should note that Aristotle's conception of happiness as the life of virtue can be expanded beyond a life perfected by the natural virtues to a life perfected further by the supernatural virtues. The value of his definition is not limited to the virtues that he personally recognized and discussed. The happiness achieved through the supernatural virtues will be greater than the happiness arising from the natural virtues alone, but it will still remain true, though in a new and more profound way, that happiness is found in rational activity perfected by virtue. The definition can be extended even further, by analogy, to the beatific vision, in which the human intellect, strengthened by what is called the "light of glory," is able to see God, not as in a similitude, but face to face. For, as Aquinas states, this created light empowers the human intellect to see God in the way that a habit makes a power more able to act.[17] What is essential to human happiness, therefore, is that it be an activity of the rational or intellectual faculty strengthened by whatever habits or qualities are necessary to enable it to act or to act more perfectly.

## Virtue Ethics and Natural Law Ethics

If we were to continue following the pattern of the *Nicomachean Ethics*, we would be pursuing what is called "virtue ethics." This would seem to be the way to proceed, for if the end is a rationally appropriate life and if the virtues enable us to live this life well, then ethics should be developed and perfected through a detailed study of the virtues. It is true that we must examine the fundamental principles of right reason, since these are the starting points for determining the mean of virtue. But since the application of right reason will differ from one virtue to another—achieving the mean in courage, for example, will differ from achieving the mean in temperance—it would seem appropriate to discuss the principles of right reason in the context of discussing particular virtues.

Moreover, Aquinas proceeds this way in his detailed study of the virtues in the *Summa Theologiae*. For example, he treats of suicide and the killing of innocent people under justice, and of fornication, adultery, and unnatural sexual practices under chastity.[18] This seems both convenient and appropriate to the subject matter, since our main interest is to acquire and practice the vir-

---

17. *ST* I, q. 12, a. 5, ad 1 and ad 2.
18. For suicide, killing the innocent, etc., see *ST* II-II, q. 64. For sins against chastity, see *ST* II-II, q. 154.

tues. Furthermore, in his treatise on law in the *Summa*,[19] Aquinas focuses on general questions—what is law, what is the natural law, how is it related to other forms of law, can it be changed or abolished, etc.—not on particular natural law precepts. However, later in the treatise, when discussing the Ten Commandments, he does give some consideration to particular precepts.[20]

This does not mean, however, that natural law ethics is of no importance for virtue ethics. If the principles of right reason are to have an objective binding force when applied to particular virtues, they must be derived in some way from the natural law. For without law, there are no objective or unqualified obligations, only such obligations as we choose to impose on ourselves. Furthermore, since we practice the virtues in order to be happy and happiness is the end to which the natural law is ordained, its precepts will be the first principles of right reason for all the virtues.

From this it appears that virtue ethics and natural law ethics are not really different ethics. Natural law ethics focuses on the first principles of right reason, principles that are essential for virtue ethics. A complete virtue ethics would contain within it the whole of the natural law, but divided among the virtues, while a complete natural law ethics would set forth, in a unified way, the first principles of right reason for all the virtues. In this way natural law ethics complements virtue ethics and clarifies it.

The virtue ethics approach, however, seems to me more suited to the subject matter of ethics than the natural law approach. First of all, it is closer to life, since it focuses on the principles of particular virtues. Moreover, the way we ought to live is revealed especially in the lives of virtuous persons, living out the demands of particular virtues in particular situations. By knowing such persons, by seeing that they are good and that their lives are good, we come to appreciate what makes for human happiness. It is by tasting the virtuous life, even vicariously, that we come to desire

19. *ST* I-II, q. 90–108.
20. *ST* I-II, q. 99–100.

it, for we are more easily persuaded by example and experience than we are by argument. Virtue ethics follows this natural way more than natural law ethics does.

Nevertheless, there are important reasons for advancing the study of natural law ethics as well. For we live in an era of moral relativism, where many people think that moral principles, even principles that they themselves approve and follow, are the result of cultural conditioning or religious faith and cannot be shown by reason to be universally valid. Again, even those who recognize the truth of certain commonsense moral principles can be perplexed about controversial issues, especially those in which common sense leads or seems to lead to contradictory results, as in what are called "moral dilemmas." To these kinds of difficulties, a developed natural law ethics provides a clear and profound response. Finally, if the natural law is not developed as a coherent system, its precepts cannot be effectively defended against other approaches to normative ethics.

CHAPTER 5

# The Natural Law

We have seen that the purpose of our existence is to achieve happiness and that happiness lies essentially in the life proper to human beings by nature: the life of virtue. But a life is virtuous only if it is guided by the principles of right reason. If we are to achieve happiness, therefore, we must investigate what these principles are.

The principles of right reason must be natural, since they direct us to our natural end. Furthermore, they must be legal principles. For if the purpose of our existence is to achieve our natural end, we are unconditionally obligated to follow the principles that will guide us to it. But only laws can bind us objectively and unconditionally; our personal rules of conduct, considered as such and independent of law, have only such force as we choose to give them. Therefore, the principles that we are seeking must be legal precepts belonging to a law to which we are subject by nature, a law appropriately called "the natural law."

In this chapter, we shall be concerned with the natural law in a general way, clarifying what it is and how it is related to human law, following the first part of Aquinas's treatise on law in the *Summa Theologiae*.[1] We will begin with the general definition of law and the application of this definition to the natural law. This will be followed by a discussion of the primacy of the common good and of the dependence of human law on the natural law. We will then turn to Aquinas's formulation of the first principle of the

1. *ST* I-II, q. 90–97.

natural law and to his division of natural law precepts according to three levels of natural inclinations. This division will provide the organizing principle for the discussion of particular precepts in the following chapters. We will then consider the first and most important principles of the natural law, the commandments to love God above all things and our neighbor as ourselves. I will conclude with a note regarding a common objection to natural law theory: that it attempts to derive moral precepts from factual statements about human nature, the is/ought fallacy.

## The Definition of Law

To understand Aquinas's definition of law, it is helpful to begin with two characteristics of law that are evident from ordinary experience. The first is that law is a rule of conduct imposed on us from above. We are "under the law." The second is that it is our duty to obey the law. Otherwise, how could the authorities be justified in demanding obedience to the law and punishing disobedience? A satisfactory definition of law must be able to account for these characteristics.

One might object that the law does not demand obedience, but rather proposes an alternative: either obey the law or suffer the punishment; the choice is yours. And indeed, the law does speak this way to those who have no scruples about disobeying it, because such persons must be coerced by the fear of unpleasant consequences. But this is not the way the law first speaks to us. It expects us to understand its purpose and our obligation to obey it. The threat of punishment is there to deter the wicked.

With the two characteristics mentioned in mind, let us turn to Aquinas's definition of law, which is this: *Law is a rule of reason for the common good established by the proper authority and promulgated.*[2]

---

2. *ST* I-II, q. 90, a. 4, c. The parts of the definition are explained in the four articles of Question 90.

We can clarify the elements in this definition most easily in human or positive law.

First of all, law must be a rule of reason. This is because law is intended to direct human conduct to an end, and only reason is capable of ordering means to an end. This would be true in a sense even if a law were unjust, because an unjust law might be well adapted to its purpose. However, such a law would not be a true rule of reason, since it would not be directed to the true human good. It would not be rational without qualification. Nor would it really be a law, since we cannot be obligated to obey a rule of conduct that is not ordered to the true human good. An unjust law is called a law not because it really is a law, but because it has the appearance of being a law, having been enacted by the appropriate authority in legal form, just as we speak of a corpse as a dead man, not because it really is a man, but because it looks like the man who once existed.

Must we refuse to obey unjust laws? Certainly, if they require us to cooperate directly in doing something wicked. Nevertheless, there are laws that we should obey out of a general respect for the rule of law, even if they are in some respects defective. Examples would be paying our taxes when the tax burden is not equitably distributed or when the taxes used to support practices contrary to the natural law—abortion, for example—represent only a very small portion of the total tax revenue.

The second requirement is that a law be directed to the common good—that is, not to an individual good but to the good of the political community that imposes the law. For the law requires us to prefer this good to our individual goods. Consider, for example, the provisions that the positive law makes for the common defense. The citizens may be forced to join the army and to stand firm in battle for the good of the community, even though they might better secure their personal safety by dodging the draft or by fleeing the enemy. But if the law requires us to prefer the common good to our individual goods, even to the risking of our lives, it is clearly ordained to the common good.

The same point can also be seen negatively, if we consider what it would mean for the law to be aimed at the good of a particular individual. Suppose, for example, that it were aimed at my individual good, not for any reason related to the common good, like a veteran's benefit or a welfare payment, but simply because it is me. Of what interest, then, would it be to others in the political community? For them it would be an alien good, a good in which they have no share. But the law cannot reasonably be imposed on all of us unless it is ordained to a good in which we are all meant to share, and this is the common good. Furthermore, because the common good is not an alien good, but a good for all the members of the community, a law directed to the common good is fully consistent with human dignity. For both the individual good and the common good, properly understood, pertain to the individual's "own good," as I explained in chapter 1.

The remaining two elements in the definition are also easily illustrated in human law. Since law is ordained to the common good, it must be established by an authority responsible for the common good, and this is public authority. Hence, the law appears as something imposed on us from above. A private individual has the right to seek his individual good, but he does not have the right to establish laws binding on others. Even a public commission charged with preparing a legislative proposal cannot make that proposal a law. However well adapted to promote the common good, such a proposal is not a law until it has been enacted by the appropriate legislative authority. Finally, a law must be promulgated, since the members of the community are bound to obey it, and no one can be bound to obey a legislative enactment that has not been made public.

### The Definition of Law applied to the Natural Law

Does the natural law satisfy all the conditions specified in the general definition of law? It is clear that the natural law is a rule of reason, for if its precepts were not appropriately ordered to the attainment of our natural end, they would not constitute a law that binds us by nature. But what is the common good to which it is ordained? By what authority is it established? And how is it promulgated? The answers to these questions are not as obvious as they are in the case of human law. But if Aquinas's general definition of law is correct, all the elements in this definition must be present in the natural law. Otherwise, it will not really be a law, but perhaps only a set of moral intuitions.

Because it is directed to our natural end, the natural law must be addressed to every member of the human race. For happiness is not a good meant just for me or for you or for any one people or nation. Moreover, we can attain happiness only if we cooperate with each other, for none of us is individually self-sufficient. Hence, the natural law obligates us to facilitate the achievement of the life of virtue as a good meant for everyone and to seek an abundance of the external goods and services that are valuable instrumentally for virtuous actions. The common good to which we are ordained by the natural law, therefore, is the happiness of the human race,[3] and this not just for the present generation but for future generations as well. It follows that the authorities in a particular political community, although concerned first of all with the happiness of their own citizens, must also be willing to cooperate with other such communities for the sake of the greater and more ultimate good, the happiness of the human race as a whole.

When considering justice in chapter 4, I defined the common good, following John XXIII, as comprising all those conditions of social living whereby individuals are enabled to achieve their perfection. Here I define it as the happiness of the human race. How are these definitions related? Briefly, the definition in terms of happiness is the primary and essential definition. For happiness is desirable simply for itself, not as a means to anything further.

3. *ST* I-II, q. 90, a. 2, c. Aquinas is here speaking of happiness as the common good of a particular community, but I think the idea can be extended to the human race as a whole.

But how is happiness to be achieved? Obviously, no one can be forced to live virtuously; this depends on personal choice. Nevertheless, the political community can help its members achieve happiness by establishing or encouraging appropriate social conditions: everything from protecting persons and property and ensuring that necessities like food, shelter, and medical care are readily available to facilitating the development of initiatives and institutions for education, culture, and religion. These conditions define the common good in an instrumental or practical sense; they are not the end itself, which is happiness, but a means to it.[4] We shall frequently make use of this practical definition in subsequent discussions.

The authority who established the natural law must be God, the Author of nature. For every law is established by the authority responsible for the common good to which the law is ordained. But the common good to which the natural law is ordained is the happiness of the human race, the end to which we are ordained by nature. Hence, the authority who established the natural law must be the one who established human nature. This is God, the Author of Nature.

If it belongs to the essence of the natural law that it be established by God, then, if God does not exist, the natural law will not exist. In chapter 1, I argued for the existence of God as the Author of nature, proceeding a posteriori from our unqualified condemnation of a heinous crime. For to condemn that crime without qualification, we had to assume that we exist by nature for our own good. But this means that there is finality in nature, and finality can be established only by an intelligent cause. We confirmed this a posteriori argument by showing, in chapter 2, that

---

4. John Finnis has proposed a similar view of the practical common good. He states that the point of the political community would be "to secure the whole ensemble of material and other conditions, including forms of collaboration, that tend to favor, facilitate, and foster the realization by each individual of his or her personal development." See Finnis, *Natural Law and Natural Rights*, 2nd ed. (New York: Oxford University Press, 2011), 147.

all living creatures, including man, are ordained by nature to their appropriate ends. This allowed us to conclude by a more direct argument that there exists an intelligence, the Author of nature, who ordains us to our natural good by creating us to be what we are. It follows that there exists an authority who has established the natural law and therefore that it truly is a law.

Hugo Grotius, a seventeenth-century jurist and legal philosopher, strongly affirmed the existence and providence of God, but maintained, nevertheless, that natural laws would have some status ("*locum aliquem haberent*") even if God did not exist.[5] This, I think, is false; there could be no natural law without a divine lawgiver. But it contains an element of truth. For we can be aware of the *fact* that we have moral obligations before we have clarified the ultimate *source* of these obligations, and this is to be aware of the natural law, though imperfectly. If we begin from our experience of life, we can easily see that there are principles that we ought to follow simply because we are human beings, prior to the dictates of human law and sometimes even in opposition to them. It is in seeking to understand the source of these principles that we are led ultimately to the Author of nature.

How is the natural law promulgated? Since it is imposed on us in virtue of our nature, it will become known to us through our life experiences, as a law written upon the human heart. We know, for example, that we ought to respect our parents, to avoid injuring our neighbors, to tell the truth, to keep our commitments, to make our contributions to the good of our communities, and many other such principles. However, the precepts of the natural law are not all equally known. Everyone knows the most general principles—for example, that we ought not to harm our neighbors—but not everyone knows all the specific precepts that follow from these principles. The degree to which the natural law is known will obviously be affected by the customs, positive laws,

5. Hugo Grotius, *The Law of War and Peace*, trans. Francis W. Kelsey, with the collaboration of Arthur E. R. Boak et al., in *De jure belli ac pacis libri tres/Hugo Grotius*, vol. 2, *Prolegomena* (Oxford: Clarendon Press, 1925), § 11.

and popular teachings current in a particular society at a particular period of its history. Thus, many natural law precepts may not yet be fully apparent to barbarous and uncultivated peoples, and the knowledge of some of these precepts may be obscured or distorted among more civilized peoples because of false teaching or moral decline.

Aquinas defined the natural law as *the rational creature's participation in the eternal law of God.*[6] This definition assumes that the natural law is part of a larger law, called the "eternal law," by which God governs the whole of creation. By this law, all creatures, rational and nonrational, are ordained to their proper ends. We participate in this eternal law in a more perfect way than nonrational creatures do, since we are capable of understanding the law and of freely directing ourselves by its precepts. Our participation in the eternal law, therefore, is not a purely natural or instinctive participation, but rather a *rational* participation.

## The Primacy of the Common Good

We have seen that law is ordered to the common good and that, for the natural law, the common good is the happiness of the human race. We saw also that an individual person cannot achieve happiness unless he cooperates with other individuals in a political community and that he must prefer the common good of the political community to his individual good. We can get a clearer idea of the primacy of the political common good by contrasting it with the common goods of associations formed for particular purposes.

Imagine first a company of men who discover the wreck of an ancient merchant ship with a cargo of silver and gold. They cooperate with each other in the work of bringing up the treasure with a view to selling it and dividing among themselves the money thus acquired. The bringing up of the treasure is a kind

6. *ST* I-II, q. 91, a. 2, c.

of common good, and while this activity is actually taking place, the good of each of the cooperating men *as such* lies in his specific contribution to the common effort. But this common good is not ultimately prior to the private goods of those participating in it, since each of them is thinking primarily of personal gain. For we are assuming that without the prospect of profit, the men would not be interested in the shipwreck. We see a similar motivation in games of chance, where each participant is intent on winning something for himself or, in a somewhat different way, in business contracts, where each party seeks primarily his private advantage.

Consider now an athletic team—say, a football team. The players cooperate with each other for the sake of victory over the opposing team. The victory, if it results, will not be the good of any individual player as such, although every player will share in it. It will be essentially a common good, the team's good, and the good of each player will lie in his specific contribution to the execution of the game plan. Thus far, the cooperating football players are similar to the cooperating members of the company raising the sunken treasure. But their fundamental motivations are different. The treasure seekers desire the success of their common endeavor for the sake of private gain, whereas the football players desire victory for its own sake. Hence, victory has more the character of a common good, since many can share in it without diminishing or dividing it. But the money gained from the sale of the treasure is essentially a private good that can be shared only by being divided up.

Although the football players desire victory for its own sake, they do not desire it as an ultimate end. It is a common good of limited scope and duration, prior to the individual goods of the team members insofar as they are teammates, but not insofar as they are human beings. As we have seen, the common good to which human beings as such are naturally ordained is first of all the happiness of the political community to which they belong— ultimately, of course, the happiness of the whole human race.

But is human happiness really a common good? It is certainly common in the sense that it can be participated in by many without being diminished. For no one who achieves the life of virtue deprives anyone else of it. In this it differs from purely private goods, like a house or a yacht, where possession by one person excludes possession by others. However, the life of virtue does not seem to be a good achieved by cooperative activity, like victory in an athletic contest or success in bringing up a sunken treasure. Each person achieves his own individual happiness by the way he personally chooses to live. Your happiness lies in your good life, my happiness in mine. So, it might seem that the life of virtue is not really a common good.

On the other hand, it is clear that none of us can achieve happiness apart from a community that seeks happiness as a common good. For no individual can achieve the life of virtue by himself alone. As we have seen, the life of virtue requires bodily goods like health and strength as instruments for virtuous actions and external goods like food, water, clothing, shelter, and health care that are required for bodily well-being. No individual could provide these goods sufficiently by himself alone. Furthermore, how could individuals secure their personal safety or acquire the moral and intellectual virtues necessary for true happiness without the public offices, institutions, and programs available only in a community with resources sufficient for these purposes—that is, in the political community? We may conclude, therefore, that the life of virtue is indeed a true common good, not in the sense that cooperative action by itself alone can make anyone happy—we have seen that individual happiness depends ultimately on individual choice—but in the sense that it can help or facilitate the achievement of happiness. The ensemble of the social conditions that facilitate the achievement of happiness for the community's members is what we have called the practical or instrumental common good.

If human beings can achieve their natural end only in cooperation with other human beings in a political community, they will naturally be parts of a political community, though not necessarily parts of the particular community in which they were born. And since a part that belongs naturally to a whole always belongs to it, human beings will belong to a political community not momentarily for some special purpose, as one belongs to an athletic team, but permanently. As we shall see more fully in chapter 10, the political community is man's natural home.

If the individual is part of the political community, and if the good of the part, as such, lies in its contribution to the good of the whole,[7] then the good of the individual citizen, as such, will lie in his contribution to the common good.[8] We saw this in the example of the football team, where the good of the individual player as such is ordered ultimately to the victory of the team. Furthermore, inasmuch as the individual is a *natural* part of the political community, he is united to it much more closely than a player is united to his team. This unity can be compared to the way in which arms, legs, and other bodily organs are united to the living substance of which they are parts. As the acts of bodily organs are ordered to the good of the living substance, so the acts of individual human beings, insofar as they are parts of the political community, are ordered to the good of the community.

There is a fundamental difference, however, between the way in which the organs of the body are related to the living substance and the way in which human beings are related to the political community. The difference is this: individual human beings exist for their own good, whereas the organs of the body exist for the good of the living substance. Hence, as we have seen, the common good of the political community must be the good of its members. Insofar as he is a part of the community, the individual person dedicates his efforts to establishing and maintaining the social conditions that facilitate the achievement of happiness for everyone. But he also benefits from these efforts and from the efforts of

---

7. *ST* I-II, q. 109, a. 3, c; *ST* II-II, q. 58, a. 5, c; *SCG* III, cap. 17, n. 6.
8. *ST* I-II, q. 90, a. 3, ad 3, and q. 92, a. 1, ad 3.

others, because his own happiness depends on them. On the other hand, if the state were to use its citizens as instruments for purposes other than their own good or attempt to exercise total control over them in the way that a living substance uses and controls the organs of its body, this would be tyranny and totalitarianism.

When a political community is organized and functioning according to the natural law, the citizens, through their cooperative efforts, seek happiness as a good in which they are all meant to share. Everyone contributes and everyone benefits. Public authority is closely linked to these efforts; its purpose is to protect the community from outside attack, to maintain order within it, and to welcome, encourage, and supplement the efforts of individuals and local communities for the happiness of all. In this way, the true political common good is achieved and maintained.

The primacy of the common good in the political community explains why individual citizens attain their perfection especially in service to the community. For human perfection is found essentially in the life of virtue, and it is better and more virtuous to prefer the greater good. But the common good is a greater good than the good of any one individual. Therefore, to serve the common good is better and more noble than to serve one's individual good.[9] A sign of this is the fact that we regard those who make great sacrifices for the sake of the common good as excelling in virtue and as worthy of the highest honors.

Service to the community is not just public service, however. Those who devote themselves to the care of a family serve the community by raising the children who will form the next generation of citizens. Those who produce or make available the necessities of life or who serve their fellow citizens in the professions and in other ways, if they dedicate their efforts to the common good, also serve the community. However, distinguished public service, since it is related more immediately to the common good, is especially praiseworthy.

9. *NE* I.2.1094b 6–11.

Insofar as they are parts of the political community, individual human beings are perfected by their service to the political common good. But they are not parts of the political community totally and in every way.[10] This is shown by the fact that the social conditions established through cooperative action are not sufficient to make anyone actually happy; this depends ultimately on each person's own efforts. It is shown even more clearly by the religious quest. For to seek God is to seek an eternal good, a good that goes beyond the temporal common good to which the political community is ordained. It follows that a religious community is not, strictly speaking, a part of the political community. However, the members of a religious community are also members of a political community, and are therefore obligated by the natural law to seek the temporal common good. Since the natural law comes from God, this will be a religious duty. So long as both church and state are faithful to the natural law, therefore, there need not be conflict between them, although questions and issues may arise that require negotiation.

Let us conclude these reflections by noting that we begin as children with a primary focus on our individual good. But as we make progress in the life of virtue, we come to realize that we are parts of a local and national community, and ultimately of the community of mankind, and that we are meant to take our part in promoting the good of these larger communities. Beyond this, when we reflect on the fact that the human race is part of a yet larger whole, the universe with its many creatures of all kinds, we can see that the good of the human race is part of a still greater good, the common good of the universe, which reveals the glory of the Creator. For the Creator is the supreme common good, the first cause of the good of every creature.[11]

10. *ST* I-II, q. 21, a. 4, ad 3.
11. *ST* I, q. 65, a. 2, c.

## The Dependence of Human Law
## on the Natural Law

The definition of law is more easily illustrated in human law than in the natural law. For positive law is imposed on us by a visible authority that enforces it and punishes disobedience. It is established after rational deliberation. We all understand that a law is supposed to be directed to the common good, although, in practice, it often reflects the undue influence of special interests. It is promulgated by public announcements and in statute books and the records of court decisions that anyone may consult.

But none of this proves that human law is really law unless we also assume that it is composed of precepts that we are obligated to obey. Now most human laws, especially the most fundamental ones, do seem to meet this criterion. We do not question the rightness of laws forbidding crimes like murder, rape, theft, and perjury, or requiring parents to take care of their children, or citizens to pay taxes for the common welfare. But the question remains: why are we *obligated* to obey these laws? Or again, how could we be justified in *disobeying* a law? For it is clear that there can be laws that we must refuse to obey.

With respect to the first question, it is clear that a human law cannot be binding in conscience unless it receives this binding force from the natural law. For the fact that a positive law is established by a human authority in juridical form does not of itself prove that we are morally obligated to obey it. It must be directed to the true human good. But it is by the natural law that we are directed to this good. It follows that if a law is opposed to the natural law, it will not be directed to the true human good and so will not be binding in conscience. Ultimately, therefore, it is only through the precepts of the natural law that we can establish the obligation to obey human laws.

To this, someone might reply that we are obligated to obey the laws of the state, *not* because of the natural law, but because we have agreed to bind ourselves to the terms of a social contract specifying the citizens' rights and duties. But even on this assumption, our obligation to obey will depend on the natural law. For the obligation to respect the terms of a social contract depends on the general obligation to keep agreements. But this is a principle of natural justice, on which the force of all contracts depends.

On the second question, let us suppose that there were human laws requiring us to deny our religion or to cooperate in state-sponsored genocide. We would refuse to obey such laws. But how could we justify this disobedience? On what grounds could we maintain that measures duly enacted in legal form by those in authority are not truly laws? Would we not have to appeal to such basic human rights as the right to life and the right to practice one's religion? But these are based on principles of natural law. It is on the basis of the natural law, therefore, that we judge unjust human laws to be null and void. On the other hand, if there were no natural law, these wicked enactments would have as much claim to obedience as any other human law.

Furthermore, an unjust law cannot be ordained to the common good. For the common good is a good in which every member of the community is meant to share, whereas injustice means violating the rights of at least one member. But it is of the essence of law to be ordained to the common good. Therefore, an unjust law cannot really be a law.

Could we justify our refusal to obey wicked laws on the basis of our personal moral convictions, especially if these convictions are widely shared? There would then be no need to call upon the natural law. The problem with this is that personal moral convictions do not, as such, have the force of law, and they have no power to show that a law is null and void. Nullification is possible only on the basis of a higher law, proceeding from a higher authority. We see this within the sphere of human law when a legislative enactment is nullified by a Supreme Court decision on the basis of constitutional law. Similarly, a wicked law, even one approved by the supreme juridical authority of the state, is nullified by the natural law. Nevertheless, people who refuse to obey a law because it violates their conscience can be justified not only subjectively, but also objectively, when their moral convictions are in fact based on precepts of the natural law, even though they do not think of them as such.

## Deriving Human Laws from the Natural Law

If true human laws are derived from the natural law, how does this derivation takes place? Is it by a process of deduction? Sometimes this is possible. In laws against grave injustices like murder, rape, and theft, we can see a straightforward deduction from a general principle of natural law: that we ought not to injure our neighbor. But, as Aquinas points out, a human law is often a kind of invention or determination, like a work of art. An architect, for example, has in mind the general idea of a house, but he cannot deduce from this the precise design of the house he is going to build. He must create a design that is adapted as well as possible to the climate, the location, the available materials, the cost, etc. Similarly, a human legislator, beginning with a general idea from the natural law, must determine a specific way of realizing it in accord with many relevant circumstances. Thus, the punishment of crime and the levying of taxes are contained in the natural law as general principles, but what punishments shall be inflicted for what crimes and what system of taxation shall be adopted must be determined by human law.[12]

If human law depends on the natural law, and if the natural law aims at happiness, then human law must aim at happiness as well. But obviously there are limits to the power of human law. It cannot forbid all evils, but only the evils that appear in external

12. *ST* I-II, q. 95, a 2. For a discussion of these two ways of deriving positive law from natural law, see Finnis, *Natural Law and Natural Rights*, 281–90.

actions—and not even all of these, but only such as it is possible to forbid according to the conditions of time and place, emphasizing especially public order and the security of persons and property. Nor is human law able to bring about all of the social conditions that facilitate the achievement of happiness, although it should seek to promote them as much as possible.

Moreover, as we have seen, the natural law aims not just at the happiness of this or that particular human community, but at the happiness of the human race as a whole. Consequently, international law should seek to establish the conditions necessary for the happiness of all peoples. We will return to this topic when we consider the universal common good and subsidiarity in chapter 10.

## The Content of the Natural Law

In a much discussed article in his treatise on law, Aquinas asks whether the natural law contains many precepts or only one.[13] He responds that the precepts are many, but that they are all founded on one first principle. Because this first principle is important and needs clarification, and because our discussion of the particular precepts of the natural law in the following chapters will follow Aquinas's way of distinguishing them in this article, it will be helpful to consider it in some detail.

Aquinas teaches that the first and most evident precept of the natural law is this: *Good is to be done and pursued and evil is to be avoided*. It is first because it is founded on nothing more than the general concepts of good and evil. For good is what we desire and seek to obtain, and evil is what we try to avoid. When we want to understand how we should act, we begin with this principle, just as when we want to understand anything at all, we begin with the principle that the same thing cannot be simultaneously affirmed and denied.

13. *ST* I-II, q. 94, a. 2.

There is, however, a difficulty about this first precept of the natural law. For there are good things that we sometimes ought *not* to seek. Sexual intercourse, for example, is a good thing, yet we ought not to seek it in adultery. This difficulty is touched upon indirectly in the second objection in the article we are considering. According to this objection, if there were many precepts of the natural law pertaining to the different parts of human nature, then even the inclinations of the concupiscible appetite (the faculty by which we desire and seek sensual pleasures) would belong to the natural law. But if this were true, what would be wrong with seeking sexual pleasure whenever we desire it? The natural law directs us to seek what is good, and sexual pleasure is good. Therefore, we ought to seek it.

Aquinas's reply contains the key to answering our difficulty. He states that the inclinations of the concupiscible appetite belong to the natural law *insofar as they are ruled by reason*. This is the answer we would expect, since happiness consists in living according to reason. Therefore, if sexual intercourse is not sought in accordance with reason, it is not really good for man. Or we may say that sexual intercourse in adultery is good in a certain respect—that is, insofar as it is sexual intercourse—but not good without qualification. For what is good without qualification must be good in all relevant respects, while a thing can be evil because of a single significant defect, just as bad health can result from any one of many diseases or infirmities. This is why we can achieve the mean of virtue only if we do the right action, at the right time, in the right way, for the right reason, etc. Therefore, if sexual intercourse is good when considered abstractly, but contrary to reason when gotten through adultery, then adulterous intercourse is not a good to be sought after, but rather an evil to be avoided.

We are categorically obligated by the natural law to do and to seek what is good and to avoid what is evil. This means doing and seeking what is really good, not what is only apparently good. It means doing and seeking what is good here and now, satisfying all the requirements of right reason, not what *would* be good if circumstances were different. It means doing and seeking what is good without qualification, not doing or seeking what is good in some respect, but evil absolutely speaking. For if the first principle of the natural law did not obligate us to do what is really good, it would not really be a law; for no law can obligate us to do what is evil. Of course, someone might think that what he wants to do is good when really it is not good, and so derive a false conclusion from the first principle of the natural law. But a mistake in its application does not destroy the truth of a principle. With these clarifications, the precept directing us to do and seek what is good and to avoid what is evil becomes the first principle of the natural law.[14]

## Natural Goods

What things are naturally good and what things are naturally evil? According to Aquinas, those things to which we have a natural inclination are good, and their contraries evil. He then divides our natural inclinations into those that we share with all things, those that we share with the animals, and those that are proper to ourselves. With all things, and especially with living things, we share a natural inclination toward existence. Hence, we recognize life, physical health, bodily integrity, and whatever preserves these as good and death, sickness, bodily mutilation, and whatever causes these as evil. With the animals—the higher animals at least—we share a natural inclination to mating and to the care of offspring,

14. For a different interpretation of Aquinas's first principle of the natural law, see Germain Grisez, "The First Principle of Practical Reason: A Commentary on the *Summa Theologiae*, 1–2, Question 94, Article 2," *Natural Law Forum* 10 (1965): 168–201. Grisez argues that this principle should not be understood as a moral principle, but as a principle that directs us to pursue the basic human goods. How we should pursue the basic goods—that is, what moral principles should guide us in this endeavor—is considered later. The new natural law theory began with this way of thinking about Aquinas's first principle of natural law, which is also called "the first principle of practical reason." For the development of this theory, see Germain Grisez, Joseph Boyle, and John Finnis, "Practical Principles, Moral Truth, and Ultimate Ends," *American Journal of Jurisprudence* 32 (1987): 99–151.

and we therefore see these activities as good. Finally, we possess inclinations proper to ourselves based on our rational nature. Thus, we recognize truth as good, especially the truth about God and about our origin and destiny, and falsehood as evil. Again, we see that living peacefully with others in society is good, and that harming those with whom we live is evil.[15]

If these are our natural goods, the objects of our natural inclinations, it might seem that we would never have any desires or inclinations opposed to them. But in fact, we do have such desires and inclinations. How this is possible?

Speaking generally, we may say that a natural inclination is an inclination that is in accord with what reason recognizes as appropriate to our nature as rational animals. These are the inclinations toward the natural goods distinguished by Aquinas. For reason sees at once that personal existence is naturally good for man because it is the foundation of every other human good, that mating and the care of offspring are naturally good for man and other animals because these activities preserve the existence of the species, and that seeking the truth and living peacefully with others in society are naturally good for man as a rational being. When these goods are considered in themselves, according to what they are, objectively, and in a sense abstractly, apart from our individual desires and habits, it is clear that they are precisely suited to man as a rational animal. Hence, our inclinations toward these goods are natural, and the inclinations opposed to them are unnatural.

When considered concretely, however, as they appear within the lives of individuals, the things that reason understands to be naturally good do not always appear so. This happens because powerful emotions can make what is good seem evil or what is evil seem good. Consider, for example, a desire opposed to the natural good of life. A person suffering great pain may perceive life as evil and death as good, and so be moved to suicide. Of course, it is not

15. *ST* I-II, q. 94, a. 2, c.

life itself that is evil, but rather sickness and pain, and it is the desire to escape these that makes life appear evil. Again, adultery and assault are opposed to the natural inclination of reason to respect others and to avoid harming them, but sexual passion can make *this* act of adultery here and now seem good, and uncontrolled anger can make *this* assault seem justified. Those whose emotions move them to act unreasonably usually regret it afterward. For emotions are momentary, and when they have passed, reason reasserts itself, and what seemed good at the moment no longer seems good. That there should be this opposition between our reason and our emotions, a kind of fracture within human nature, is something of a mystery, a mystery whose explanation belongs to theology, however, rather than to philosophy. But the fact of this opposition is clear, and it explains why desires contrary to reason are possible.

When someone is moved by an uncontrolled passion to act against reason, we may speak of reason being momentarily overcome, but not yet of a definite inclination contrary to our rational nature. For an unnatural inclination, as distinguished from a momentary aberration, is a determinate and lasting tendency toward actions that are opposed to reason. These inclinations arise from bad habits or vices. For just as good habits or virtues incline us to act in ways that are in accord with reason and make good actions connatural and pleasing to us, so vices incline us to act against reason and make bad actions connatural and pleasing. For habits, as we saw in chapter 4, are a kind of second nature. Through bad habits, therefore, a person becomes inclined to act in a way that, absolutely speaking, is not natural, but is natural in a way. For such actions are well suited to that sort of person.

Some inclinations are unnatural because they are opposed to our animal nature. Such are the inclinations opposed to normal eating and drinking, to sleeping, and to the natural sexual intercourse of man and woman, the acts that preserve us as individuals and as a species. These are what we usually have in mind when we speak of unnatural inclinations. They incline us to actions that are unnatural or perverse, turned away from their natural purpose, as we see especially in unnatural sexual practices. Such practices are doubly unnatural, being contrary both to reason and to our animal nature. For we are not disembodied rational substances; we are rational animals.

What are the causes of the inclinations opposed to our animal nature? When discussing unnatural pleasures, Aquinas states that they arise from some kind of natural corruption, either on the part of the body or on the part of the soul. On the part of the body are those that arise from sickness, as in persons suffering from fever who experience sweet things as sour and vice versa, and those that arise from a bad physical constitution, as in persons who enjoy eating earth or coals or other unnatural foods. On the part of the soul are those that arise from bad habits or customs—cannibalism, for example, and bestiality.[16] Since unnatural pleasures arise from unnatural inclinations—for we enjoy what we are inclined to—the causes of unnatural pleasures will also be the causes of unnatural inclinations.

Although the primary causes of unnatural inclinations on the part of the soul are bad habits and bad customs, there may be other causes as well. For example, in regard to homosexuality, we might ask whether something in the physical constitution of the body might make someone more susceptible to same-sex attraction than most people. What psychological experiences or traumas might lead someone to homosexuality? Questions like these cannot be considered here.[17] For our purposes, what is important to emphasize is that the homosexual attraction is not in and of itself opposed to the natural law, provided that is not deliberately chosen or fostered. As we shall see in chapter 8, it is homosexual acts that are opposed to the natural law.

16. *ST* I-II, q. 31, a. 7, c. Aquinas does not specifically mention homosexuality in this article, but he does mention it, together with bestiality, in *ST* II-II, q. 154, a. 12, c.

17. For an introduction to these issues, see John F. Harvey, *The Truth about Homosexuality* (San Francisco: Ignatius Press, 1996).

To conclude this section, let us note again that Aquinas's threefold division of natural inclinations—those we share with all things, those we share with the animals, and those proper to ourselves as rational beings—will provide the organizing principle for the following chapters. Thus, in chapters 6 and 7, we will consider the life issues; in chapters 8 and 9, sexual morality, marriage and family; and in chapters 10 and 11, the search for truth, cooperation with others in the political community, and natural rights.

## The Love Commandments

In chapter 4, I considered the love commandments—the commandments to love God above all things and your neighbor as yourself—in relation to Aristotle's theory of friendship in the *Nicomachean Ethics*. We shall consider them here insofar as they are precepts of the natural law. As we shall see, these commandments are prior to and of greater dignity than all of the other precepts. For this reason, it seems appropriate to consider them here, before turning to more specific precepts in the following chapters. We can most easily accomplish this by looking at how Aquinas explains the place of the love precepts within the natural law in his discussion of the Ten Commandments.[18]

Of the Ten Commandments, the first three concern our relationship with God, and the other seven, our relationship with our neighbor. Taken together, according to Aquinas, they contain all of the precepts of the natural law, but not all in the same way.[19] The precepts that most people can see with relatively little reflection are the ones that are stated explicitly. But the first and most universal precepts—for example, that we should not wrong anyone—are not expressly stated, because they are imme-

---

18. *ST* I-II, q. 100.
19. *ST* I-II, q. 100, a. 1, c.

diately evident to natural reason. They are contained in the Ten Commandments as principles are contained in their conclusions. Thus, anyone who understands that we ought not to murder or steal or commit adultery obviously understands that we ought not to wrong our neighbor. Other precepts are contained in the Ten Commandments as conclusions in their principles, conclusions that are not quickly and easily seen, but require more careful reflection.[20] For example, the natural law precepts prohibiting prostitution and homosexuality are added to the commandment against adultery as corollaries.[21]

The love commandments are first among the universal natural law precepts and are therefore contained in all of the other precepts, as principles are contained in their conclusions.[22] This is because the love commandments are ordered immediately to friendship with God and with our neighbor, and friendship is the end of all the commandments.[23] For while it is good to render to someone what is due to him, it is even better to render it to him *for his sake*. But to seek the good of another for the other's sake springs from the love proper to friendship. Hence, the ultimate end of the commandments is to bring us into friendship with God and with each other. Also, the goal of every commandment is that it be observed as completely and perfectly as possible, and this results from friendship. For the other commandments either forbid what is evil, like murder and adultery, or enjoin what is good and obligatory, like honoring God and our parents, and these are all observed spontaneously and with pleasure through friendship. Again, the purpose of the commandments is to bring order and peace into our relationships, and this is most perfectly realized when we are in friendship with God and with each other.

We experience the meaning and the beauty of friendship when we become aware that someone is concerned with our good

20. *ST* I-II, q. 100, a. 3, c.
21. *ST* I-II, q. 100, a. 11, c.
22. *ST* I-II, q. 100, a. 3, obj. 1, ad 1.
23. *ST* I-II, q. 99, a. 2, c.

*for our sake* and not simply for his own benefit. We see in this a recognition of our dignity as persons, as beings who exist for their own good. This is true love and the beginning of friendship, because to love us in accord with our dignity is to love us as human beings should be loved. If, on the other hand, someone treats us well for his own benefit or simply in order to follow a moral precept, desiring our good materially perhaps, but not desiring it for our sake, we feel that something is missing, even that the main thing is missing. Friendship, therefore, is the fulfillment of the natural law.

A sign of this is the common belief that morality means transcending selfishness and having a concern for others. For selfishness arises from a kind of self-love that excludes this concern. But to seek the good of others out of a concern for them is to seek the good of others for their sake, and this, as we have seen, is true love. However, the good we seek for others must be their true good, what genuinely contributes to the life of virtue, not just what they might happen to want. Furthermore, since we naturally love ourselves more than we love our neighbor,[24] we should begin by seeking the true good for ourselves. To love our neighbor rightly, we must first love ourselves rightly. As we saw in chapter 4, this is how we should understand the second love commandment: that we should love our neighbor as ourselves.

The first love commandment, however, does not command us to love God as we love ourselves, but to love God more than we love ourselves, to love him above all things. To see why this is so, we must recall what was said earlier about the primacy of the common good. As we have seen, the good of the part is for the sake of the good of the whole, the common good. This is why the good citizen loves the common good of the political community more than his individual good. Therefore, since we are parts of a yet larger whole, the universe containing all that God has created, we should love the common good of the universe more than we love our indi-

24. *ST* II-II, q. 26, a. 4, c.

vidual good. This good is found in the order of the universe—that is, in the relation of its parts to the whole and to each other. Within this order, each part finds its proper place and the purpose of its existence, the way in which it is meant to contribute to the good of the whole. We should love the order of the universe, therefore, more than we love ourselves.

This argument leads us directly to the first love commandment. For if we love the order of the universe more than we love ourselves, still more will we love God. For the order of the universe is not the ultimate good; it exists for the sake of the divine good. An analogy proposed by Aristotle helps to clarify this. An army is a whole composed of many different parts—infantry, armor, artillery, etc.—that must be ordered properly in relation to the whole army and to each other if the army is to operate effectively. But this order, important as it is, is not the ultimate good; it is for the sake of a yet greater good, the good sought by the commander, victory in battle. Similarly, God established the order of the universe not ultimately for its own sake, but for the sake of a yet greater good, the divine goodness and wisdom, which is revealed especially through this order. Because the greater good is more worthy of love and the first and highest good is worthy of the greatest love, God should be loved above all things. Furthermore, just as the commander is the cause of the order of the army, so God is the cause of the order of the universe. Therefore, if we love the order of the universe on which our individual good depends, we will love God, the first cause of this order, even more, as our greatest benefactor.[25]

We will love ourselves rightly, therefore, if we understand that we are parts of the universe, meant to assume our proper place in God's creation in accordance with the natural law. From this comes our natural friendship with God, provided, of course, that

25. Aristotle, *Metaphysics* XII.10.1075a11–15; Thomas Aquinas, *Commentary on Aristotle's "Metaphysics,"* Book XII, Lectio 12; *ST* I, q. 103, a. 2, c, ad 3; *ST* I, q. 44, a. 4, c. On the natural love of God above all things, see *ST* I, q. 60, a. 5, c, and *ST* I-II, q. 109, a. 3, c.

we love God primarily for his sake, since this is the love proper to friendship. Of course, it is also natural for us to love God as our supreme benefactor, the first cause of all our good; indeed, if no good came to us from God, we would not have any reason for loving him.[26] But to love God merely because of the good we receive from him is not yet to love him as one should love a friend.

This friendship between God and man is a natural friendship, a friendship founded on God as the Author of nature. Beyond this natural friendship, Christianity speaks of a more perfect and more intimate friendship with God, a friendship that comes to fruition when we see God as he is in himself in the beatific vision. Since we cannot see God as he is in himself through our natural powers, this friendship becomes possible for us, as I also noted in chapter 4, only through supernatural grace.[27] This is a theological teaching, however, and beyond the scope of the present work, although I will have to say something further about it when discussing the contemplative life in chapter 10.

I would like to summarize these brief reflections on the love precepts and their relation to the other precepts of the natural law with a comment on why all the natural law precepts are necessary. The precepts other than the love precepts are necessary because they specify in detail what the love of God and of our neighbor requires of us. Without them, our efforts to love our neighbor might actually lead to harm, as happens, for example, when compassion moves someone to recommend abortion to a woman with a problem pregnancy or suicide to a person suffering from an incurable disease. But the observance of these precepts, important as they are, can lead to legalism, the tendency to obey laws simply because they are laws, without looking to their ultimate meaning. As we have seen, the ultimate meaning of the specific precepts of the natural law lies in the friendship that results when we obey them out of the love of God and of our neighbor. It is clear, then, that

26. *ST* I, q. 60, a. 5, ad 2.
27. *ST* I-II, q. 109, a. 3, ad 1.

the love precepts and the more specific precepts of the natural law are complementary and that all of them are necessary.

## A Note on the Is/Ought Fallacy

Before beginning our study of the precepts of the natural law, we should consider a common criticism of natural law theory: that it attempts to derive moral precepts from facts about human nature and that this is fallacious, since statements of obligation cannot be deduced from statements of fact. In the following chapters, we will be deriving precepts of the natural law from the fact that human beings are ordained to the life that is proper to them according to their nature—that is, the life of reason perfected by virtue. Does this procedure commit the is/ought fallacy?[28]

To respond to this question, we must consider, first of all, that when we say that someone is obligated to act in a certain way, we are presupposing a statement about an end or goal.[29] If someone wants to be a professional musician, for example, we say that he ought to practice. This, of course, is only a conditional or qualified obligation, since no one is obligated to become a professional musician. Or rather, if someone *is* obligated to become a musician, this will result from some moral obligation, like the obligation to

28. The is/ought fallacy (also called the "naturalistic fallacy") is usually traced back to David Hume; see Hume, *A Treatise of Human Nature*, Book III, Part I, Section I, 2nd ed., ed. L. A. Selby-Bigge, text rev. P. H. Nidditch (Oxford: Clarendon Press, 1978), 469. For a critique of natural law theory emphasizing this fallacy, see Kai Nielsen, "An Examination of the Thomistic Theory of Natural Law," *Natural Law Forum* 4 (1959): 63–71. See also Nielsen, "The Myth of Natural Law," in *Law and Philosophy: A Symposium*, ed. Sydney Hook (New York: New York University Press, 1964), 122–43. For a natural law response to the is/ought fallacy, see Steven J. Jensen, *Knowing the Natural Law: From Precepts and Inclinations to Deriving Oughts* (Washington, D.C.: The Catholic University of America Press, 2015). For a brief discussion of some philosophical developments after Hume's statement of the is/ought fallacy, see Ralph McInerny, *Ethica Thomistica: The Moral Philosophy of Thomas Aquinas*, rev. ed. (Washington, D.C.: The Catholic University of America Press, 1997), 48–56.

29. *ST* I-II, q. 99, a. 1, c; *ST* II-II, q. 44, a. 1, c.

make the best use of one's special talents. But if it is a fact that a person wants to be a professional musician—not an idle wish but a definite commitment—then he must practice, and the obligation to practice will remain as long as the commitment on which it is based remains.

It seems then that we have derived an obligation from a fact—in our example, the fact that someone wants to be a musician. This is true, but the obligation we have derived is not unqualified, because its force depends on a commitment to an end that is not obligatory. If we are to derive absolute or unqualified obligations, therefore, we must begin from an end that by its very nature is obligatory—that is, absolutely obligatory. This must be the ultimate end, since the achievement of this end is the purpose of our existence. For if we were to reject the end for which we exist, we would treat our existence as pointless. From our unqualified obligation to seek the ultimate end, the life of virtue, we can deduce an unqualified obligation to follow the precepts that guide us in achieving it. These are the precepts of the natural law.

The obligation to follow the precepts of the natural law, therefore, does not depend on whether or not I *want* to live in accord with reason and virtue. In this it differs from my obligation to develop my musical skills, which depends on my wanting to be a musician. It differs also from obligations that follow from false ideas of happiness; these also have force only because of what I happen to want. The obligation to follow the natural law, however, is not dependent on what I happen to want; it is absolute and unqualified, just as is our obligation to seek the life of virtue.

In summary, it seems evident that a being who exists for the sake of an end, if he knows the end and is able to seek it, will be obligated to seek it. Therefore, if we exist in order to live the life of virtue, we have an obligation to seek this life. But this implies an obligation to follow the precepts that will guide us in living virtuously. Hence, we are obligated to follow the precepts of the natural law.

# CHAPTER 6

# The Life Issues

## Part 1

Because the inclination to existence is shared by all living things, and because without life no other good is possible, we begin our study of the content of the natural law with the precepts concerned with life, including also those concerned with health and bodily integrity, that are closely related to life.

It is not difficult to see that the natural law obligates us to respect human life. If we have an unqualified obligation to seek the ultimate end, and if this is the life of virtue, and if the life of virtue is impossible without existence, it is clear that we must protect and preserve our lives. This does not mean that there are no limits to what we must do to preserve our lives, as we shall see when discussing extraordinary medical treatments. Nor does it mean that we should not risk our lives when necessary for the sake of the common good. For although life is the most fundamental good, it is not the highest good. But to kill ourselves or to refuse or neglect reasonable means to preserve our lives would clearly be contrary to the natural law. And we must respect the lives of others as well, since they also exist for their own good, the life of virtue, and therefore must not be used as a means to an alien good. This is why the nephew, in the example discussed in chapter 1, is obligated to respect his uncle's life.

Similar arguments apply to health and bodily integrity. For there are many virtuous actions that we cannot perform or perform well if we lack good health or the appropriate bodily organs and capacities. It follows that our obligation to seek the life of virtue requires us to protect and preserve these natural goods just as it requires us to protect and preserve life itself.

Although these obligations are clear enough in general, there are many points of controversy, especially regarding the precepts that absolutely forbid suicide, the killing of the innocent, euthanasia, and abortion. For while most people believe that it is usually wrong to commit suicide or to kill innocent human beings, many doubt that such actions must *always* be wrong. What if there is no other way to alleviate terrible suffering or to prevent a disaster? Proponents of abortion often argue that unborn human beings, though innocent, are not yet persons, so that killing them can be justified, at least in the early stages of pregnancy. There is controversy also about the destruction of healthy bodily capacities. Is sterilization, for example, always opposed to the natural law, or can there be exceptions?

It seems appropriate to begin with a discussion of the absolute prohibitions concerned with human life. In this chapter, therefore, I will argue that suicide, the killing of the innocent, euthanasia, and abortion are always opposed to the natural law and that the same is true for the destruction of bodily parts and capacities, although here there are certain exceptions, as we shall see. In chapter 7, we will consider indirect killing—that is, when someone is killed as a side effect of an action aimed not at him but at something else. I will then turn to the more difficult questions of capital punishment and war and conclude with some reflections on the killing of animals. I shall not be concerned with all aspects of these questions or with practical recommendations for social and political action, but only with fundamental principles of natural law.

## Suicide

Suicide is an action or omission chosen for the purpose of ending one's life.[1] It is not suicide to face the danger of death for some other purpose. A soldier on what is called a "suicide mission" may foresee that his heroic action will cause his death, but he does not aim at killing himself. His sole intention is to carry out his mission. He accepts death as a consequence but does not desire it or cause it by his own action. A sign of this is that he will certainly not be disappointed if he survives, and will not begin looking for some other way of ending his life.

Since it destroys the most fundamental natural good, suicide seems unnatural and irrational. Nevertheless, there are situations in which it may appear justifiable. An obvious example is a person experiencing extreme and irremediable suffering, when the benefits of continued existence seem outweighed by its burdens. Another example is an elderly, totally incapacitated person who wishes to avoid being a burden to others. Further examples are the spy who kills himself to avoid revealing secrets under torture and the zealot who sets himself on fire to call attention to the oppression of his people.

Besides the arguments justifying suicide in particular situations, there is a more general line of argument that goes something like this. If I am not hurting anyone else, why can't I dispose of my life as I wish? After all, it's *my* life! Perhaps it would be wrong to commit suicide if I had family obligations to fulfill or if I had some serious public duty to discharge. But if my affairs are in order and no one is likely to be harmed by my death, why should I not be able to decide whether to live or die?

But what does it mean to say "it's my life"? The expression might mean simply that I am the one whose life is in question. From this, nothing follows. Or it might mean that I own myself and can therefore destroy myself as I would a piece of unwanted

1. On suicide: *ST* II-II, q. 64, a. 5.

property. But how can I own myself, if there must be a distinction between an owner and what he owns? Or shall we say that "it's my life" means that I have authority over my life, not only the right to make use of it, but also the right to determine whether or not it shall continue? But I did not cause my existence; it was given to me in order that I might attain the life of virtue. How could I have the right to destroy it?

A more plausible case can be made for suicide in extreme situations. Can these suicides be justified, or does the natural law forbid suicide altogether? The answer turns on whether or not suicide can be ordained to the human good, for we have seen that human beings exist by nature to attain their own good as an ultimate end. Now the human good must be either one's individual good or the common good. We must therefore consider whether suicide can be ordained to the individual good of the person who commits suicide and whether it can be ordained to the common good.

Suicide clearly cannot be ordained to the individual good of the person who commits suicide. For the good to which every human being is ordained as an ultimate end is the life of virtue. It follows that all human actions must be directed to this end. But an act of self-destruction cannot be directed to the life of virtue, since it is opposed to this life, rendering its continuation impossible. Therefore, suicide for personal reasons is opposed to the natural law.

It might be replied that suicide must surely be justified for someone facing the imminent prospect of a mental decay so severe that he will no longer be able to live rationally. For when the capacity to reason is lost, virtuous actions are impossible, and life is no longer useful for attaining the ultimate end. It has become worthless, like a tool that we discard because it can no longer serve its purpose. One who can no longer live a properly human life is of no use to himself and is a burden to others. Why should a person facing this prospect not kill himself while he is still in control of his actions?

This argument proceeds as if the value of a human being were a utility value. But the good that defines a utility value is the good of something else; for a thing is said to be useful in relation to what uses it. It retains its value, therefore, only so long as it is good for the user. As we have seen many times, however, human beings exist for their own good, ultimately for the life of virtue, and what exists for its own good retains its value even when it can no longer actually achieve its good. To destroy it, therefore, would be to treat it in a way that is directly opposed to its true value. This is why we respect the lives of those who are mentally handicapped and senile. It is not what they can presently accomplish, but what they are naturally meant for, that is the source of their value as persons.

Attempts to justify suicide as a release from suffering proceed as if the purpose of human life were to avoid pain. But relief from pain is not the ultimate end; it is a means to the end. Since pain, especially severe and protracted pain, impedes our activities, pain relief can be directed to the life of virtue. But suicide cannot be so directed. Moreover, the true human good is possible even while we are suffering, for it is an act of great virtue to bear suffering patiently, thus giving witness to our true value as human beings. And since the natural law comes from God, we can confidently expect that he will give us the strength to remain faithful to it.

There remains the question of suicide for the sake of the common good. An example of this, mentioned earlier in this section, is the spy who kills himself to avoid revealing secrets under torture. If the spy's suicide is to be justified, it must be authorized by public authority, since no private citizen has the right to put anyone to death for the sake of the common good. In this respect, the situation of a spy is similar to that of an executioner; for the executioner does not administer the death penalty on his own authority, but on the authority of the state. But does the state have the power to authorize the spy to kill himself? The answer depends on whether the state has the authority to kill innocent persons for the sake of the common good. As we shall see in the next section, the state does *not* have this authority. Therefore, the spy's suicide cannot be justified either by the common good or by his individual good and is therefore necessarily opposed to the natural law.

## Killing the Innocent

According to the natural law, the killing of an innocent human being is intrinsically wrong.[2] No individual or community has the right, under any circumstances or for any reason, to intentionally kill an innocent human being.[3]

Part of the argument for the absolute prohibition against killing innocent persons has already been considered in the discussion of suicide. We have seen that the killing of a human being cannot be ordained to that person's individual good. This argument does not depend on whether the person is innocent or guilty of some serious crime, for in neither case can killing a person advance his individual good. But when we ask whether the killing of a human being can be ordained to the common good, we must distinguish between the guilty and the innocent. The question of whether the natural law permits the killing of persons guilty of heinous crimes will be considered in chapter 7. For the present we are concerned only with innocent persons.

That the killing of an innocent person cannot be ordained to

2. On killing the innocent: *ST* II-II, q. 64, a. 6.

3. Did Abraham violate the natural law when he resolved to sacrifice his innocent son, Isaac? He did not, because he was obeying God's command. The natural law precept forbidding the killing of the innocent reflects the limits of human power and authority. We cannot benefit a fellow human being by killing him; we can only do him harm. But God's power and authority are unlimited; he can bring a greater good out of the evil of Isaac's death, a good that can more than compensate Isaac for the loss of his earthly life. The natural law is a law for man, not a law for God. Just as a local official cannot act beyond his limited powers and responsibilities without the command or permission of a higher authority, so human beings cannot act beyond the limits established for them by the natural law without the command or permission of the Author of nature.

the common good follows from the very essence of the common good *as common*—that is, as a good in which everyone is meant to share. Life is clearly such a good, for no one can achieve happiness without it, and the common good of the political community is the happiness of its citizens. For this reason, the common good authorizes every member of the community to demand that his life be respected—subject, however, to the condition that he respect the lives of others. This condition is essential because if I could demand that my life be respected while refusing to respect the lives of others, I would be making a unilateral demand, a demand based solely on my private advantage, not on the common good. A person is said to be innocent because he satisfies this condition—that is, he is not guilty of murder or of some other very serious crime. It follows that an innocent person possesses an unqualified right, based on the common good, to demand that his life be respected. Public officials cannot violate this right without exceeding their authority, which arises precisely from the common good and is therefore limited by it.

It might seem that this right, however valid under ordinary circumstances, may reasonably be set aside in what are called "disastrous consequences" cases. In such cases, the authorities are confronted with two alternatives: either kill an innocent person or suffer terrible consequences. There is no third alternative. Imagine, for example, a situation in which a war or a serious riot can be averted only by hanging an innocent man. Given such a dilemma, it is tempting to think that the killing of the innocent man, however regrettable, is preferable to allowing many innocent people to be killed in the war or riot. To clarify our understanding of the meaning and consequences of the absolute prohibition against killing innocent persons, we can imagine increasingly terrible consequences, involving the painful deaths of millions of innocent men, women, and children. At some point we may feel that the injustice of killing an innocent person cannot possibly be worse than the disaster.

This argument, however, is not based on the common good,

but on the good of persons other than the one to be killed. Suppose the public authorities were to order the destruction of a minority race for the benefit of the majority, as happens in genocide. Leaving aside the question of how the destruction of a minority could *really* benefit a majority, we can see clearly that the killing of the minority is not for the common good. It is intended to benefit a faction, a faction that includes the greater part of the community, but a faction nonetheless. The case is not essentially different if we continually enlarge the majority and shrink the minority until the latter consists of one individual only. To destroy him for the benefit of the others may look like it is ordained to the common good, since the majority in this case includes all but one. But the common good, by its very nature, is the good of all. Therefore, however terrible the impending disaster, the killing of an innocent person cannot be justified on the basis of the common good.

It is true that the death of one innocent person is *as such* preferable to the death of many. For example, suppose that in a fire I can rescue either a single individual or a group of individuals, but not both. Other things being equal, it seems clear that I should try to rescue the group, even if, as a consequence, the single individual will perish. But I am not guilty of having killed him, either by a positive act or by a culpable omission; he dies because I could not get to him in time, given that saving the group had to be my first priority. It would be an altogether different matter, however, if I were to actually *kill* one person in order to save others. That would make the one I kill a mere means to the advantage of those I wish to save, as if he existed for an alien good, a good in which he has no share, rather than for his own good. This is what happens when we kill an innocent person to avoid disastrous consequences.

Furthermore, it is false to say that the disaster is worse than the injustice of killing an innocent person. For if happiness consists essentially in the life of virtue, then physical life, though desirable for itself, will not be the highest good. It will be valuable ultimately because it makes virtuous actions possible. It follows that virtuous actions are much more valuable than life and that wicked actions are much worse than the loss of life. Suffering a disaster means losing lives and bodily and external goods, whereas committing an injustice means acting contrary to virtue. Committing an injustice is therefore worse than suffering a disaster. Just as a soldier in battle may not desert even to save his life, so the state may not act unjustly even to save the lives of its citizens.

Let us conclude these reflections by imagining the worst possible case. Suppose that the very survival of the human race were at stake. Must we follow the dictum "Let justice be done, though the world perish"?[4] If we refuse to kill one innocent person, all must die, including the innocent person whose life we have spared. If we spare the innocent person, do we not then become responsible for our own extinction?

Our difficulty with this dilemma arises from a failure to reflect on what it means to be under law. Just as, under human law, there are matters that exceed the authority of private individuals and are the responsibility of public officials, so, under the natural law, there are matters that exceed all human authority and are the responsibility of the Author of nature. The natural law does indeed require us to promote the survival of the human race, but only in a way that respects the dignity of all human beings. Beyond this, we must place our trust in divine providence.

However, if human dignity were a value that we ourselves invented, then we might indeed kill an innocent person for the survival of the human race. For on that assumption the value of a human being would not be naturally superior to the value of an animal. Consequently, just as we sacrifice individual animals for the survival of the animal herd, so we might sacrifice individual human beings for the survival of the human herd. For if human dignity were no more than a cultural construct, why would we not be free to set it aside whenever this seemed expedient? But if human dignity is a reality in the nature of things, we must al-

---

4. *Fiat justitia et pereat mundus.*

ways respect the lives of innocent human beings, whatever the consequences.

## Euthanasia

Euthanasia may be defined as an act or omission intended to bring about the death of a person for what is believed to be his benefit. When death is brought about by administering a fatal injection or by some other positive action, it is called "active euthanasia" or "mercy killing"; when brought about by withholding medical care or treatment, it is called "passive euthanasia." It may be voluntary, when the person himself requests it, or involuntary, when he refuses it, or nonvoluntary, when his desires are unknown because he is unconscious or senile. We shall be considering euthanasia here as it may occur in a medical context, but the principles involved will apply also in other contexts.[5]

Those who support active euthanasia typically argue that it may be the only way or the best way to end extreme suffering in a terminally ill patient. Some supporters of euthanasia appeal also to individual freedom or "autonomy," insisting that individuals should have the right to terminate their lives, at least in situations like this. But if suicide and the killing of innocent persons are opposed in principle to the natural law, then these arguments cannot justify active euthanasia, even in its voluntary form.

Although voluntary euthanasia proceeds from the patient's suicidal decision, it is not exactly the same as suicide, since someone other than the patient is responsible for his death. This raises some new questions. First of all, it is dangerous to allow the killing of persons whose lives are thought to have lost their value. We may easily move from voluntary euthanasia to nonvoluntary or even involuntary euthanasia. What at first required the patient's

5. For a natural law perspective on euthanasia, see CDF, *Declaration on Euthanasia* (May 5, 1980).

explicit request, repeated often over a period of time, with many safeguards, later requires fewer formalities, as we begin to assume that euthanasia is what any rational person would want under the circumstances. Eventually, the patient himself may begin to think that if he refuses his consent, he will be an unreasonable burden to others.

A further question arises if physicians are called upon to administer euthanasia. For the vocation of the physician is to sustain life and to restore health. Hence, there are professional reasons why physicians should not be involved in killing patients, just as they should not be involved in executing criminals. Nor does physician-assisted suicide escape this professional objection. For although the physician does not kill the patient himself, he makes his own the patient's intention to commit suicide and cooperates with him in achieving it.

Passive euthanasia, like active euthanasia, is contrary to the natural law, if we understand it properly as an omission *intended to bring about death*. But while the intention in active euthanasia is plain from the external action, the intention involved in omitting treatment is not always evident. It is true that there are some omissions that, if they are not due to incompetence or gross negligence, seem clearly intended to bring about the patient's death. But this is not true of all omissions. Sometimes a medical treatment can reasonably be judged to be excessively burdensome or relatively useless under the circumstances. If it is withheld or withdrawn for this reason and not in order to bring about the patient's death, this is not passive euthanasia.

Since happiness is impossible without life, we are clearly obligated by natural law not only to avoid what destroys life but also to provide what sustains it. What must always be provided are the natural means for sustaining life, like food and water and other forms of basic care. But *medical* means—that is, interventions going beyond these natural means—may sometimes be withheld or withdrawn. For these measures may be more or less burdensome for the patient or for the community that must provide them, and they may be more or less useful in curing disease or in warding off death. Sometimes a medical means may be so burdensome or so futile as to be beyond what is required by the natural law. It then becomes what is called an *extraordinary means* and need not be administered.

It is important to note that when a medical treatment is judged extraordinary, what is being judged is the value of the treatment, not the value of a human being. For while the essential value of a human being always remains unchanged, whatever his physical or mental condition, the value of a particular medical treatment may be greater or less depending on conditions. Thus, a treatment may be useless under the circumstances or it may impose burdens in suffering or even in expense that are greater than what the patient or his family can reasonably be expected to bear. Extremely expensive treatments of marginal benefit may also impose a disproportionate burden on the community, which must be concerned primarily with the ordinary medical needs of the people. When we reject treatments for such reasons, the death of the patient, even if foreseen, remains entirely outside our intention.

One might think that if suicide and euthanasia are always wrong, then human life must have an absolute value—that is, a value such that everything must be done to protect and maintain it. But suicide and euthanasia are not wrong because life has an absolute value, but because all of our actions must be directed to our ultimate end, the life of virtue, and suicide and euthanasia cannot be so directed. Furthermore, if life were an absolute value, we would be obligated not only to make use of extraordinary medical procedures, but even to betray our country or deny our religion, if our lives depended on it. Only the ultimate end has an absolute value. But life, although it is a fundamental human good and desirable for its own sake, is not the ultimate end, since it is ordered to a higher good, the life of virtue.

It can be difficult to determine when a medical treatment is extraordinary. But we should note that this kind of difficulty is not unique to medical decisions. Consider the obligation to give to people in need. How much must we give? Presumably not so much that we are unable to maintain a decent standard of living. But it is not easy to know where to draw the line between what we are morally obligated to give and what goes beyond this. In the same way, it is not easy to draw a line between ordinary medical interventions, which are obligatory, and extraordinary interventions, which are beyond the call of duty. The demands of the natural law are satisfied if we make these decisions conscientiously as best we can.

## Abortion

Abortion is the intentional killing of an unborn human being by physically assaulting it or by preventing it from implanting in the womb. The destruction of an embryo produced through in vitro fertilization, though not called an abortion, raises essentially the same moral questions.[6]

We have seen that the intentional killing of an innocent human being is always opposed to the natural law. Therefore, if a human embryo or fetus is an actually existing human being, then abortion is always wrong. Moreover, since all innocent human beings have an equal personal dignity, it will be wrong to kill an embryo or fetus even to save the life of the mother, just as it would be wrong to kill the mother in order to save the life of the embryo or fetus. An innocent human being may not be killed for any reason at any stage of life.

But is the embryo or fetus an actually existing human being? Proponents of abortion often maintain that an embryo or fetus is not fully human, but only *biologically* human, or that it is not an *actual* person, but only a *potential* person. To be an actual person, according to these arguments, one must be capable of conscious

6. For a natural law perspective on abortion, see CDF, *Declaration on Procured Abortion* (November 18, 1974).

desires or interests. But we do not see evidence of this capability in an embryo or fetus, at least not in the early stages of its development. But if an embryo or fetus is not yet an actual person, it might seem that it does not yet have an actual right to life.

This objection raises a question about the meaning of the word "person." Traditionally, a person has been defined as an individual rational substance. This rationality becomes known to us through signs of rational activity as they appear in mature human beings. But the *existence* of a rational substance does not depend on our perceiving its rational activity. Nothing prevents an embryo or fetus from being a rational substance before it shows any outward signs of rationality, or before it has any internal rational experience, or even before its sense powers have developed sufficiently for it to be able to exercise its rational powers. The rational substance possesses the capacity to reason by its very nature from the beginning of its existence. Otherwise, how could activities manifesting rationality appear later?

It might be objected, however, that an embryo, at least in the earliest stages of its development, may not possess the rational capacity that is manifested later in a mature human being. For it may not yet be a rational substance. It may be a pre-human form of life that only later becomes a human being. But the theory that there is a change from a pre-human substance to a human substance somewhere during the process of embryonic and fetal development is implausible in the light of contemporary scientific knowledge of conception and embryology. There is no point in the continuous development from conception to birth that marks or appears to mark a substantial change. The embryo is therefore likely to be a human being, and so we ought to assume that it is and spare its life.[7] Otherwise we seriously risk killing a hu-

---

7. For a detailed defense of the humanity of the embryo, see Robert P. George and Christopher Tollefsen, *Embryo: A Defense of Human Life* (New York: Doubleday, 2008), chapter 2. See also the authors' refutation of the claim that an early embryo is not a human individual because it is not sufficiently unified or because of the possibility of twinning; ibid., 144–58.

man being, just as would a hunter who fires at something moving without making sure that it is not another hunter. Furthermore, even if the embryo *were* a pre-human substance, we would still be obligated to respect its life. For the embryo would be in the process of becoming a human person, and to destroy it would be to deprive the person who is coming to be of a life that he was naturally meant to inherit.

These arguments assume the traditional definition of personhood. But someone might object that personhood should not be defined in this way, at least not for the purpose of assigning rights. No one should be called a person until he has reached a certain stage of development. Just as a human being becomes an artist or a physician when he has attained a certain level of knowledge and skill, so a human being becomes a person when he has attained at least some level of meaningful conscious activity.[8] Only then can he have conscious desires or interests that we are obligated to respect.

To respond to this objection, it is first of all necessary to distinguish conscious desires from interests. A human being has an interest in whatever is useful for the attainment of his well-being, whether he knows it or not. Even in the embryonic stages of its development, a human being has interests, in particular an interest in staying alive, since without life it cannot attain its natural end. Of course, an embryo is unaware of its interests, but this does not mean that we do not have an obligation to respect and promote them. A child is often unaware of his true interests, but we promote them nevertheless, sometimes even against the child's desires.

Why are we obligated to respect the embryo's interest in remaining alive? As with all the life issues, the answer lies in human dignity, in the fact that human beings, unlike plants and animals, exist in order to attain their own good as an ultimate end. It is

8. I have seen the expression "becoming a person" used in relation to childhood development, the idea being not that the child is becoming a human being, but that he is becoming a more mature human being.

unjust to sacrifice them to an alien good. Human dignity does not begin when a human being becomes aware of it or when he has attained a certain level of development. It is present from the beginning of life. For the process of human development, from its very beginning, is for the sake of the new human being who, through this process, is developing and coming to maturity. Like all members of the human community, therefore, the embryo or fetus has rights to whatever is necessary for its survival and well-being.

Let me conclude by noting that the right-to-life argument is not the only argument against abortion. It is the most compelling, since it is founded on the most fundamental human right. But there are many other arguments, some concerned with the nature of pregnancy, others with the nature of marriage and the role of mothers and fathers, yet others with the deleterious cultural consequences of the abortion mentality. But we shall not consider these arguments here.

## Bodily Integrity

The precepts concerning health and physical integrity are similar to the precepts concerning life. For good health and physical integrity are valuable instrumentally for virtuous actions, and when they are lacking, the possibilities for such actions are correspondingly diminished. The man missing a limb or suffering from a physical disability will find many external activities difficult or impossible, and the man in poor health may not be able to continue with his life's work. Of course, such persons can live useful and praiseworthy lives, for virtuous persons always make the best use of their circumstances, but they will not be able to do all that they would otherwise wish to do. It follows that actions intended to ruin one's health or to destroy one's bodily integrity cannot be ordained to the ultimate end and that a failure to take reasonable measures to preserve these goods shows an inadequate respect for them.

Although the amputation of a *healthy* limb or organ, except in certain emergencies, cannot be ordained to the ultimate end, the same is not true for the amputation of a *diseased* limb or organ that threatens the life of the body. For the part exists for the sake of the whole, and while a healthy part of the body completes and perfects the whole, a diseased part may threaten to destroy it. Therefore, if the survival of the whole is at stake, a diseased part that cannot be cured must be amputated. In certain emergencies, however, even a healthy limb, trapped and unable to be dislodged, might have to be cut off to save a person immediately threatened by enemy explosives or by fire or rising water. This is justified by the same fundamental principle: that the part exists for the sake of the whole.

While the destruction of a healthy part of the body normally strikes us with horror—the pitiful story of Van Gogh cutting off his ear comes to mind[9]—it is frequently maintained that an exception should be made for the reproductive organs under certain circumstances. For example, if a further pregnancy would seriously threaten a woman's life, should she not be sterilized? For it would not be reasonable for her to again become pregnant.

Nevertheless, even in these circumstances, to destroy a woman's reproductive power would be contrary to the natural law. For sterilization is necessarily a diminishment of the woman who undergoes it, since it is opposed to the fullness or completeness of her womanhood, just as vasectomy is opposed to the fullness or completeness of manhood. But a procedure that diminishes the human body makes it less capable of being an instrument of virtuous actions. Such a procedure cannot be ordained to the life of virtue and is therefore contrary to the natural law.

But how can the sterilization of the woman in this case be opposed to the life of virtue? For we are assuming that, because of the danger to her life, it would no longer be reasonable for her

---

9. I use this story because it is well known, although I am told that it may not be true.

to become pregnant. But if it is unreasonable for her to become pregnant, her reproductive power can no longer be used as an instrument of virtuous actions. Therefore, it would seem that sterilization is not always opposed to the life of virtue.

This objection arises from a failure to appreciate the significance of the diminishment of the woman resulting from sterilization. Her procreative power is not merely an instrument she uses, like an external tool; it is part of her very nature and completes and perfects her. Respect for her dignity means respect for her in her integrity, including all of her natural powers. For these powers have been given to her to be used in virtuous actions. As we have seen, the life of virtue is the ultimate end, the end to which everything she does and everything done to her must be directed. But the destruction of her procreative power cannot be directed to the life of virtue, because it does not maintain or expand, but rather contracts the possibilities for virtuous actions. Just as the value of the woman remains even when she is permanently unconscious or senile and can no longer live or live well the life of virtue, so the value of her procreative power remains, as part of her natural integrity, even when, because of circumstances, it is not reasonable for her to make use of it. Similar arguments apply to male sterilization.

This completes our consideration of the absolute prohibitions regarding life and physical integrity. As we have seen, every intentional destruction of an innocent human being or part of a human being—except when the part must be removed to save the whole—is opposed to the natural law. But what of lethal actions that are not directed at innocent persons, but nevertheless do kill them? And what about the killing that takes place in capital punishment and war? These are the main issues to be considered in chapter 7.

# The Life Issues

## Part 2

In chapter 6, we saw that the directly intended killing of an innocent human being is absolutely prohibited by the natural law. In this chapter we will be concerned first with what is called "indirect killing" and then with two kinds of direct killing, capital punishment and killing in war, which require special consideration. I will conclude with some thoughts on the killing of animals.

## Indirect Killing

Killing is direct when we aim a lethal act at someone either as an end, because we want him dead, or as a means to an end, because we want something else that the lethal act will enable us to obtain. In indirect killing, we do not aim a lethal act at the one we kill; rather, his death is a side effect of an act that we have aimed at something else. A sign of this is that our act would accomplish its purpose even if the one in danger of being killed indirectly were somehow able to escape harm. The death of a person killed indirectly is therefore unintended, though it may be foreseen.

War provides typical examples of indirect killing. A commander directing an attack against enemy soldiers may also kill noncombatants who are in the area. But he does not aim to kill noncombatants either as an end, since they are not fighting against him, or as a means to an end, since the fact that they are harmed contributes nothing to his purpose. Their death is the side effect of a military action aimed entirely at enemy soldiers. The same thing occurs when air attacks aimed at military installations or war plants cause the death of noncombatants—so-called collateral damage.

Is indirect killing opposed to the natural law? Not necessarily, since it does not violate human dignity per se. For since the lethal act is not aimed at the person himself, but at something else, he is not being used as a mere means to the good of others. Nevertheless, an act that kills someone indirectly will violate the natural law unless it can be justified by what is called the "principle of double effect."

An indirect killing is justified by the principle of double effect when it satisfies four conditions. These conditions, as they apply to indirect killing, may be stated as follows: (1) the killing of the person is not the end intended by the agent; (2) the lethal action is not aimed at the person as a means to an end; (3) the results of not performing the action will be worse than the results of performing it; and (4) the bad results cannot be avoided. The first two conditions express the definition of indirect killing; the last two are relevant to determining when an action that indirectly kills someone can be justified. For an action that endangers the life of a person without adequate reason is clearly a violation of the right to life.

When the principle of double effect does *not* apply, it is often because the second condition—the condition that forbids directing a lethal act at a person as a means to an end—is not satisfied. For when a lethal act is aimed precisely at a person, he is killed directly. Only when the killing is indirect does the principle of double effect allow us to consider the third and fourth conditions.

The principle of double effect has been used to justify certain procedures that result in the death of an embryo or fetus, procedures that are called "indirect abortions." If a pregnant woman is in danger of death from cancer of the uterus, the surgical removal of this diseased organ can be justified, even though it will result in the death of the fetus as a side effect. Similarly justifiable is the surgical removal of a fallopian tube in an ectopic pregnancy, since, if it is not removed, the tube will rupture with very serious consequences for the mother. In neither case is the act that causes the death of the fetus aimed at the fetus itself.

Another important example is the administration of pain-killing medication to a dying patient. Although this medication may have the effect of shortening life, the use of it is not opposed to the natural law if the purpose is to alleviate significant pain, not to bring about death, and if the medication itself and the doses administered are an appropriate means to this end. The earlier death of the patient, should it occur, is an unintended side effect that is tolerable under the circumstances. Speaking more generally, medications typically have undesirable side effects. Following the principle of double effect, we can justify the use of such medications when the good effects outweigh the bad effects and no better alternative is available.

## Killing in Self-Defense

Killing in self-defense, properly understood, can also be justified by the principle of double effect. The argument is difficult and controverted, however, and will require some discussion. The first thing to note is that only public authority has the right to directly kill a guilty person, as we shall see later in the section on capital punishment. From this it follows that a private individual does not have the right to directly kill his attacker. He may, however, take whatever measures are necessary to defend himself, even if these should result in his attacker's death.

To be justified, therefore, an act of self-defense must not aim to kill the attacker either as an end or as a means to an end. The action taken must be essentially defensive, intended to prevent injury to the one being attacked rather than to do harm to the attacker. The harm to the attacker will then be the result of his own aggression, since he attacks in spite of the potential victim's defenses, so that what happens to him will be his own fault. Since an innocent person may put his own safety ahead of the safety of his attacker, the third double-effect condition is satisfied. And if the defensive measures employed do not involve more risk to the attacker than is necessary to secure the safety of the person being attacked, the fourth condition is also satisfied.[1]

But is it really the case that the potential victim's action is purely defensive and not aggressive? Consider a case in which I stop my attacker by firing a gun at him. Am I not protecting myself by directing a lethal act at my attacker, and isn't this direct killing? But if a private person does not have the right to directly kill anyone, how can my action be justified?

The problem in this and similar cases is the difficulty of distinguishing a defensive action from an aggressive one. For whether I act aggressively or defensively, I fire the gun, and the result is the same. However, aggressive and defensive actions are essentially different. If I choose to kill or harm my attacker as a means to an end, I act aggressively, and his death is due to me. But if I choose to defend myself, the death of the attacker, if it results, is due to him, since he continues the attack in spite of my defense. The attacker is like the man who insists on going into a snake-infested area and dies from a snake bite. No one would deny that he is responsible for his death. Similarly, the attacker dies not because I am trying to kill him, but because he enters a danger zone that I have established for my protection. My gun will fire only if he continues his attack. His death or injury is therefore clearly his own fault.

Because I fire the gun at him, my action looks more like aggression than would an action in which I am less immediately involved. Imagine that between me and a murderous attacker is an electric fence, which, if I turn it on, will electrocute anyone who touches it. If the attacker persists, he will die because I have

1. *ST* II-II, q. 64, a. 7.

turned on the fence, just as he will die if I fire my gun. Or suppose I am in a room that I have booby-trapped so that a gun will fire if the door is opened. Turning on this booby trap will kill the attacker when he opens the door, just as would happen if I were to fire at him with my hand gun. Firing a gun, therefore, is not essentially different from activating any other potentially lethal defensive measure.

It is true that once I turn on my fence or activate my booby trap, I need not be further involved, but if I defend myself with a gun, I must myself choose when and where to fire. But is this a significant difference? Just as I decide when to fire, so I decide when to activate my fence; and just as I decide where to point my gun, so I decide where to aim the gun in my booby trap. In all of these cases, I determine the when and the where according to what will be most effective in stopping the attack. In the fence and booby-trap cases, I can usually give a warning, since the danger to me is not quite so immediate. But what if I do not have time to turn on the fence before the attacker is already touching it or to activate the booby trap before the attacker is actually pushing open the door? Furthermore, it is not clear that a warning is always obligatory. Suppose, for example, that the fence is my only defense and that if I warn the attacker, he will be able to get at me in another way. Every attacker must recognize that the person defending himself will use whatever defense he has and that he will not necessarily reveal what that defense is. For these reasons, I think that these various ways of defending oneself are not significantly different. They are all essentially defensive, not aggressive. The problem, I think, is with our imagination.

Since in all of these cases the defensive measures are lethal or potentially lethal, one might question whether I have not gone beyond the bounds of legitimate self-defense. For if my measures for defense are more harmful to the attacker than what is reasonably necessary for my safety, I am, to that extent, acting aggressively rather than defensively. I agree that this would be a serious question in cases where the attacker could be stopped with less violence. Here I am just assuming that the defensive measures in my examples are the only ones available. My concern has not been to analyze self-defense cases in detail, but simply to clarify the distinction between aggressive and defensive actions.

## Capital Punishment

As we saw in chapter 6, the natural law does not permit the direct killing of innocent persons under any circumstances. But what of persons who are guilty of murder or of some other crime of equal or greater danger to the community? Does the natural law permit the execution of such persons?

This topic involves three questions that must be considered in sequence. The first is whether capital punishment violates the right to life. For if it does, it will be absolutely forbidden by the natural law. If it does not, then we must consider a second question: whether persons guilty of capital crimes *must* be put to death. If this is not absolutely necessary, we can turn to a third question: whether capital punishment is helpful or harmful to the community.

Does capital punishment violate the right to life? If human beings exist by nature for their own good, and if this good is found essentially in virtuous actions, and if life is necessary for such actions, then all human beings have a natural right to life. From this it would seem to follow that even murderers have this right. It is true that a murderer has violated his victim's right to life. But does this make it right for the community, in its turn, to violate the murderer's right to life? Two wrongs do not make a right.

Must we say then that capital punishment violates the right to life? Or can we say, as has traditionally been said, that a murderer forfeits his right to life and, therefore, that capital punishment is not opposed to the natural law, at least not per se?[2]

---

2. *ST* II-II, q. 64, a. 2. On the debt of punishment, see *ST* I-II, q. 87, a. 1.

Let us approach this question by reviewing what was said earlier about human beings existing for their own good as an ultimate end. We have a tendency to think of a person's "own good" as that which is good for him only—that is, his individual good, not shared with others. This would mean that I exist only to enjoy *my* life, think *my* thoughts, pursue *my* ambitions, and so on. If this were all that human dignity meant, then capital punishment would necessarily be opposed to the natural law. For capital punishment is clearly opposed to the individual good of the person executed.

However, the individual's "own good" includes the common good as well as his individual good. For the common good, as we have seen, is not the good of the majority or the sum total of individual goods; rather, it is the good of every individual person in the community, though not of any one person exclusively. Thus, public security, adequate supplies of food and water, help in time of need, and institutions for education, cultural enrichment, and religion are all parts of the common good. Every individual in the community benefits from them directly or indirectly. But since they are realized only through cooperative action, no individual can claim the benefits resulting from them as belonging to him exclusively.

To understand how this applies to capital punishment, we must begin by clarifying the idea of a right. A right may be defined roughly as what is legally due to a person from one or more other persons. Since what is legally due can be claimed by the one to whom it is due (or by another on his behalf), a right may also be defined as a legally authorized claim on the conduct of others. Since claims of right are authorized by law and laws are established for the common good, it is necessary that such claims be essentially bilateral, not unilateral. By this I mean that no one is entitled to demand, on the basis of the common good, the enjoyment of a benefit that he refuses to let others enjoy. Respect for life is such a benefit. Hence, the natural law authorizes every person to demand that his life be respected *on condition that he respect the lives of others*. This is why an innocent person has a right to life and why this right is inviolable. But a murderer, since he refuses to respect the lives of others, can no longer reasonably demand that his life be respected as a matter of principle. His execution, therefore, does not violate the right to life.

To see this more clearly, imagine a man who has just killed a fellow human being and who demands that his life, nevertheless, must absolutely be respected. We see immediately that he is asking for a privilege. He is demanding that an exception be made for him so that he may take the life of another while his own life remains inviolable. But to ask for something as a privilege is not the same as to demand it as a right. The murderer has deprived himself, by his own action, of the right to demand that his life be absolutely inviolable. He has forfeited his right to life.

Moreover, if the murderer is executed on the basis of the common good, it is clear that he is not executed on the basis of an alien good, but on the basis of his own good. For the laws against murder and the punishments for murder were intended for his benefit as much as for the benefit of others. If his execution furthers the common good, therefore, the murderer cannot reasonably protest it. For, as we saw in chapter 5, the common good takes precedence over private advantage.

While this argument shows us that capital punishment is not opposed to the natural law per se, it does *not* show us whether it *furthers* or *hinders* the common good. Before we can discuss this question, however, we must consider another line of argument, associated especially with Kant, that holds that capital punishment need not be justified by an appeal to deterrence or to any other aspect of social utility. A murderer deserves death as retribution for his crime, and the courts have a duty to sentence him to death.[3]

---

3. Immanuel Kant, *Metaphysical First Principles of the Doctrine of Right*, in *The Metaphysics of Morals*, trans., ed. Mary Gregor (Cambridge: Cambridge University Press, 1996), Public Right, § 49E. However, Kant does admit the possibility that the executive authority might pronounce a sentence less than death in a particular

The premise in this argument is true: the murderer does indeed deserve to die. For he has injured not only his victim and his victim's family, but the community as well. This is because the order of justice is a common good and its support and vindication a public matter. By violating the order of justice, the murderer has created an inequality or unbalance for which he deserves to suffer something against his will equal to the evil that he has willfully caused. He deserves, therefore, the punishment of death.

But this does not prove that murderers *should* be executed. For it is one thing to show that a murderer deserves to die and another thing to determine who has the right to execute him and for what purpose. The right to execute murderers does not belong to private citizens, for the citizens are all equal and none has authority over any other. Parents, of course, have authority over their minor children, but this is a strictly limited authority. Only public authority, to which all the citizens are subject, has the right to pass judgment on a murderer and to execute him. But the state's right to execute murderers is not unconditional. It depends on the common good, that is, on whether the execution of murderers promotes the welfare of the people. As Aquinas notes, the punishments of the present life are medicinal, intended for the good of the individual or of the community.[4] It is in this context that the appropriateness of capital punishment must be evaluated.

We come therefore to our third question, the question of the usefulness of capital punishment. Here my remarks must be more exploratory, since I do not have the qualifications and experience necessary for a sophisticated response to the issues involved.

Does capital punishment promote the common good by deterring others from committing murder? Opponents of capital punishment often point to studies that show that its abolition does not affect the murder rate. Proponents claim that such stud-

---

case by right of majesty. *Metaphysical First Principles of the Doctrine of Right* is the first of the two parts of Kant's *Metaphysics of Morals*; *Metaphysical First Principles of the Doctrine of Virtue* is the second part.

4. *ST* II-II, q. 66, a. 6, ad. 2, and *ST* II-II, q. 68, a. 1, c.

ies are inconclusive, because capital punishment, even when legal, is not frequent enough or expeditious enough or visible enough to constitute an effective deterrent.

There are also psychological arguments. It would seem that a punishment as fearful as the death penalty must deter many potential murderers. On the other hand, if murderers act either in a fit of passion, not caring what will happen to them, or with careful calculation, expecting to get away with it, how will capital punishment be an effective deterrent? But wouldn't capital punishment, administered promptly and publicly, increase social solidarity by assuring law-abiding citizens that their rights are being zealously safeguarded? Or are executions, especially public executions, nothing more than spectacles that satisfy blood lust or arouse morbid curiosity?

Nor are deterrence and respect for law and order the only issues. There is also the problem of miscarriages of justice, when persons are executed and later discovered to have been innocent. And even if a person is guilty, wouldn't it be better to punish him with imprisonment, thus giving him the opportunity to repent and be reintegrated into society? Further problems arise when only a fraction of those guilty of murder are executed and when a disproportionate number of these are poor and minorities. Perhaps these problems could be remedied somewhat by reforming the institution of capital punishment. However, when we look at the cruel mass killings that took place under Nazism and Communism and the indiscriminate terrorist killings taking place today, perhaps it would be better to abolish the death penalty altogether. Furthermore, although in times past capital punishment was generally regarded as a socially useful institution, today it has been abolished or greatly restricted in most countries. From this it would seem that the abolition of capital punishment, like the abolition of slavery, reflects a fuller appreciation of human dignity and is a sign of human progress.[5]

5. John Paul II, *Evangelium Vitae*, Encyclical Letter (March 25, 1995), nos. 9, 27, 56. See also the *Address of His Holiness Pope Francis to Participants in the Meet-*

Although I favor the abolition of capital punishment, my purpose here has not been to prove that it should be ended, but to distinguish it from the killing of innocent human beings, which, being intrinsically wrong, is far more serious. Therefore, if the abolition of capital punishment shows an increased respect for human dignity and is a sign of progress, would not the ending of abortion and euthanasia show this respect even more and be an even greater sign of progress? The killing of innocent human beings is not progress but regression.

## War

A discussion of the morality of war must be concerned with two fundamental questions. The first is a question of principle: on what conditions can war be justified? The second and more difficult question concerns the application of these conditions. How should they be applied in the contemporary world? To what extent is war a suitable means for maintaining or restoring justice today? Only the first question is directly relevant to the present study, but I shall nevertheless make a brief comment in response to the second one as well.

Aquinas taught that the natural law permits killing in a just

---

*ing promoted by the Pontifical Council for Promoting the New Evangelization* (October 11, 2017). Following Pope Francis, the Catholic Church teaches, in the light of the gospel, that "the death penalty is inadmissible because it is an attack on the inviolability and dignity of the person"; Holy See Press Office, Summary of Bulletin, *New Revision of Number 2267 of the Catechism of the Catholic Church on the Death Penalty* (February 8, 2018). Since this teaching is proposed in the light of the gospel, its discussion belongs more to moral theology than to philosophy. However, if we grant that capital punishment does not advance the common good, I think it can be defended philosophically. For human dignity means that human beings exist for their own good, the individual good and the common good. But capital punishment does not advance the individual good of the person executed. Therefore, if we assume that it does not advance the common good either, how can it be consistent with human dignity? As we have seen, the fact that a murderer has forfeited his right to life does not imply either that he must be executed or that the state has an unconditional right to execute him.

war. A war is just when three conditions are satisfied: (1) that the war be declared by public authority; (2) that the cause be just; and (3) that the intention be right.[6] We will first consider these conditions and then turn to a special problem, the killing of enemy soldiers who are fighting in a war that is in fact unjust, but who do not recognize the injustice, and think that they are only doing their duty. Finally, I will turn, very briefly, to the question of how these conditions should be applied today.

Aquinas's first condition, that war must be waged by public authority, follows from the fact that war involves direct killing. For, as we have seen for capital punishment, direct killing can be authorized only by the authority responsible for the common good. Ideally, just wars should be declared or authorized by an international public authority, since they are fought in order to maintain or restore the international order of justice. But when such an authority does not exist or cannot act effectively, individual states must themselves judge the justice of their cause and declare war when peaceful efforts to maintain their rights (or the rights of other states or persecuted peoples) have failed. Furthermore, an individual state always retains the right to defend itself from an unjust attack, since such aggression is clearly contrary to the international common good.

Aquinas explains his second condition, that wars must be fought for a just cause, by stating that the cause is just when the enemy deserves it because of some fault. He then quotes Augustine, who mentions cases in which a state refuses to make reparations for harm done by its subjects or to restore what it has seized unjustly. These statements suggest that a just cause for war can arise from any serious violation of the order of justice. Examples would be an attack by a state against its innocent neighbors, the refusal by a state to remedy serious injustices that it has committed against other states or their citizens, and the subjecting of a people to genocide or to intolerable oppression. International

6. *ST* II-II, q. 40, a. 1, c.

positive law may establish more restrictive conditions—for instance, that a state must not interfere in the internal affairs of another state. Such restrictions have pragmatic justification insofar as they prevent an aggressive state from using tensions or disturbances within a neighboring state as an excuse for military intervention. But in extreme situations they could be unreasonably restrictive.

The third condition, according to Aquinas, is that those who propose to fight a just war must have the right intention: that they act to promote good and to prevent evil. He quotes two texts in this connection. The first is a canonical text stating that wars should not be waged out of cupidity or cruelty, but for the sake of peace, to restrain the wicked and support the good. The second, a text from Augustine, condemns wars fought out of a passion for inflicting harm, a cruel vengefulness, an implacable spirit, a savage rebelliousness, a lust for domination, and the like. In summary, then, the intention is right when the war is fought in order to promote good and to prevent evil and is conducted throughout in a way that reflects this purpose.

Of these three conditions, the third is the most difficult to apply, since many factors related to the decision to go to war and to the fighting of the war must be taken into consideration. Many specific limitations and cautions that have been proposed in discussions of just war theory seem to me to be related to right intention. For no matter how just the cause, a war cannot be justified unless it is reasonable to expect that it actually will promote the common good. Before going to war, therefore, a state must consider whether the injustice can be remedied by peaceful means; for it may be better to tolerate some injustices with a view to gradually resolving them peacefully than to engage in a war that may cause even greater evils. The state must also consider whether the war has a reasonable prospect of succeeding, whether it can be fought in such a way as to avoid disproportionate harm to noncombatants, whether it will lead to a humanitarian crisis for civilian populations, whether it is likely to lead to a just peace or merely sow the seeds of future wars, etc. In conducting the war, the state must respect truces and cease-fires and generally keep faith with the enemy, minimize harm to civilian populations (a difficult matter when military installations are concealed among civilian populations), and treat prisoners of war and civilians in occupied territories humanely. Finally, the state must make plans for building peace after the war by not making excessive demands on a defeated enemy and by helping so far as possible with reconstruction. The whole point of war is peace, and a lasting peace requires reconciliation and the reestablishment of friendly relations.

## Treatment of Enemy Combatants

Let us turn now to the special problem I mentioned earlier: is it possible to justify the killing of enemy combatants who believe— sincerely, let us suppose, but erroneously—that they are fighting in a just war? Killing in war is direct killing. Soldiers engaged in combat intentionally kill the enemy, just as executioners intentionally kill prisoners condemned to death. But whereas the criminal who is executed is guilty of a capital crime, the enemy soldier may believe that he is acting justly. Deceived perhaps by propaganda, he may see himself as fighting for the rights of his country. Moreover, he is easily persuaded that whatever the original cause of the conflict, defeat will result in injustices being inflicted upon his people by the victors. Killing in war, therefore, would seem to lack the justification possible for capital punishment. It might seem to violate the absolute prohibition against killing innocent persons.

To resolve this dilemma, we must consider, first of all, that the soldier fighting in an unjust war is actively opposing the international order of justice. It is clear, therefore, that he is acting unjustly. But if he does not realize this, he is guilty of injustice only in a qualified sense. For he has not himself chosen to act unjustly; rather he has chosen to serve as an instrument of his commander's will. But the commander's will is unjust. Therefore, while the soldier is actually engaged in battle, he is acting unjustly and forfeits for the time his right to life. But if he surrenders, he ceases to be an instrument of his commander's will, and his life should be respected.

But how can a soldier who is unaware that he is acting unjustly forfeit his right to life even for a limited time? The answer lies again in the primacy of the common good. For since a soldier fighting for an unjust cause is attacking the order of justice, and since the order of justice is an essential part of the common good, he is attacking the common good itself. But, as we saw when discussing capital punishment, the right to life is a claim based on the common good, not on one's private advantage. Therefore, since the common good cannot authorize a claim of right opposed to itself, the soldier who is fighting in an unjust war necessarily forfeits for the time his right to life.

## Applying Just War Theory Today

How should just war theory be applied today? It is obvious that we must deliberate very carefully before resorting to armed conflict, taking many things into consideration. As everyone recognizes, weapons of mass destruction pose the greatest danger. The possible use of such weapons raises the specter of total war, with consequences so terrible that war appears as an outmoded way of rectifying injustices. From this, I think we may draw two very general conclusions. The first is that the universal common good requires us to make every effort to ameliorate the conditions that lead to hatred and hostility between peoples and nations, thus sowing the seeds of war. Just as the international common good can be harmed more grievously today by war, so it can be promoted more effectively by appropriate trade and development policies. The second conclusion is that war should be undertaken, if at all, only with the greatest caution and, so far as possible, with international approval. Although the United Nations realizes the ideal of an international authority only very imperfectly, it is nevertheless important that wars be fought under its auspices or, at the very least, with due respect for world opinion.

## Killing Animals

Should we not recognize a right to life in animals as well as in human beings? For the animals—the higher animals at least—are much like us. They experience fear and pain just as we do, and they recognize danger and make efforts to save themselves from harm. They are sometimes thought to have a greater right to life than human embryos and fetuses, since these latter have little or no awareness of what happens to them. Would the right to life extend to all animals? Probably not to insects and other primitive forms of life. Would it forbid all killing of animals? That too is unlikely. But it would certainly require greater justification for the killing of animals than has traditionally been required.

The question of recognizing a right to life in animals must be distinguished from questions about preserving species of animals threatened with extinction and, more generally, from questions about caring for the natural environment. When we seek to protect wolves, for example, we are not typically concerned with the welfare of this or that individual wolf, but only with maintaining a viable wolf population. The same is true generally for all species of animals and plants; our concern is not with individuals, but with populations. And the purpose of our concern is largely our own benefit. We feel that an abundance of different kinds of plants and animals is a valuable resource for ourselves and for future generations.

To go beyond a concern for preserving species, however, and to extend a right to life to individual animals would be a mistake. There is no natural foundation for such a right. An animal does not understand the ends for which it acts, does not rationally order means to these ends, and does not freely choose what to do. It is moved to action by a natural instinct. But what is moved by instinct is moved not so much by itself as by something other than itself, by the cause of its nature and instinct. It follows that an individual animal does not exist ultimately for its own good, like a human being, but for its usefulness. It has the character of an instrument, a thing to be used by a rational agent. Since a being cannot have dignity and rights unless it exists for its own good, it is clear that an animal cannot have a right to life.[7]

To see this more clearly, consider that every living thing is naturally oriented to its individual survival and to the survival of its offspring *as an immediate or proximate end*. In this sense, we can speak of an animal having desires and interests. But what is the animal's ultimate purpose? To ascertain this, we must look at the natural world as a whole, observing the interrelationships of the different species of plants and animals. Such observations show that higher animals naturally make use of lower animals and plants for food and sometimes for other purposes. We can reasonably conclude, therefore, that plants naturally exist for the use of the animals that feed upon them, that prey animals naturally exist for the use of their predators, and that all the animals and plants exist ultimately for the use of man. For while the animals make use of only a limited number of species of plants and animals and use them only in limited ways, according to their various natural instincts, man is able to use all the species of plants and animals in an unlimited variety of ways—for food, clothing, work, play, scientific research, etc. Therefore, everything in nature other than man exists ultimately for its utility; man alone exists simply for his own good.

Nevertheless, our right to use animals and plants for our good does not imply a right to kill them wantonly or uselessly or to treat them with cruelty. They are intended for our use, not for

7. *SCG* III, caps. 111–12.

our abuse. Abusive behavior is irrational, and irrational actions are opposed to the life of virtue. Furthermore, plants and animals are intended for the benefit of all members of the human race, including future generations. Inasmuch as it deprives some human beings of resources that are meant for all human beings, the excessive or pointless destruction of plants and animals, whether directly intended or resulting indirectly from industrial and commercial development, is opposed to the common good of mankind and so is clearly unjust.

Does this view of plants and animals, the idea that they exist ultimately to be used by us for our benefit, necessarily give rise to a domineering and exploitative attitude toward nature? This need not result if we recognize that we ourselves are not outside of the natural world, but are a part of it—the highest part, the part that completes the whole, but a part nonetheless. The natural world is our world. This should lead us to a recognition and respect for all of our fellow living creatures in all of their wonderful diversity and interrelationships. For they all, even the humblest, have a value or status not completely captured by their usefulness to us, since each is interesting in its own way and makes its unique contribution to the common good. To approach the natural world in this way is to approach it in a spirit of natural piety rather than in a spirit of domination, which can easily lead to hasty and destructive interventions for the sake of immediate gain.[8]

The importance of this natural piety can be more fully appreciated if we recall our reflections in chapter 5 on the commandment to love God above all things. There we saw that man, being a part of the universe, naturally loves the common good, the good of the universe as a whole, more than he loves himself. But the common good of the universe lies in the order of its parts to each other and to the universe as a whole. Therefore, it is natural to man to love the order of the universe more than he loves himself. What is

8. For a contemporary discussion on care for the environment, our common home, see Francis, *Laudato si'*, Encyclical Letter (May 24, 2015).

especially wonderful about this order is that it manifests the wisdom of the Creator and so leads to a love of the Creator himself. We then see clearly that we should love ourselves as a part of the universe, assuming our proper place within it in accord with the natural law and contributing, together with our fellow creatures, each in its own way, to the order established by the Creator.

This completes our consideration of the life issues, the issues pertaining to the natural inclinations we share with all things, especially with living things. In chapters 8 and 9 we shall be concerned with issues pertaining to the inclinations we share with the higher animals: the union of male and female and the care of offspring.

CHAPTER 8

## Sex, Marriage, and Family

### Part 1

We turn now from the natural law precepts concerned with the preservation of life to those concerned with its transmission. While common to all living things, the transmission of life takes place in a special way in animals that have a natural inclination to the union of male and female and to the care of offspring. As Ulpian phrased it, these are the things that nature has taught all animals.[1] Because we are animals, these inclinations belong to us as well, although the manner in which we express them must be suitable to our dignity as rational beings.

Human procreation brings about a kind of earthly immortality, and this gives it a special significance and dignity. For the individual man and woman, it means continuing to have a place in the world through their offspring. For mankind as a whole, it means the continuation of the human race. Hence, the procreation necessary to ensure human survival falls under a precept of natural law, a precept not addressed immediately to individuals, but rather to the human race as a whole. Normally, enough people choose to marry and procreate to ensure a viable population. Only in an extreme situation could the duty to procreate fall on specific individuals.

When discussing the natural law precepts regarding life, I

1. *The Digest of Justinian*, trans. ed. Alan Watson, rev. English ed. (Philadelphia: University of Pennsylvania Press, 1998), I.1.

132

said very little about the precepts that require us to nourish our bodies, because these precepts, though not always intelligently observed, are not controversial. We may eat and drink more than we should, but we do not typically think that eating and drinking should be sought merely for their own sake, apart from any relation to their natural end, the preservation of life and health. But the case is not the same with sexual activity. While everyone knows that sex can be used for procreation, not everyone thinks that it is essentially related to procreation as eating and drinking are essentially related to life and health. For by the use of contraceptives and in other ways, sexual activity can be separated from the generation of new life, so as to be sought for itself alone. It is this especially that gives rise to the questions and controversies about sexual morality.

To understand the natural law precepts concerning sex, marriage, and the family, it is necessary first of all to have a clear understanding of the nature of the sexual act. So we will begin with this. We will then consider masturbation, sodomy, homosexual acts, and contraception, which are opposed to the natural sexual act, and then artificial procreation, which is opposed to the natural mode of human procreation. We will also consider the difference between contraception and natural family planning. In chapter 9, we will consider marriage and the associated topics of adultery, fornication, and premarital sex. I will conclude with some thoughts on the concept of homosexual marriage.

## The Sexual Act as an Act of Love

What is sex? More precisely, what is the sexual act? More precisely yet, what is the *natural* sexual act? For sex is not something we invented; it is something we discovered. Hence, we must begin by seeking to understand the sexual act as nature has revealed it to us.

The most obvious fact is that man and woman, by their very

nature, are physically and emotionally disposed for the sexual act. Moreover, it can easily be seen that the human sexual act has several essential dimensions: physical, emotional, and personal. The personal dimension, which expresses our rational nature, conditions the physical and emotional dimensions, giving human sexual intercourse a unique character, distinguishing it essentially from intercourse in animals. This uniquely human aspect of the sexual act is of profound importance, since this determines its relational or interpersonal meaning. Depending on the personal relationship between the man and woman, a sexual act may be an act of love or an act of lust or a conquest or a commercial transaction or a means to some other end—to gain a position, for example, or to facilitate a crime, or perhaps even to hurt someone.

Most of us believe that the sexual act should express true love, although we do not always live up to this ideal. For this reason, the expression "making love" seems more meaningful than the expression "having sex." Unless bad experiences have made us cynical, we are all attracted by the idea of romantic love with its promise of a delightful and enduring relationship. Of course, there can be an element of deception or illusion in romantic protestations of undying love; they may express more the enthusiasm of the moment than the reality of a genuine commitment. Even so, the attractiveness of romantic love is a convincing sign of a natural connection between sex and love. Nature herself seems to be teaching us that the sexual act is meant to be an act of love.

That the sexual act is naturally meant to express and foster a love relationship between a man and a woman becomes clearer if we reflect more carefully on its physical and emotional dimensions. Both of these dimensions express unity, each in its own way. The physical dimension of the sexual act consists essentially in a union of the bodies of man and woman. Two bodies become as one body, performing a natural act in which both share. The emotional dimension climaxes in a feeling of oneness, a feeling of each belonging to the other, a feeling of each being part of the other. Because the physical and emotional dimensions of the sexual act are expressions of unity, they are naturally meant to express and to foster a personal unity. But what unites persons is personal love, a love in which each seeks the good of the other for the other's sake. From this it follows that the sexual act, according to its nature, is an act of love. If it does not express genuine personal love between the man and woman, it is essentially false, the outward expression of a unity that lacks the inner reality that gives it its full human meaning.

## The Sexual Act as Procreative

Everyone knows that the sexual act can be used for procreation. But this fact by itself does not prove that there is an essential connection between sex and procreation. By means of contraceptives we can separate procreation even from sexual acts that are otherwise natural. Moreover, nature herself might seem to separate them, for procreation is neither an intrinsic part of the sexual act nor its necessary result. It is not intrinsic because procreation consists essentially in the union of sperm and ovum, and this takes place *after* sexual intercourse. Nor is procreation a *necessary* result. But if two things are essentially related, there must be a necessary connection between them. It would seem then that sex is not essentially connected with procreation.

On the other hand, it would certainly be odd to think that sex and procreation are only incidentally related, as if procreation resulted from sex by accident. In fact, they are essentially related, not in the sense that a natural sexual act always results in procreation, but in the sense that it is essentially oriented toward procreation. For by its very nature, the sexual act brings the sperm to where they are naturally apt to fertilize an ovum. This orientation toward procreation is of the very essence of the sexual act and is always present.

We should not confuse the natural orientation of the sexual act toward procreation with the intentions or purposes of the couple who are making love. They may not want to procreate at all. They may try in various ways to prevent procreation. But none of this changes the nature of the sexual act so as to make it something other than what it is. Whatever their intentions, the couple making love are engaging in an act that, in the sense explained, is essentially procreative.

It does not follow from this that the sexual act is ordained *only* to procreation. As we have seen, the sexual act is naturally apt to express and foster a love relationship between a man and a woman. These two purposes, love and procreation, are obviously complementary. For a strong love relationship between the man and woman is valuable not only for them but also for their children. Parents who love each other are much better prepared to extend love to their children.

Furthermore, the love expressed in the sexual act not only encompasses the man and woman, closely uniting them to each other, but also transcends them, celebrating the goodness of life and especially of new life, of new beginnings. This seems to be why lovers often feel that their love is something greater than themselves. And it really is, because an act naturally ordained to procreation is naturally meant to express a love of new life. And this love of new life must not be a desire to gratify ourselves, but a love that seeks the good of a new human being for its own sake. For only this kind of love can be the right motive for bringing a child into the world. Hence, it is appropriate and natural that the sexual act should express an overflowing love, a true human love that unites a man and woman not only to each other but also to the children who may come to be from their love.

In summary, then, the sexual act is an expression of personal love between a man and a woman and, at the same time, by reason of its procreative orientation, an expression of the love of new life. These dimensions belong to its very nature. We can refuse to recognize them, we can dishonor them, but we cannot change them.

## Human Sexuality and Natural Law

Before considering the sexual practices opposed to the natural law, it will be helpful to return once again to human dignity, our starting point. We have seen that human dignity implies an unqualified obligation to live in accordance with reason. As we saw in chapter 3, actions can be rational in relation to a particular end without being rational without qualification. For an action to be rational without qualification, it must be suitable to our nature as rational animals. For it is in actions of this kind that we achieve our ultimate end, the life proper to a human being as such. The natural sexual act, as we have seen, is the sexual act proper to man and woman as rational animals. It is the basis, therefore, of the natural law precepts concerned with sex and procreation.

To anticipate what will be considered in the remaining sections of this chapter, we should note that our analysis of the natural sexual act clarifies the appropriate use of the sexual organs, the orientation of the sexual act toward procreation, and the natural mode of human procreation. As we shall see, masturbation, sodomy, and homosexual acts are opposed to the natural law because these acts misuse the sexual organs in the sexual act itself; contraception is opposed because it does not respect the procreative orientation of the sexual act; and artificial procreation is opposed because it is an unsuitable mode of procreation for rational animals.

## Masturbation, Sodomy, and Homosexual Acts

To show that masturbation, sodomy, and homosexual acts are contrary to the natural law, we must proceed somewhat differently than we did when discussing the life issues. There I argued that acts directed against life, health, and physical integrity diminish the possibilities for virtuous actions or eliminate them altogether. It was therefore immediately evident that such acts could not be directed to the life of virtue. But the actions we are considering in this section are not concerned with the destruction or diminishment of the body, but rather with its *misuse*, specifically with the misuse of the sexual organs in the sexual act.[2] Hence, they are not opposed to virtuous actions in general, but rather to particular virtuous actions—that is, to actions that use the sexual organs appropriately.

It is not difficult to see that masturbation, sodomy, and homosexual acts are opposed to the natural use of the sexual organs. For in masturbation, the act takes place without a partner; in sodomy, without a union of the appropriate organs; in homosexual acts, without a partner of the opposite sex. Hence, the use of the sexual organs for these acts is a misuse of them. But no misuse of the sexual organs can be a virtuous act, since a virtuous act must be rationally appropriate in all of its essential dimensions. It follows that the use of the sexual organs for masturbation, sodomy, and homosexual acts is contrary to the natural law.

It might be objected that if these practices can be useful for expressing deeply felt emotions or for relieving sexual tension, they might well be rationally appropriate, at least for some persons and under some circumstances. They may be a misuse of the sexual organs in the sense in which we say that a tool is misused when it is used for a purpose other than that for which it was designed. But sometimes such misuse can be appropriate—for example, we might use a table knife to pry open a window in an emergency. Similarly, a misuse of the sexual organs might sometimes seem to be an appropriate use of them.

The misuse of our sexual organs may indeed be a rational use of them *in a sense*—that is, in relation to a particular end. But it cannot be rational without qualification. For, as we have seen, an action that is rational without qualification must be suitable to us according to our nature. It must be an action appropriate to us precisely as rational animals. But a misuse of our sexual organs is

2. *ST* II-II, q. 154, a. 11 and 12; *SCG* III, cap. 122, n. 5 and n.9.

not suitable to us according to an essential part of our nature—
that is, our animal nature. Therefore, any use of our sexual organs
that is opposed to their natural use, even if useful in view of some
particular end, will be contrary to the natural law.

But could not actions that are opposed to our animal nature
be in accord with our nature in a higher sense, insofar as we are
rational beings? This might be true if it were possible to understand man as a purely rational being, reducing his animal nature
to a subhuman status, as if man were a mind using a body that
was not actually a part of himself. For then the body would not
share in human dignity, and its misuse, like the misuse of a tool,
might be appropriate in some situations. But we really are animals, and our bodies and their organs are really part of ourselves.
Therefore, a misuse of our sexual organs is opposed to our nature
properly understood. It is a misuse not just of our bodies but of
ourselves.

## Contraception

Contraception raises an issue different from the one posed by the
practices we have just considered. Take, for example, the use of
contraceptive pills. They are opposed to conception, but they do
not involve a misuse of the sexual organs in the sexual act itself,
as in the unnatural sexual practices we have just considered. Although some forms of contraception do involve a misuse of the
sexual organs—the use of condoms, for example, is a kind of
masturbation—those who use such methods use them not for
their own sake, but only as a means to an end. They would prefer
methods that prevent procreation without interfering at all in the
sexual act itself. This is why contraception does not seem to be as
unnatural as sodomy or homosexual acts.

The word "contraception" is used in a very general sense for
any method that seeks to prevent or avoid procreation from sexual intercourse. Some methods accomplish this by actively in-

tervening to prevent the sperm from fertilizing an ovum or to prevent a newly conceived embryo from implanting in its mother's womb. Natural family planning methods, on the other hand, avoid procreation by abstaining from intercourse during the fertile part of a woman's cycle. Contraceptive methods that prevent implantation are abortifacients—that is, they cause early abortions. Such methods violate the right to life of a new human being and are therefore far more serious than methods that prevent fertilization. Because natural family planning does not involve any active intervention opposed to procreation, it will be treated separately in the next section.

Contraception is usually promoted by arguments based on utility. Some of these arguments emphasize the undesirable consequences for a woman who ought not to become pregnant, at least not at a particular time. Others call attention to the social consequences of unwanted or excessively numerous pregnancies: neglected children, welfare costs, overpopulation, etc. If it is argued that contraceptive pills may have undesirable effects on a woman's health, proponents of contraception typically reply that the benefits outweigh whatever risks there may be.

Furthermore, when it is considered from the point of view of the natural law, contraception gives rise to a moral dilemma. Because it is used to prevent sexual intercourse from achieving its natural result, it would seem to be opposed to the natural law. However, natural family planning methods, which are also used to avoid procreation and are also called "contraception," are *not* said to be opposed to the natural law. To resolve this dilemma and to grasp clearly the moral issue involved, we must consider contraception more carefully.

To begin with, we need a definition of contraception that signifies precisely the sort of practice that is contrary to the natural law. Let us therefore define contraception as *a physical or chemical intervention opposed to the procreative orientation of the sexual act, introduced before, during, or after voluntary sexual intercourse.* The phrase "physical or chemical intervention" distinguishes contraception from natural family planning methods that make use of the natural periods of infertility. The phrase "opposed to the procreative orientation of the sexual act" distinguishes contraception from medical interventions that are undertaken for other purposes, but that cause sterility (temporary or permanent) as a side effect. The phrase "voluntary sexual intercourse" distinguishes contraception, as here defined, from measures intended to prevent the sperm from fertilizing an ovum in rape victims. For such measures, provided they do not destroy an embryo already conceived or prevent it from implanting in the womb, fall under the natural right of every human being to resist assault. A similar argument applies to measures taken to prevent ovulation when this is necessary to protect women working in areas where they are in danger of being raped.

From this definition, it is clear that our question does not concern the sexual act itself, but rather the contraceptive act—taking a contraceptive pill, for example, or inserting an IUD. But, as we have seen, contraception does not constitute a misuse of the sexual organs, at least not to the same extent as sodomy or homosexual acts. Why, then, is it contrary to the natural law?

The contraceptive act is opposed to the natural law because it is opposed to an essential dimension of the sexual act, its natural orientation toward procreation. This means that it is opposed to the sexual act itself, since to be opposed to what is essential to a thing is to be opposed to the thing itself. Therefore, a man and woman using contraception are both engaging in a sexual act and acting in opposition to that act. This is like using speech that is naturally meant to express truth while undermining it by lying. Since the natural sexual act is the act appropriate to human beings as rational animals, the contraceptive act, which opposes it, is necessarily opposed to the natural law.

Although the sexual act is naturally oriented toward procreation insofar as it is the act of bodily organs, someone might object that insofar as it proceeds from a higher power, from reason, it should be considered in the light of its utility. Would it not sometimes be useful to oppose the orientation of a bodily act in order to deal with serious physical, psychological, and social problems? It might seem, therefore, that contraception could sometimes be rationally appropriate.

This objection is similar to the objection that we considered in our discussion of masturbation and sodomy. It would have some force if we were purely rational beings and our bodies were not essentially part of ourselves. For, if that were true, the body and its faculties would merely be things that we use, and the procreative orientation of the sexual act would not belong to us but only to our bodies. But, as it is, we are essentially rational animals, not rational beings using an animal body that is essentially different from ourselves. Hence, it is not just our bodies but we ourselves who are oriented toward procreation in the sexual act. When we oppose this orientation through contraception, we are not acting against a thing that we use, but against ourselves.

Furthermore, the contraceptive act is opposed to the sexual act not only insofar as it is a procreative act, but also insofar as it is an act of love. For in the act of love, the man and woman seek to become two in one flesh. But this unity is possible only if they give themselves to each other freely, in a human way, each as a gift to the other. But if they withhold their fertility, they cannot fully give themselves to each other; and to give oneself only partially is not really to give oneself, but only to give *something* of oneself. By the contraceptive act, therefore, the man and woman contradict the love by which they give themselves to each other and so fail to achieve the unity that the act of love is naturally meant to foster. Just as contraception undermines the sexual act by contradicting its procreative orientation, so it undermines the sexual act by contradicting its full meaning as an act of love.[3] This is not surprising, since, as we have seen, these two dimensions of the sexual act are intimately related. Moreover, the complete

3. John Paul II, *Familiaris Consortio*, Apostolic Exhortation (December 15, 1981), no. 32.

fulfillment of the couple's desire to become two in one flesh is found in their children, where they are united even more closely than they are in the act of love itself. Contraception, however, is opposed to this fulfillment.[4]

Finally, contraception is opposed not only to the good of the individual couple, but also to the common good of the family, the political community, and the human race as a whole. For it is through sexual acts open to procreation that the family comes to fulfillment and thus makes its essential contribution to the survival and flourishing of the larger communities to which it belongs. But as we saw in chapter 5, individual human beings, as parts of these larger communities, are obligated to order their activities ultimately to the larger common good. It follows that contraception is not entirely a private matter. Since it has implications for the common good, it is also a matter of public concern.

But would contraception *necessarily* be opposed to the common good of the political community and the human race? The common good does not seem to require that all sexual acts be open to procreation—only enough to maintain a suitable population. But this argument misses the essential point: that the sexual act is ordered by its very nature to the common good, not only of the family, but also of the political community, and that an attack upon its procreative orientation is an attack upon this order. When sex is no longer seen as being essentially related to the common good, it appears as something altogether private. This gives rise to a culture more concerned with satisfying sexual desires here and now than with founding families and seeking a better future for one's children. For it is especially because of our children that we are concerned with what happens in the political community after our death.

4. For a different kind of argument against contraception based on the idea that it is contralife, see Germain Grisez, Joseph Boyle, John Finnis, and William May, "Every Marital Act Ought to be Open to a New Life: Toward a Clearer Understanding," *Thomist* 52, no. 3 (1988): 365–426.

## Natural Family Planning

Natural family planning (NFP) is similar in a way to the contraceptive acts we have just considered, since it enables a couple to avoid pregnancy in voluntary sexual intercourse. Because of this, NFP is often classified as a form of contraception. But it is not contraception as defined above, since it is not a positive action, a physical or chemical intervention opposed to conception, but rather an abstention from intercourse during the fertile part of a woman's cycle. Therefore, while NFP is certainly a form of birth control, it is better to think of it not as one among many possible contraceptive methods, but as an essentially different way of avoiding procreation.[5]

Natural family planning methods are not in themselves contrary to the natural law, because they do not involve any action opposed to the natural orientation of the sexual act toward procreation. They make use of certain signs to determine the period of fertility in order to avoid intercourse at that time. This is simply knowledge or awareness, not intervention. There is, consequently, no contraceptive act to evaluate, and the moral problem we have been considering does not arise. Of course, NFP can be used for the same purpose as contraception—that is, to avoid pregnancy. But the intention to avoid pregnancy at certain times or under certain circumstances may be rationally appropriate. Contraception is contrary to the natural law not because it seeks to avoid conception, but because of the *way* in which it seeks to avoid it.

To understand the moral difference between contraception and NFP, it is necessary to distinguish clearly between the sexual act itself and the intentions of the man and woman who engage

---

5. In his encyclical letter *Humanae Vitae* (July 25, 1968), Paul VI considers the nature of the marriage act, contraception, natural family planning, and the grave consequences to be expected from the use of artificial methods of birth control. For an in-depth study of this encyclical and the reactions to it, see Janet E. Smith, *Humanae Vitae: A Generation Later* (Washington D.C.: The Catholic University of America Press, 1991).

in it. Contraception is intrinsically wrong not because the man and woman wish to avoid pregnancy, but because they choose the contraceptive act as a means to this end. The couple using NFP intend the same end, but do not choose the contraceptive act. And there is nothing intrinsically wrong with having sexual intercourse during an infertile period or with avoiding it during a fertile period.

NFP differs from contraception also in another way, because it can be used to achieve pregnancy as well as to avoid it. For an awareness of the fertile and infertile periods of the woman's cycle allows a couple to choose either one. It thus appears that fertility awareness is not directed against procreation per se. Contraception, on the other hand, since it is an intervention opposed to conception, is necessarily directed against procreation and can only be used against it.

Although NFP is not in itself opposed to the natural law, it can be misused. For example, a couple might want to use it to avoid having a family altogether. But this is opposed to the very nature of the sexual relationship and to sexual love. For, as we have seen, the love expressed and fostered through the sexual act is naturally meant to expand into the love and care of offspring. The use of NFP is appropriate for the spacing of children and for limiting their number according to family circumstances. It is not meant to frustrate the natural orientation of the marriage relationship to new life. For just as the marriage act is orientated to new life, so also is marriage itself.

It might be objected that if sexual love is naturally meant to extend to the love and care of offspring, then couples who discover that they are sterile ought not to engage in sexual intercourse at all. But if they are disposed to welcome children and would have children if this were possible for them, then their sexual relationship does express a love of new life. A sign of this is the fact that such couples often wish to adopt children.

## Artificial Methods of Procreation

The sexual act is the natural way of human procreation, but it is not the only possible way. A woman may conceive and bear a child through artificial insemination using sperm from her husband or from a sperm donor. Or she may have her ovum fertilized in vitro and subsequently transferred to her womb or even to the womb of a surrogate mother. Some of these practices are further removed from natural human procreation than others, but since they all depart from the way indicated by nature and rely on techniques that human beings have invented, they may all be classified as artificial methods of procreation.

These artificial methods do not involve a misuse of the sexual organs in the sexual act itself, except insofar as sperm are obtained through masturbation. Nor are they opposed to conception—quite the contrary. The questions they raise concern the manner or mode of procreation. Are these methods of procreation suitable to the dignity of human parents and their offspring? This is the question on which we must focus our attention, setting aside questions about the destruction of spare embryos, the possible damage to embryos fertilized in vitro, and the use of sperm donors and surrogate mothers. These are important questions, but they will not be our concern here.

Artificial procreation is opposed both to the dignity of the man and woman who procreate and to the dignity of their child.[6] To see why this is so, we must first have a clear understanding of the excellence of the human procreative act as compared to the reproductive acts of other living things. Sexual reproduction, which consists essentially in the union of the male and female

---

6. CDF, *Instruction on Respect for Human Life in Its Origin and on the Dignity of Procreation—Donum Vitae* (February 22, 1987). For a helpful discussion of this *Instruction*, see William May, *Marriage: The Rock on Which the Family Is Built*, 2nd ed. (San Francisco: Ignatius Press, 2009), chapter 4. New problems concerning procreation are considered in CDF, *Instruction "Dignitas Personae" on Certain Biological Questions* (September 8, 2008).

germ cells, takes place in many ways, according to the way of life, more or less perfect, proper to each kind of living thing.

Thus, plants, which have only vegetative life, have relatively little control over their germ cells and often depend on outside agents like wind or insects to bring them together. But the higher animals are aware of their environment and of each other, and so, corresponding to their more advanced way of life, they have a better way of uniting their germ cells, through the sexual act of male and female. Human beings, who surpass the animals by their capacity to understand and reason, unite their germ cells in a yet more perfect way, by an act that recapitulates the physical and emotional dimensions of the animal act and adds the new and uniquely human dimension of personal love. From this it is clear that the human sexual act, when all of its dimensions are respected, is more excellent and more beautiful than the modes of reproduction found in other living things. This is why we honor it with a special name, often referring to it as procreation, rather than simply as reproduction.

In artificial procreation, however, whether by artificial insemination or by in vitro fertilization and implantation, the man and woman no longer procreate through the act that is proper to them as man and woman. Their germ cells are brought together by technicians, who assume the role of principal agents, reducing the parents to the status of providers of materials (the germ cells) and of a place for implantation (the womb). The parents assume a secondary and inferior role in the procreation of their own children. But in natural human procreation, they themselves unite their germ cells, and not as technicians, but as man and woman. Only the natural mode of procreation, therefore, corresponds appropriately to their dignity as human beings who exist to achieve fulfillment in actions proper to them as such.

It might be objected that couples who are willing and able to care for children have a right to children and therefore a right to procreate artificially if they cannot procreate naturally. But a child cannot be the object of a right. For a right is something we claim for ourselves, something due to us, whereas a child exists for its own sake, not for ours. Parents have a right to the natural procreative acts through which their children are conceived, but this is not a right to the children who come to be through these acts. Children are a gift from nature and from the Author of nature, entrusted to their parents, who have the duty to care for them. It follows that parents have the right to nourish and educate their children, but not a right to the children themselves.

A question might be raised about whether we must also respect the modes of reproduction proper to the various species of animals. For animals also exist by nature for the way of life that is proper to them according to their species. But whereas a life in accord with human nature is the ultimate end for human beings, it is not so for animals. As we saw in chapter 7, animals do not exist ultimately for their own good, but for the good of human beings and for the good of the other living things that make use of them. Hence, just as we need not respect their lives, so we need not respect their natural mode of reproduction. We are free to reproduce them artificially when this is useful for us.

Artificial procreation is opposed not only to the dignity of man and woman whose natural act it supplants, but also to the dignity of the child thus conceived. This can be seen most clearly in in vitro fertilization, where technicians assume the role of producers and the embryo is reduced to the status of a thing produced. But it is also true in artificial insemination, where a technician, in cooperation with a woman who provides for him an ovum and a place of fertilization, introduces sperm to produce a child. But these modes of procreation are not consistent with the dignity of the child, for the status of a product is inferior to the status of its producers, whereas all human beings possess an equal personal dignity.

Procreation through the natural sexual act, however, fully respects the dignity of the child conceived by it. For in the natural sexual act, the man and woman do not act as technicians making a product, but as natural agents who, in cooperation with the Author of nature, procreate a new human being like themselves. The child no longer appears as a product made for his parents but as a child begotten of them, equal to his parents in personal dignity. Moreover, as we saw earlier, the sexual act is naturally meant to express a personal love between a man and woman, a love that overflows into the love of the child conceived, welcoming him into a new community of persons, the family. Artificial procreation cannot express this kind of love, but only the love of a product successfully made according to specifications.

Of course, good parents who procreate a child artificially will welcome it into the family and love it for its own sake. The question is not about the parents' love for their child or their desire to respect its dignity after it has been born, but about the way it came to be. The child is their child, their flesh and blood, yet it did not spring intimately from their love for each other as would a child naturally conceived. No doubt the parents can seek to compensate for this, refusing to think of their child in the image of a product made for them. Yet this is the way the child was conceived.

The inferior status of the embryo is particularly evident in in vitro fertilization. For in this procedure, not only the manner but also the place of fertilization—outside the womb—serves to reduce the embryo to the status of a product. Furthermore, the embryos produced in vitro are not produced for their own sake, but for the purpose of bringing about a pregnancy. An individual embryo is not valued for itself, but for its potential to give rise to a viable pregnancy with minimal danger of birth defects. This is why some embryos may be selected for transfer to the womb, others frozen (thus exposing them to new risks), yet others discarded or used in nontherapeutic experiments. In this way, in vitro fertilization gives rise to even more serious violations of human dignity.[7]

7. In *Embryo: A Defense of Human Life* (New York: Doubleday, 2008), Robert P. George and Christopher Tollefsen are chiefly concerned with the destruction of human embryos in scientific research. In their concluding chapter, they present political, technical, and cultural principles for dealing with this problem.

This concludes our consideration of the natural law precepts regarding practices opposed to the nature of human procreation. There are many relevant questions that I have not discussed here: questions about various methods of assisting natural procreation, about experimentation on human embryos, and about cloning and other forms of genetic engineering. I have touched only on the most obvious questions and concerns, those that arise immediately from an analysis of the sexual act as nature has revealed it to us.

# CHAPTER 9

# Sex, Marriage, and Family

## Part 2

In chapter 8, we considered the natural sexual act and the acts opposed to it: masturbation, sodomy, homosexual acts, contraception, and artificial procreation. In this chapter we shall be concerned with marriage and with the associated topics of adultery, sex outside of marriage, and homosexual marriage. We shall not be concerned with rape, pederasty, seduction, sexual trafficking, and the like, since these are generally recognized as evil. We shall be concerned only with the sexual activity of consenting adults.

A question might be raised about why we considered the natural sexual act and the practices opposed to it before discussing marriage and extramarital sex. For these latter might seem to be the main issues in sexual morality, because of the social problems that arise when children are born outside of marriage and when marriages and families become unstable. Contraception, unnatural sexual acts, and artificial modes of procreation, on the other hand, are often seen as matters of private choice, not of public concern.

However, these private choices are not without public consequences. For since they tend to separate sex from procreation, they tend also to separate it from marriage or from any kind of stable union. Couples begin to see procreation as incidental to their relationship and perhaps undesirable. Marriage appears as a conventional arrangement, useful for the economic and other benefits it brings, and easily dissolved when it becomes unsatisfying. In this way, private choices transform culture, giving rise to ways of thinking and to patterns of behavior that lead to public problems.

There are two principal reasons why we considered the nature of the sexual act and the practices opposed to it before considering marriage. The first is that practices opposed to the natural sexual act are more opposed to the natural law than adultery and extramarital sex.[1] As we shall see, adultery and extramarital sex are opposed to the natural law because the man and woman are not in the kind of relationship appropriate for sexual activity. But sexual practices contrary to nature dishonor the sexual act itself, the act upon which the marriage relationship is founded. Hence, they are opposed to the natural law in a more fundamental way than sex outside of marriage.

The second reason for postponing the discussion of marriage until now is that an understanding of the nature of marriage presupposes an understanding of the sexual act and its various dimensions. For the essence and properties of marriage depend on the nature of the sexual act and on the natural complementarity of man and woman. This is why marriage is primarily and essentially an institution of natural law and only secondarily an institution of human law. For although the positive law can and should provide for the public recognition of marriages and establish positive norms supporting marriage and protecting the rights of the spouses, it did not create marriage and has no power to change its essential nature.

## The Nature of Marriage

What, then, is marriage? Setting aside for the moment the idea of homosexual marriage, most people would agree that marriage is a union between a man and a woman that is appropriately ex-

1. *ST* II-II, q. 154, a. 12.

pressed in sexual acts. But we have seen that the sexual act is essentially ordered toward love and procreation. It follows that marriage also is naturally oriented toward procreation and toward fostering the love of the man and woman for each other and for their children. As a consequence of this love, they nourish and educate their children and cooperate with each other in maintaining their household. This defines marriage as an institution of natural law, prior to and more fundamental than its institution by human law.

Marriage is like the partnerships found in those species of animals where the male and female remain together to care for their offspring. But it differs from these animal unions in that it is not instinctive but freely chosen, resulting from mutual promises or vows. Through these vows, the man and woman give themselves to each other, forming a union that is uniquely human.

Because it is oriented toward procreation, marriage is a permanent union.[2] For children have a natural right to the care of their parents, a care that requires that the parents remain together. Moreover, as we saw earlier, the sexual act expresses a love that extends to the welcoming of children and includes a commitment, rooted in that love, to care for them and to guide them toward a life of virtue. The marriage union is therefore meant to endure, and to endure not just while the children are young, but for a lifetime. For parental love does not come to an end when the children are grown. The care of a family is a life's work, and parents are concerned to offer their love and support to their children even after they have reached maturity. Finally, the permanence of their parents' marriage fosters stability in their children's lives and marriages.

A question might be raised about the marriages of couples who discover that they are unable to have children. Why should such marriages be permanent? The answer lies in the nature of marriage itself, not in its fruitfulness. For marriage is ordered to

2. *SCG* III, caps. 122 and 123; *ST* Suppl, q. 67, a. 1.

procreation and family by its very nature, and this is the cause of its permanence. A marriage that is not blessed with children remains a marriage, and neither spouse has the right to repudiate the other.

There is also a deeper reason. To understand why all marriages, including childless marriages, are permanent, we must reflect further on the nature of the act of love. In this act, the man uses the woman's body as part of himself and she uses his body as part of herself. They take possession of each other, not as property, but as the natural completion of each other. For unless the man's body is completed by the woman's and the woman's body by the man's, neither of them can engage in a procreative act. But this taking possession of each other can be consistent with human dignity only if the man and woman, in complete freedom, make gifts of themselves to each other, so that they come to belong to each other. This mutual self-giving is the vow of marriage. It follows that the bond created by the marriage vows is not like the bonds created by ordinary contracts; rather, it is like the natural bond that unites each of the spouses to his or her own body. But a bond of this kind is naturally permanent, since no one has the right to cut off a part of his or her body. Therefore, the bond of marriage is a permanent bond, enduring until death.

It is easy to misunderstand the way in which the spouses become part of each other or come to possess or belong to each other. For whenever we think of possession, we think of property, and by property we understand something that we value not for its own sake but for the use we can make of it. So if a man were to take possession of the body of a woman as property, then, since the body is part of the person, the woman would be, to that extent, a thing that is being used. The same would be true if a woman were to take possession of the body of a man as property. But this kind of possession is clearly contrary to human dignity. It might seem then that the spouses cannot really belong to each other.

Kant recognized this difficulty and tried to respond to it. He thought that the man and woman who marry do take possession of each other and that this possession is like the possession of a thing. To be possessed as a thing obviously means a loss of status, for a thing possessed is inferior to the person who possesses it. But since the one who possesses the other as a thing is, in turn, possessed by the other in the same way, equality is restored. Furthermore, although the man and woman possess each other as things, they are obligated to make use of each other in a way that is suitable for persons. Kant therefore introduced a special category of possession: the possession of an external object as a thing and the use of it as a person.[3]

But even if the spouses relate to each other as persons, how could they endure the thought that they belong to each other as property? To belong to each other as things owned, even under terms of equality, would clearly be opposed to their dignity as persons. But, as we have seen, the spouses do not belong to each other as property, but as their mutual fulfillment or completion. To belong to each other in this way is not a loss for either one, but rather a gain for both, since they are now able to go beyond their individual lives, bringing new life into the world and forming a new community of life and love. This way of belonging to each other is fully consistent with human dignity.

These reflections on the nature of the marriage bond can help us to understand married love more clearly. The love that moves the man and woman to give themselves to each other is by nature an enduring love. For as the gift endures, so the love is meant to endure. Moreover, the love of man and woman in marriage is a fully human and honorable love, since it is rooted in their equal personal dignity. For as the woman is completed by the man, so the man is completed by the woman. And this love is meant not only to endure but to grow stronger over the years, as the couple's relationship matures.

---

3. Immanuel Kant, *Metaphysical First Principles of the Doctrine of Right*, in *The Metaphysics of Morals*, trans., ed. Mary Gregor (Cambridge: Cambridge University Press, 1996), Private Right, § 22–27.

Not that true married love grows effortlessly. For true friendship between husband and wife is based on virtue, and, as we have seen, virtues are not innate, but must be acquired through repeated actions. Even those who marry with good intentions are likely to begin marriage by loving their spouse rather selfishly—that is, for the benefits they expect for themselves. But true love, as we have seen, seeks the good of the other for the other's sake, and only such love corresponds adequately to the dignity of persons. To learn to love as we should takes good will, determination, time, and experience, but the reward is great, as appears in the happiness of couples who have brought their love relationship to fulfillment.

In conclusion, we might raise a question about whether marriage vows should be publicly witnessed. For if these are vows that a man and woman make to each other, they might seem to be a private matter. However, since the legality and stability of marriages are of vital concern to society, the positive law reasonably requires that marriage vows be publicly witnessed. This allows the authorities to enforce the rights established by the marriage laws. Furthermore, a public ceremony serves to unite the families of the spouses and offers to the spouses themselves the opportunity to demonstrate the reality of their commitment to each other.

### Monogamy

The discussion up to this point has shown that marriage is a permanent union between a man and a woman ordered toward love, procreation, and family. But we have not considered whether marriage is by nature monogamous. If not, then polygamy might also be acceptable. Of the two forms of polygamy—polyandry (one woman with more than one husband) and polygyny (one man with more than one wife)—the former seems clearly opposed to the natural law. For if a woman has more than one husband, fatherhood becomes uncertain. But the father as well as the mother must be definitely known, since both parents are responsible for raising their children. In polygyny, this problem does not arise. A man who is able to provide adequately for a very large household might enter into permanent relationships with many women. Why, in these circumstances, would polygyny be contrary to the natural law?

Insofar as it is a permanent relationship ordered toward procreation and family, polygyny does not seem contrary to nature. But it is not fully in accord with the natural law. For marriage is ordered not only to procreation and the raising of children, but also to fostering love and cooperation between husband and wife and to maintaining good order in their household. But there must inevitably be controversies and jealousies among wives sharing a single husband, each concerned with her position and the position of her children. Furthermore, how can one man establish close relationships with many wives and with the many children born of these wives? The decisive point, however, is the equal personal dignity of man and woman. In polygyny, each wife gives herself exclusively to her husband, but her husband does not give himself exclusively to her. Her status as a wife is thus inferior to his status as a husband, and this does not respect the equality of the gifts that they give to each other in their marriage vows. Polygyny, therefore, does not adequately respect the nature and purposes of marriage.[4]

To this we might add that nature itself seems to have taught us monogamy, since, unless we interfere, men and women tend to be born in roughly equal numbers. If polygyny were widespread, therefore, some men might find it difficult or even impossible to exercise their natural right to marry. And the same would be true for women, if polyandry were widespread.

4. *SCG* III, cap. 124; *ST* Suppl, q. 65, a. 1.

## Divorce

While a separation of the spouses can sometimes be justified, divorce is clearly impossible under natural law if by divorce we understand the breaking of a natural marriage bond. For the marriage bond, as we have seen, is permanent. Questions might be raised, however, about the permanence of childless marriages and about deficiencies in the marriage vows.

If marriage is naturally ordered to children and family, then it might seem that the marriage of a couple who are unable to have children because of infertility should be dissoluble. For if one of the spouses is the cause of the infertility, the other spouse might be able to realize his or her desire for a family with someone else. But, as we have seen, the marriage bond is by its very nature permanent and cannot be dissolved even when the couple cannot have children. Furthermore, marriage is not a contract for having children. The spouses do not promise each other children; they promise each other the sexual acts from which children may be conceived. This is why the marriage contract can be voided because of preexisting impotence, the inability to engage in sexual acts, but not because of infertility.

A second question concerns deficiencies in the marriage vows. Not everyone who goes through a marriage ceremony understands or intends a true marriage commitment, especially when divorce and remarriage are permitted by human law. It is therefore important to distinguish between marriage as an institution of natural law and marriage as it may appear under the civil law of a given society at a given time. Couples entering a civil marriage where divorce is permitted may form a bond that, while permanent in their hope and expectation, may not be permanent in their commitment. As the civil marriage laws become more and more lax, the marriage bond becomes more and more tenuous, until one wonders whether there is any bond at all. Therefore, while divorce is contrary to the natural law, it is sometimes possible to judge that, in a particular case, a natural marriage does not really exist, because one or both of the spouses could not or did not make a true marriage commitment.

Nevertheless, we should not forget that there is an ideal of permanence underlying the civil institution of marriage, however lax the marriage laws may be. For everyone recognizes the advantages of stable marriages and families. Therefore, even if the civil law does not require the permanent commitment of natural marriage, a couple should make every effort to grow in love and to preserve their marriage. For they belong to each other in a union naturally meant to endure, and they will find happiness in its success.

## Adultery and Sex outside Marriage

Adultery is not the breaking of the marriage bond but a violation of it, and it is everywhere condemned. For it is utterly destructive of marriage. When a man and woman marry, they promise each other sexual intimacy and sexual fidelity. For adequate reasons and by mutual consent, they may agree to forgo sexual intimacy or to live apart from each other, even for extended periods of time, without violating their marriage vows. But they cannot for any reason set aside sexual fidelity, even by mutual consent. For the spouses have given themselves to each other through their marriage vows, and the one who commits adultery violates this vow by giving to another what belongs to his or her spouse. This is true whether marriage is understood in its full natural reality or as it appears in the imperfect forms of civil marriage that allow divorce.

Sex between a man and woman who are both unmarried does not constitute the breaking of a marriage vow. Is it then permissible by mutual consent, at least for mature couples? Or is unmarried sex intrinsically wrong, so that it is always against the natural law? The answer depends on whether or not there is an essential connection between sex and marriage. For if sex and marriage are not essentially connected, then unmarried sex, although it might be wrong in some circumstances, would not be wrong in itself.

That sex and marriage are indeed essentially connected is clear from our reflections on the permanence of marriage.[5] Because the sexual act is oriented essentially toward procreation, the man and woman who make love must be prepared to accept the responsibilities that procreation entails. From this it follows that they must be united in a relationship that is stable and lasting, the relationship we call "marriage." This will be true even if the couple is unable to have children. For the essential connection between sex and marriage depends on the nature of the sexual act itself, not on whether or not procreation actually results.

The same conclusion follows from the fact that the man uses the body of the woman in the sexual act as the completion of his own body and that she, similarly, uses his body as the completion of hers. As we have seen, this use of each other's body cannot be consistent with human dignity unless they have freely given themselves to each other. Otherwise, they are merely using each other. But this mutual self-giving is the substance of the marriage vows. Sex apart from the commitment of marriage, therefore, is essentially false, an act that has the appearance of mutual self-giving without the reality.

In every act of unmarried sex, the man and woman use each other as external objects or things and therefore not according to their dignity as persons. This is most obvious in prostitution, where a woman (or man) allows herself (or himself) to be used as a sex object in return for money. It is also obvious, though less venal, when they use each other for mutual pleasure without any kind of commitment. A sexual act resulting from the passion of romantic love seems less reprehensible, since the couple give themselves to each other in a kind of momentary imitation of married love.

Closer to marriage is the practice of couples who are seriously

5. *ST* II-II, q. 154, esp. a. 2, 3, and 8.

thinking of marriage but want to live together first in order to assess their compatibility with each other. The experience of living together experimentally, however, is not the experience of living a permanent commitment. Rather, what is needed before marriage is a clear understanding and a firm acceptance of what marriage means and of what each partner has a right to expect from the other. Such an understanding does not come from living together before marriage, but from time spent getting to know each other as persons, from serious conversations, and from listening to couples and counselors who have learned from experience what makes for a successful marriage.

What is called "premarital sex" is even closer to marriage, if the couple are engaged and definitely intend marriage. But it is unmarried sex, nonetheless, since the intention to marry is not the same as marriage itself and is no guarantee that it will actually take place. Also, it seems a bad sign and rather disappointing that a man and woman could not wait until they had actually given themselves to each other through their marriage vows.

Can there be a permanent commitment of a man and woman to each other when they live together without marriage? Perhaps not at first, but when the relationship has continued for a long time, and especially when there are children, they may come to see themselves more and more as belonging to each other in a union naturally meant to endure. But without the marriage vows, their commitment to each other remains imperfect.

## Homosexual Marriage

From the preceding discussion it is clear that homosexual marriage is impossible. For persons of the same sex lack the complementary organs necessary for engaging in the natural sexual act. It is therefore impossible for them to form a natural sexual union. Their relationship can be called marriage only by equivocation.

Could we say that homosexual couples *do* engage in natural

sexual acts—that is, in sexual acts that are natural for them, even though they appear unnatural to heterosexuals? However, this also would be an equivocation. Heterosexual acts are natural in themselves, whereas homosexual acts are not, but only seem so because homosexual persons are emotionally inclined to them. Nor is a homosexual inclination natural if it appears early in life, for this can be true of many unnatural or abnormal conditions, both physical and psychological. Whether present from the beginning of life or not, the homosexual orientation is unnatural, since it inclines people to use their sexual organs in ways that are opposed to their natural use.

Though the homosexual inclination is unnatural, it is important to understand clearly that it is not itself contrary to the natural law. For we are not responsible for physical or psychological dispositions that we have not ourselves caused and do not seek to foster. It is homosexual acts that are contrary to the natural law.

Given the essential difference between the natural sexual union of man and woman and the unnatural sexual union of same-sex partners, how is it possible for us to conceive of homosexual unions as marriages? The most obvious reason is a superficial idea of marriage. As contraception becomes widespread, we begin to think of marriage as an emotional relationship expressed in sexual acts that are no longer thought of as essentially related to procreation and family. It begins to seem like the purpose of marriage is the satisfaction of whatever sexual desires have drawn the couple together. Hence, homosexual relationships appear to be on the same plane as heterosexual relationships, as if they were just different ways in which different couples are inclined to use their sexual organs.

But isn't the unnaturalness of homosexual unions obvious to common sense? I believe that it is, but we override common sense by our conviction that, whatever the truth may be, we must recognize the right of people to define their lives as they wish. Just as we think that everyone has a right to his own opinion, so we think that everyone has a right to his own way of life. This is reinforced by an uncritical acceptance of the scientific picture of the world. For, as we saw in chapter 2, a failure to recognize the limitations of the scientific method leads people to imagine that nothing in nature can be for the sake of an end. If this were true, how could any use of the sexual organs be contrary to nature?

Closely related to this way of thinking is the idea that marriage is a human invention, which we can alter at will. For if we think of human law as altogether autonomous, not subject in any way to the natural law, what is to prevent us from defining marriage as we please? Suppose we decide to define marriage as an emotional relationship expressed sexually. This kind of relationship is possible for homosexuals as well as for heterosexuals. To deny homosexuals the right to marry would then appear to be unjust discrimination.

However, denying marriage to homosexual couples is not really unjust discrimination. For if marriage is a public institution, it must serve a public purpose. What could this be but the procreation and raising of the next generation? Homosexual unions, however, are private friendships, formed not for any public purpose, but for the satisfaction of the partners' personal desires and concerns. Why, then, do we want to give such unions a public status by supporting them through the privileges and financial benefits established by the marriage laws? Or if we do, why do we not similarly support all private friendships? Imagine a brother and sister or two close friends who truly love each other, but have no interest in a sexual relationship. Why should the community support homosexual friendships more than these? Homosexuals, therefore, cannot reasonably demand that their friendships be publicly recognized and supported as marriages.

But if homosexual unions cannot be marriages because children do not result from them, what about childless heterosexual unions? For children do not always result from heterosexual unions either, sometimes because of infertility, sometimes by deliberate choice. Therefore, if the procreation and raising of the next generation is the public purpose of marriage, how can childless heterosexual unions be marriages? The reason for this is that marriage is a public institution not because children always result, but because it is ordered by its very nature to procreation and family. But homosexual unions cannot be ordered to procreation and family, not because of infertility or human choice, but because of what they are. They are essentially nonprocreative. Hence, homosexual unions cannot really be marriages.

But is it not possible for homosexual couples to have children, either by adoption or by using sperm donors or egg donors and surrogate mothers? They can form families just like heterosexual couples do. Of course, they may not choose to raise a family, but heterosexual couples may not choose to do so either. It would seem then that homosexual unions and heterosexual unions are equally entitled to be recognized as marriages.

But if homosexual couples have children, this does not result from their union, but from adoption or from an artificial mode of procreation. In this latter case, the child is procreated outside the homosexual union, since it results from the union of one of the partners with a third person. It is this couple, the natural parents of the child, who are responsible for raising it. Since the third person is not required to accept this responsibility, the child is in effect adopted by the homosexual couple. It follows that homosexual couples can have children only by adoption. But marriage is not necessary for adoption; a child may be adopted by its relatives, by an unrelated couple, or even by a single individual. The fact that homosexual couples can and sometimes do adopt children does not prove that their relationship is or could be a marriage.

A question can also be raised about whether children should be given for adoption to homosexual couples. This does not seem to be in accord with the dignity of the child. For a child has a natural right to be cared for by its parents. If the parents are unable or unwilling to carry out their responsibility, the child should be adopted into a heterosexual family, where it can have a foster father and mother to take the place of its natural father and mother. A child adopted by a homosexual couple will not have a foster father and mother and will not be raised in a natural sexual environment. For these reasons, children should not be adopted by homosexual couples.

## Conclusion

This concludes our consideration of the natural law precepts concerned with the second level of natural inclinations, those that we share with the animals. In chapter 8, I sought to clarify the various dimensions of the natural sexual act and to show that this is the act proper to man and woman as rational animals. From this it follows that the natural law is violated by misusing the sexual organs, by opposing the procreative orientation of the sexual act through contraception, and by substituting an artificial mode of procreation for the properly human mode. In this chapter, I considered marriage as an institution of natural law based on the natural sexual act. This explains why marriage is permanent and monogamous, why adultery, fornication, and premarital sex are opposed to the natural law, and why homosexual marriage has no natural reality and cannot be anything more than a legal fiction.

CHAPTER 10

# The Contemplative Life and Life in Society

We turn now to the natural law precepts concerned with the inclinations belonging to us insofar as we are rational beings, essentially different from the other animals. According to Aquinas, we have, as rational beings, a natural inclination to know the truth about God and to live in society. As a consequence, shunning ignorance, not offending those with whom we live, and other such things all pertain to the natural law.[1]

Following the order suggested by Aquinas's words, we shall first consider the obligation to seek truth. For if we are ordained by nature to the life of reason, and if the object of reason is truth, we are clearly obligated to seek truth and to avoid error, and especially to seek the highest and most important truth, the truth about God. Because the search for the highest truth belongs to the contemplative life, we shall consider this life and the happiness to be found in it, following Aristotle's discussion of it in Book X of the *Nicomachean Ethics*.

After this, we will turn to the topic of life in society, partly in this chapter and partly in the next. As rational beings, we have a natural inclination to put order into human life, not only into our personal lives, but also into the life of the communities to which we belong. Since the purpose of putting order in things is to achieve an end, and since the end for human beings is happi-

1. *ST* I-II, q. 94, a. 2, c.

166

ness, it is clear that the life of society must be ordered to happiness, the life of virtue. We see this ordering realized first in the family, then in communities beyond the family, and finally in political communities. We shall be concerned here principally with the appropriate ordering of political life. Negatively, this means that we must avoid harming each other; positively, that we must seek to establish social conditions that foster the achievement of the life of virtue.

## Truth and Wisdom

Who would not be touched by Augustine's account of the awakening of his desire for wisdom?[2] He was reading Cicero's *Hortensius* and was delighted by his advice to love and seek and attain and hold fast and strongly embrace not this or that philosophical sect but wisdom itself, whatever it might be. "O Truth, Truth," he writes, "how inwardly did the very marrow of my soul sigh for You."[3] That the desire for truth, once aroused, should be so intense and all-consuming is not surprising, for it is especially in our intellectual life that we surpass the other animals and are most truly ourselves.

The truth that Augustine was seeking was not just any truth. He was not seeking truths about contingent things, things that may or may not exist. Although a knowledge of particular contingent things often has practical relevance, it does not satisfy our deepest desire for truth. What Augustine longed for was unchanging or eternal truth, especially the truth about the first cause or causes of the universe and the ultimate meaning of human life.

The search for truth, insofar as it is attainable by natural reason, is the task of philosophy and indeed of all the sciences, especially the natural sciences, since they all contribute to the search for

2. Augustine, *Confessions*, trans. F. J. Sheed, rev. ed. (Indianapolis: Hackett, 1993), III.iv.
3. Ibid., vi.

wisdom. But not all truths are of equal importance. The desire for truth is above all a desire for the first truth, the truth about the first cause or causes upon which the being of things ultimately depends. Until we have attained this truth, the truth that alone can satisfy our desire for wisdom, we remain fundamentally unsatisfied.

## The Contemplative Life

We search for wisdom in order to be happy, for this is the ultimate goal of all of our activities. As Aristotle shows in Book X of the *Nicomachean Ethics*, the happiness to be found in the contemplation of the highest truth is greater than the happiness to be found in the exercise of the moral virtues in the active life. It follows that we ought to seek the happiness of the contemplative life even more than the happiness of the active life, preferring the search for wisdom to practical activities. But when there are things that have to be done, practical activities must obviously take precedence. What is best absolutely may not be what is best at the moment.

Aristotle offers six arguments for the greater happiness of the contemplative life.[4] The first of these focuses on the excellence of contemplative activity. If happiness lies in rational activity, it will lie especially in the highest activity of which reason is capable. This will be the activity by which it attains the highest reality— that is, the first or highest truth. But this is essentially a contemplative activity perfected by philosophical wisdom, the wisdom by which we understand the universe in the light of its first cause or causes. Therefore, if happiness lies in rational activity perfected by virtue, it will lie especially in rational activity perfected by the virtue of philosophical wisdom.[5]

---

4. *NE* 10.7.1177a20–b25. Two additional arguments can be formulated on the basis of Aristotle's further discussion of the contemplative life from 1177b26 to 1178a8; see *ST* II-II, q. 182, a. 1.

5. Philosophical wisdom is an intellectual virtue. The distinction between the

Also, if happiness must be an enduring good, then the contemplative life will be happier than the active life. For contemplative activities are less tiring than practical activities and can be sustained for a longer time. However, contemplation cannot be sustained indefinitely, since it requires the use of the sense powers that exist in bodily organs that eventually grow tired. Moreover, the demands of practical life set limits to the life of study and contemplation. Hence, the happiness to be found in contemplation can be realized only imperfectly in the present life.

Again, the pleasures of contemplation would seem to surpass all other pleasures. For spiritual pleasures are purer than bodily pleasures. Thus, for example, we speak of "pure joy" or "sheer joy" when we unexpectedly encounter a long-lost friend or hear a musical composition of surpassing beauty. This purity of pleasure is found in all virtuous activities, but especially in contemplation, where we are taken out of ourselves, so to speak, and our minds find joy in the knowledge of the highest truth. Furthermore, the pleasures of contemplation have a greater stability than bodily pleasures, since they are concerned with what is unchanging, whereas bodily pleasures, the pleasures of eating and drinking, for example, quickly come to an end as the disposition of the body changes.

Also, the contemplative life requires less in the way of external resources than the active life. For a person can study and contemplate by himself alone, although, of course, he will benefit much from conversations with colleagues. But a person primarily engaged in the active life will require many more resources as instruments for practical action. This is especially true for people in political and military careers, engaged in difficult and complex activities essential for the common good. Hence, the contemplative life will be more self-sufficient than the active life.

Again, contemplative activity is more desired for its own

---

moral and intellectual virtues was considered in chapter 4. As we saw there, prudence also is a kind of wisdom—not wisdom without qualification, but *practical* wisdom.

sake than practical activity. For the acts of the moral virtues are desired not only because they are excellent and praiseworthy in themselves, but also because they bring about good results. Thus, we value heroic actions in war both because of the courage they display and because of the victory they make possible. But contemplative activity, especially as it attains the highest truth, is desirable for itself, apart from whatever practical value it may have.

Finally, contemplation is a leisure activity, not like the activities of the active life that are chosen out of necessity. For if there were no tasks to carry out or practical problems to solve, we would certainly not create them so as to have an opportunity to exercise the moral virtues. We would not start a war so that we might act courageously or allow people to fall into poverty so that we might generously come to their aid. Practical activity aims at solving problems and getting things done so that we can be at rest, as war aims at peace. Leisure is the end or goal of practical activity. Therefore, since contemplation is a leisure activity, the happiness of the contemplative life will be more ultimate than the happiness of the active life.

Of course, contemplation is not the only leisure activity. There is also play. But play is for the sake of serious activities, since its purpose is to relax and restore the body, which is wearied by the demands of practical life. It would be childish, as Aristotle remarked, to make it our ultimate end. Moreover, endless play would bore us, since it satisfies more the needs of the body than the desires proper to a rational being as such. There are, however, some kinds of leisure activities, like literature, music, and art, that, in addition to being refreshing, are also in some measure contemplative and, at their best, dispose us to seek wisdom and even introduce us to it. But they cannot themselves satisfy the desire for ultimate truth. It is only in the attainment of the highest truth in contemplation that we can find a leisure activity that satisfies our deepest desire for happiness.

## Searching for Wisdom

Where will we find wisdom? The earliest Greek philosophers thought that the first cause was a material principle—water, for example, or air or fire—for it seemed to them that matter is the reality from which all things come to be and to which they all return, the alpha and the omega, so to speak. If this were true, to know that it is true would be wisdom. But then the first cause would be something less than what we are. For by our power to transform matter, we demonstrate our superiority to it. It would be strange, however, if we were superior to the first cause. It would seem, therefore, that matter cannot be the first cause.

Furthermore, if matter were the first cause, it would be more satisfying to contemplate the things that emerge from the first cause than to contemplate the first cause itself. For what emerges from matter is the vast and wonderful world of nature and especially of life, and it is here that we find the intelligible and the good and the beautiful, which accord with our reason. All of these are aspects of being insofar as it is actual, whereas matter, as such, is potential. But actual being is being to a greater extent than potential being, and so again, it seems that the first cause cannot be matter.

To understand what is meant by "potential being" or "being in potency" and by "actual being" or "being in act," it is helpful to consider the creation of a work of sculpture—Michelangelo's *Pietà*, for example. Before Michelangelo begins to work, the *Pietà* is in the marble *in potency*—that is, the block of marble is *able to become* the *Pietà*, although it is not yet *actually* the *Pietà*. When Michelangelo is finished working, the *Pietà* exists actually or, as we say, it exists *in act*. In a similar way, we can say that plants and animals exist in potency in the elements of the universe and that once they have come to be, they exist in act. If to exist in act is greater than to exist in potency, and if matter is potency, then the first cause will not be matter.

Where, then, will we find the first cause? If it is not found in potential being, it must be found in actual being. But it cannot be found in the living and nonliving natural substances that emerge from matter. They are actual beings, they exist in act, but they do not exist prior to the matter from which they are made. A cause, however, must be prior to its effect. For the same reason, they cannot bring themselves into existence. The first cause of the natural substances that emerge from matter must therefore be a cause that is superior in actual being to the natural substances that it brings into existence.

To see this more clearly, let us return to the creation of the *Pietà*. It is clear that the block of marble, which contains the *Pietà* in potency, does not cause it to exist in act. Nor can we say that the *Pietà* emerges from the marble by its own power. It is the sculptor, Michelangelo, who brings it from potential to actual existence. This is possible because the form of the *Pietà* preexists in his mind and guides him in his work. Since the cause of the actual existence of something has a greater and more perfect existence than the thing that it brings into existence, it is clear that Michelangelo has a greater and more perfect existence than the *Pietà*. From this it appears, by analogy, that the first cause of *all* being must have the highest and most perfect existence of all.

If, then, potentiality cannot bring anything into actual existence, and if a thing that exists potentially cannot bring itself into actual existence, it would seem that the first cause must be a cause that is fully actual, unlimited in power. For just as Michelangelo had within himself the power to bring all the works of his art into actual existence and therefore had a more perfect existence than these works, so the first cause of all being must contain within itself the power to bring all things into actual existence and therefore must have the most perfect existence of all. Furthermore, since all the things that exist show wisdom, goodness, and beauty, these perfections—indeed, all perfections—will exist without limit in the first cause. It is therefore reasonable to believe that in this cause, the cause we call God, we will find the goal of our search for wisdom.

To this we might add that if wisdom is a perfection, and if we are perfected by something better and more perfect than ourselves, then it is reasonable to expect that wisdom will be found in a first cause that is supreme in actuality and perfection rather than in a first cause that is potential and less perfect than we are. This also suggests that the goal of the search for wisdom will be found in God.

In chapters 1 and 2 I argued for the existence of God as the Author of Nature. My concern here, however, is not with God's existence but with the natural law obligation to search for ultimate truth. The argument just given is not meant to be a rigorous proof of God's existence, but rather an encouragement to search for him. What I want to suggest is that nothing less than a first cause of infinite perfection could fully satisfy our natural desire for ultimate truth. It follows that we will not be true to ourselves as rational beings if we abandon the search for God. This means that we ought not to neglect a careful study of the philosophical traditions that have proposed arguments for the existence and attributes of God.

We must also consider the religious traditions of mankind— their teachings, their works, the lives of their prophets and saints, their role in history, etc.—to see whether God has revealed himself to us. It seems plausible that he would reveal himself, for otherwise, as Aquinas noted, he would be known only by a few people and only after long study and mixed with many errors.[6] But a true knowledge of God is of the greatest importance for all human beings, since it enables them to participate in some measure in the contemplative life and to direct their practical affairs in accord with divine wisdom. Therefore, if we sincerely desire to find the truth, we should look carefully for signs of divine revelation.

Moreover, even the most careful philosophical investigations can lead us only to such knowledge of God as his effects can reveal. But to know God only in his effects is not to know him in

6. *ST* I, q. 1, a. 1, c.

himself, and so our natural desire for ultimate truth, as Aquinas argued, would still remain unsatisfied.[7] But it is implausible to suppose that a natural desire would be vain and empty.[8] How it is to be satisfied, however, God himself must reveal. Hence, for this reason also, we should search for evidence of a divine revelation.

We violate our dignity as rational beings in the most fundamental way when we place obstacles in the way of the search for God, thus limiting the horizon of our own lives and the lives of those whom we influence. For when we turn away from the search for God, we confine the meaning of our lives to the sphere of the finite and temporal, not allowing it to expand toward the infinite and eternal.[9] A life engaged in the search for God, therefore, has a far greater meaning than a life focused exclusively on worldly concerns.

It might be objected that if the contemplation of the highest truth is the ultimate end for all human beings, then all human beings should be able to attain it. But this does not seem to be possible, at least not in the present life. Of course, even if only a few people attain philosophical wisdom, many others can participate in it in various degrees through a religious culture in conformity with this wisdom. But this is not enough for perfect happiness—even philosophical wisdom is not enough, as we have seen. This raises the question of whether perfect happiness is possible in a future life and, if so, how it can be attained. Only in a divine revelation will we find complete answers to these questions.

I would like to conclude this section by noting that although the contemplative life is more ultimate than the active life, both are necessary. For we cannot devote ourselves to contemplation

7. *ST* I-II, q. 3, a. 8, c; *SCG* III, cap. 50.

8. In his *Commentary on the "Nicomachean Ethics,"* Book I, Lectio 2, no. 21, Aquinas states that a natural desire cannot be vain and empty because a natural desire is an inclination inhering in things by the ordering of the first mover who cannot be frustrated. He is commenting on *NE* I.2.1094a20.

9. An idea inspired by Kierkegaard's distinction of the aesthetic, ethical, and religious stages of life.

unless our emotions are under rational control and our practical affairs are in order.[10] Furthermore, the pure love of truth implies a strong and firm desire for what satisfies reason, so that one who seeks the highest goal of reason in contemplation will hardly be satisfied with irrationality in practical affairs. Finally, since practical duties are unavoidable and we cannot devote ourselves entirely to contemplation, the life of virtue will be more complete if we achieve it in practical action through the moral virtues as well as in contemplation through philosophical wisdom or through a higher wisdom revealed by God.

## The Political Community and Public Authority

Our consideration of the natural law approach to the political community will be in two parts.[11] In this chapter, we will be concerned with the origin and nature of the political community and public authority. Our response to these questions will be based on Aristotle's theory of the political community as the natural fulfillment of man's inclination to live in society, in contrast to Locke's theory of the social contract. We will also look briefly at three related topics: democracy, the universal common good, and subsidiarity. In chapter 11, we will consider natural rights with a view to showing how the political community might facilitate the achievement of the life of virtue.

If the topics considered in previous chapters have been treated rather summarily, still more must this be the case here. It is one thing to set forth principles of natural law for political communities; it is quite another to investigate how far and in what ways these principles can be applied in particular historical contexts.

10. *ST* II-II, q. 180, a. 2, c, ad 2.
11. The names "political community" and "state" signify the same thing, and I use them interchangeably. However, I think there is a difference of emphasis: "political community" emphasizes the people who belong to the community, and "state" emphasizes the unity of the community under public authority.

To effectively guide social development, the natural law must be supplemented by an intimate knowledge of the current state of the positive law and of contemporary customs and social conditions. Therefore, our discussion here will have to be very general, focusing on fundamental principles rather than on concrete proposals for political action.

Let us turn first to the nature of the political community. As Aristotle taught, human beings have a natural inclination to live in society, an inclination that appears first in the family, then extends to clans and villages, and reaches fulfillment in the political community. For the political community contains within itself sufficient resources to support its members and to enable them to achieve happiness. The political community is therefore natural, the goal of our natural social development, as physical maturity is the goal of our natural organic development. We are by nature parts of a whole, and the whole is the political community, and to be in the political community, therefore, is to be in our natural state.[12] Hence, Aristotle remarked, whoever does not naturally belong to the political community is either above normal humanity or below it, either a god or a beast.[13]

If membership in a political community is our natural state, it is clear that we do not need a contract to bring us from a state of nature to a civil or political state. As we saw in chapter 5, we have an unqualified obligation to seek happiness as a common good, and since we are not individually self-sufficient, we have a corresponding obligation to cooperate with each other in political communities. We have this obligation simply because we are human beings. How particular political communities come to be and what constitutional forms they take will depend on particular historical conditions. But that we should live in such communities is of natural law.

Nor is a contract necessary to legitimize public authority. For

12. Aristotle, *Politics* I.2.1252a24–53a39.
13. Ibid., 1253a1–6 and 27–28.

if we are obligated by natural law to cooperate with others in a political community to achieve the common good, and if this cooperation requires a coordinating authority, then public authority will have the power to govern by natural law. It follows that when we obey public authority, we obey a higher authority, the authority who established the natural law. We obey God more than we obey man. This assumes, of course, that public officials are acting in virtue of the authority established for them by the natural law— that is, for the sake of the common good and not for ideological reasons or for private advantage.

## Locke's Theory of the Social Contract

To see this more clearly, let us briefly consider the social contract as Locke envisioned it.[14] We should note, first of all, that Locke affirmed the dignity of the human person and certain fundamental natural rights—the rights to life, liberty, and property—that follow from human dignity.[15] Because these rights belong to human beings by nature, they are prior to membership in any particular political community. I think it was because of this, at least in part, that Locke was moved to distinguish radically between the state of nature and the political or civil state. Although he thought that the civil state is useful and even necessary, Locke did not think that man is by nature a political animal. But if man is not by nature a political animal, the state must arise from an

14. For Locke's theory of the social contract, see John Locke, *Second Treatise of Government*, ed. C. B. Macpherson (Indianapolis: Hackett, 1990). The social contract idea is developed further in Rousseau, Kant, and Del Vecchio, but Locke's theory is more useful for clarifying the argument I am advancing here. For a discussion of the development of social contract theory, see Giorgio Del Vecchio, "Su la teoria del contratto sociale," in *Giorgio Del Vecchio: Contributi alla storia del pensiero giuridico e filosofico* (Milan: Dott. A. Guiffrè, 1961), 217–74.

15. Locke states that we are not authorized to destroy one another "as if we were made for one another's uses, as the inferior ranks of creatures are for ours"; Locke, *Second Treatise of Government*, § 6.

agreement or contract, and, as Locke maintained, the individual must be free to join or not, as he sees fit.[16]

Whence comes the right of public authority to govern individuals who are by nature free from such authority? Locke's solution follows the pattern of private contracts, in which the contracting parties agree to give up something in return for something. Thus, public authority receives its power to govern from the individuals who are to be subject to it in return for the protection of their rights and the other benefits of community life. This means that the rights of public authority must originally have been possessed by individuals, for one cannot dispose of what one does not possess. Hence, for Locke, the individual is originally sovereign, possessing not only the private right to defend himself and others, but also the public right to judge and punish violators of the natural law.[17]

It is impossible, however, for an individual person to be sovereign in this way. For to judge others and to punish them is to assume authority over them, and no individual person as such has authority over any other individual person. As we saw in chapter 7, this is why an individual has a natural right to defend himself from attack, but not the right to judge and punish his attacker.[18] The rights of parents are not an objection to this, since parents have only a qualified right to punish their children, and this only in their office as parents and in virtue of the common good of the family. The power to judge and punish in the full sense belongs only to public authority.

It might be objected that an individual in Locke's state of nature has the right to act in virtue of the natural common good of the human race, there being no established authority to which he might appeal. But this would still be to assume public author-

16. Ibid., § 15 and § 95.
17. Ibid., § 7, § 8, § 11, and § 87.
18. I discussed killing in self-defense in chapter 7. The proof that only public authority has the right to execute murderers is stated later in that chapter, in the discussion of capital punishment.

ity arbitrarily. This kind of difficulty arises because we think of Locke's state of nature as having at some time actually existed. But community is so necessary and so natural to mankind that it is hard to imagine a historical situation in which people would not be living together. But people cannot live together peacefully without law—if not by the law of a fully formed political community, then at least by laws arising from local custom. However imperfect such laws may be, to act on the basis of customary laws is not the same as to act as if one were individually sovereign.

Note, however, that even on Locke's theory, the origin of public authority lies in the natural law. For if public authority is established by sovereign individuals through a contract, and if these individuals have their sovereignty by the natural law, then public authority will be founded on the natural law. Since God is the authority who establishes the natural law, the authority of public officials will depend ultimately on divine authority.

Locke affirms the traditional view that public authority is responsible for and limited by the common good.[19] But to what extent will the common good be prior to the private interests of the citizens? If the political community results from a contract made by sovereign individuals, and if people generally make contracts for the sake of their private interests, a community constituted by a social contract will likely tend to emphasize these interests. We see this to some extent in Locke's emphasis on the protection of life, liberty, and property, goods that sovereign individuals will be especially anxious to safeguard.[20] The social contract approach may therefore lead to an overly individualistic conception of the political community, hindering to some extent the full development of the social conditions necessary for achieving the happiness of all.

19. Locke, *Second Treatise*, § 131.
20. Ibid., §§ 123–24.

## Natural Law and Democracy

What is the relationship between democracy and the natural law? In approaching this question, the main thing to keep in mind is that the natural law is more concerned with the end or purpose of government than with its constitutional form. No form of government that truly serves the common good is opposed per se to the natural law. However, some forms may be more suitable than others for particular peoples at particular times. As a people advances in education and virtue, it is reasonable and in accord with human dignity that it should have a greater share in public affairs, both in electing its leaders and in holding them accountable. For education and virtue prepare a people to assume the responsibilities of democratic citizenship.

As we have seen, the power to govern belongs to public authority by natural law. It is not conferred by individual citizens through a social contract. But this is not an objection to democracy. For it is one thing to confer the power to govern as if it were something originally possessed by sovereign individuals, but quite another thing to decide who is to possess this power. In a democracy, the people decide by their votes who will hold public office. But the power of elected officials to govern does not come from the people's vote but from the political constitution of their country and, ultimately, from the natural law.

It is generally believed today that states should be democratic, and not without reason. For the leaders in democratic states must be concerned with the basic needs of the people, and this is of fundamental importance for the common good. Moreover, the civil and political institutions in modern democracies—a constitution that recognizes human rights, a separation of the legislative, executive, and judicial powers, civilian control of the military, term limits for the highest offices, universal education, a free press, etc.—serve to protect the people from tyranny. Even so, democracy is fragile and will be weakened or even corrupted when the virtue of the people declines or when the power of the state becomes excessive, especially if it is dominated by financial interests or by ideology. Hence, the importance in a democracy of stable families, good educational institutions, active associations of civil society, and strong religious communities. These all contribute to the moral and intellectual formation of the people and serve as a counterbalance to the power of the state.

## The Universal Common Good

As we saw in chapter 5, the natural law is concerned not just with the good of this or that particular community, but with the common good of the human race as a whole, including future generations. It follows that individual nations are obligated by natural law to cooperate with each other to achieve this larger good. Just as the citizens of a particular state contribute to its welfare by serving it according to their special talents and vocations, so, in an analogous way, particular states must contribute to the welfare of mankind as a whole. For this international cooperation to be fully effective, it should be coordinated through a universal public authority. This is the ideal toward which we are directed by the natural law.[21]

However, establishing a universal public authority will be a difficult process and not without danger. Will it lead to a monolithic world community organized under theories of law and human rights based primarily on the special culture of a dominant nation or region? Or will it be organized on the basis of principles that are universally valid? Clearly, it should be organized on universally valid principles. But different cultures, with different ways of life, will not always agree on what these principles are. Hence, it is of the greatest importance that the principles that

21. John XXIII, *Pacem in Terris*, Encyclical Letter (April 11, 1963), Part IV. See also Robert P. George, "Natural Law and International Order," in *In Defense of Natural Law* (New York: Oxford University Press, 1999), 228–45.

are to guide a universal public authority be developed gradually, freely, by consensus, and after a careful study of the common elements in different systems of law and rights. This process will be greatly benefitted by a renewed study of the natural law. For the precepts of the natural law direct us to a way of life precisely suited to our nature as human beings and have therefore a preeminent claim to be regarded as universally valid.

Furthermore, a universal public authority should not insert itself into the internal affairs of particular states, except perhaps when this is necessary to remedy very serious violations of fundamental natural rights. The point of a world authority is *not* to do what particular states or regional associations could do for themselves. Rather, a universal public authority should work with individual states to realize benefits, like world peace and environmental protection, that they could not achieve by themselves alone. This is demanded by the principle of subsidiarity.

## Subsidiarity

Subsidiarity means that higher levels of social organization should not take over functions that are within the power of lower levels or individuals. Thus, individuals should be active, not passive, seeking to achieve happiness and the things necessary for happiness as much as possible by their own efforts. They cooperate with others in order to achieve what is beyond their individual powers, first in families, then in local organizations and associations, and then in local government. They should call upon higher levels of social organization and government only when they lack the resources to accomplish what is needed on their own.

Subsidiarity protects and promotes human freedom and initiative. As free beings, we achieve happiness primarily by our own efforts; hence, it is natural that we should take the initiative in our lives. Of course, we cannot achieve happiness without the help of others. But this does not mean that others exist to do for us what we can do for ourselves or that higher levels of social organization exist to take over functions that can be carried out at a lower level. Thus, social policies established by political communities ought not to substitute for the efforts of individuals and local organizations, but rather to facilitate them, so that, as John XXIII taught, human beings are *enabled* more fully and more readily to achieve their perfection.[22]

## Conclusion

To conclude this chapter, let us review what we have seen thus far in our study of the precepts of the natural law and preview what remains to be considered. Since man is first of all an existing being, we began, in chapters 6 and 7, with precepts concerning life and physical integrity. Second, since man is an animal, having a natural inclination to mate and to raise a family, we considered, in chapters 8 and 9, the precepts concerning sex, marriage, and family. Finally, in this chapter, we looked at the inclinations proper to man as a rational being: the inclinations to know the truth, especially the first truth, and to live with others in a political community for mutual benefit.

What remains to be considered are natural rights, the rights that belong to human beings by nature. For if the common good of the political community is the happiness of its members, then each member of the community will have a right to share in whatever can be achieved through social cooperation to enable or facilitate the achievement of happiness. They will have rights to life, freedom, property, education, opportunity, and many others. Because these rights are ordered to the achievement of our natural end, they are all natural rights.

Chapter 11, therefore, will be devoted to natural rights, the rights that all human beings have by nature and that political

---

22. John XXIII, *Pacem in Terris*, no. 58.

communities are obligated to recognize and foster. This will complete our consideration of the political community and our consideration of the natural law. For thus far we have considered the natural law only insofar as it imposes duties. It remains, therefore, to consider it insofar as it establishes rights.

CHAPTER 11

# Natural Rights

In this chapter we shall consider natural rights, the rights that belong to all human beings by nature. We shall first consider these rights in general, relating them to the natural law and to the rights established by positive law. We will then consider particular natural rights—not all of them, but only some that I wish to emphasize. These will be grouped under three headings: (a) the fundamental rights to life, freedom, and property, (b) the rights of the family, and (c) the rights of the people with respect to morality, culture, and religion. These three groups of natural rights correspond roughly to the three levels of natural inclinations discussed in chapter 5.

Our reflections on natural rights will necessarily be quite general, concerned more with defining and clarifying them than with investigating what positive laws and public policies might be useful for promoting them. For these will depend on what is possible for a particular society at a particular time. We should note, however, that the laws and policies established by different communities will have certain fundamental principles in common. The Romans incorporated principles of this kind into what they called the *jus gentium*, the law of nations. I will say something about this law later when discussing the right of private property.

Before turning to the theory of natural rights, however, I would like to say something about the concerns of those who see problems with the contemporary emphasis on rights. There are, it seems to me, three main objections. The first concerns the way in which an overemphasis on individual rights prevents an intelligent balancing of the different interests at stake in a given controversy.[1] I would like to suggest, as an example, the controversy over university admissions policies. A highly qualified student may think that his interest in being admitted is absolutely prior (it is his right!) to a university's interest in educating a more diverse student body for the sake of the common good. It seems unreasonable to prefer the student's interest over the university's a priori, using rights as trump cards, unless, of course, an inviolable natural right is involved. But no such right is involved in a controversy like this.

A second, more specific objection concerns government entitlements that exaggerate the power of the state and increase the dependency of the citizens without a sufficient regard for subsidiarity.[2] I agree with this objection, but, as we shall see, it is not an objection to natural rights per se. For government entitlements are positive rights, established by human law, not natural rights. Although they are intended as a response to natural rights and to this extent are certainly praiseworthy, they are not an unproblematic response. Other ways may be better. This will be clearer later, especially in the section on responding to natural rights.

The third objection, far more serious, concerns positive rights that violate the natural law, like the right to abortion. Such rights are mere human inventions; they are not themselves natural rights, nor can they be a valid response to any natural right. They are, moreover, extremely dangerous, since they give public recognition to practices fundamentally opposed to right reason and human happiness. I will say something further on this topic in the section on modern natural rights theory.

1. For an extensive and well-informed discussion of this topic, see Mary Ann Glendon, *Rights Talk: The Impoverishment of Public Discourse* (New York: Free Press, 1991).

2. On the entitlement problem, see James V. Schall, "Entitlements: Unintended Paradoxes of the Generous State," in *Reason, Revelation and Human Affairs: Selected Writings of James V. Schall*, ed. Marc D. Guerra (Lanham, Md.: Lexington, 2001), 23–34.

## Natural Rights and Natural Duties

First, we should clarify the concept of a right. The fundamental idea is that a right is what is legally due to a person or association from another person or association, as when a payment is due to you or your company for a product or service or when respect for your life is due to you from me and from all other persons. By associations I mean here families, private organizations, and political and religious communities. Moreover, since what is legally due can be claimed by the right holder or by someone on his behalf, a right can also be defined as a claim that a person or association is authorized by law to make on the conduct of one or more other persons or associations.

Since rights are established by law and laws are established for the common good, the positive rights established by a human authority should aim at the common good of the political community under its jurisdiction. The various parts of a political community are in fact linked together by rights and by the duties corresponding to them. Thus, individuals, families, private organizations, and religious communities have rights and duties in relation to each other and to the public authority, which, in turn, has rights and duties in relation to them. When these rights are recognized and the duties corresponding to them are faithfully carried out, the common good of the community is effectively safeguarded and promoted.

As the natural law is prior to the positive law, so natural rights are prior to positive rights. Because natural rights belong to all human beings, they must be founded on the natural common good of the human race—that is, on happiness. Since we are directed to happiness by the natural law, it is by this law that our natural rights are established.

To understand how the natural law establishes rights, we must consider that it first establishes duties. For the precepts of the natural law show us what we must do to achieve happiness, the life of virtue. Our duty to follow these precepts is absolute and unqualified, since the life of virtue is the purpose of our existence. But the natural law cannot impose duties without simultaneously establishing rights to whatever is necessary for carrying out these duties. It follows that we have natural rights to whatever is necessary for achieving the life of virtue.[3] To fully achieve it, we must cooperate with others in communities. Therefore, we have natural rights to the social conditions that will enable us to achieve the life of virtue. As we have seen, these include everything from an adequate food supply to what facilitates the search for ultimate truth. This is why John XXIII described the common good as "the sum total of those conditions of social living whereby men are enabled to achieve their integral perfection more fully and more easily."[4]

But how can we have natural rights to whatever is necessary for achieving the life of virtue? A right is a claim, affirmative or negative, on the conduct of others. Therefore, if natural rights are really rights, there must be persons or institutions obligated to respond to them, and this, at least for many natural rights, does not seem to be possible. Our obligation to respond to claims of natural rights, therefore, does not seem to be the same as our obligation to respond to specific positive rights established by human law. We shall consider this question in the section on responding to natural rights.

To see the priority of natural duties to natural rights in another way, let us imagine that we had no natural duties. On what basis could we then demand anything from anybody as a matter of natural right? If, for example, I had no natural duty to preserve my life, how could I have a natural right to demand that you respect it? Because I want you to respect it? But the fact that

3. Jacques Maritain derived natural rights from the natural law in this way in *The Rights of Man and Natural Law* (New York: Charles Scribner's Sons, 1943), 65–66. He stated essentially the same thing in *Man and the State* (Chicago: University of Chicago Press, 1951), 95. See also Ralph McInerny, *Aquinas on Human Action: A Theory of Practice* (Washington D.C.: The Catholic University of America Press, 1992), 207–19.

4. John XXIII, *Pacem in Terris*, Encyclical Letter (April 11, 1963), no. 58.

I want something does not, of itself, authorize me to demand it from you. On the other hand, if I have a natural duty to preserve my life, and you, likewise, a natural duty to preserve your life, then each of us will have a natural right to demand that the other respect his life. For without life, no one can achieve the life of virtue. In this way, the natural right to life is established from the natural duty to preserve one's life.

Could we reverse the logic and say that the natural right to life comes first and that the duty to respect life is a consequence of this? But we are not concerned here with what follows from a natural right *once it has been established*, but rather with a more fundamental question: how are natural rights established in the first place? As we have seen, the natural law cannot impose duties without simultaneously establishing rights to whatever is necessary for carrying out these duties. Thus, if the natural law obligates us to preserve our lives, it must grant us rights to what we need to fulfill this obligation. For how could we preserve our lives if we had no right to personal safety or to food and shelter? Our natural rights therefore follow necessarily from our natural duties as determined by the precepts of the natural law.

If natural rights are based on our duty to live virtuously, what would follow if someone were to fail to carry out this duty by wasting his time and not making good use of his talents? Would he then lose his natural rights? He would not lose them, because natural rights are established on the basis of the kind of life we are *meant for*, not on how well we have actually achieved it. They open the way for us to proceed toward our fullest perfection, a constant invitation to make progress in living virtuously. Hence, the natural rights of those who fall short in their duty to live virtuously must be respected—unless, of course, they forfeit rights by committing crimes, as we saw earlier when discussing capital punishment.

## A Modern Natural Rights Theory

Although natural rights are not prior to the natural law, they are prior to the positive law and to positive rights. If, for example, we have natural rights to life and to freedom of religion, we are authorized by the natural law to demand that the positive law recognize these as positive rights. In this sense, we can speak of natural rights as prior to law—prior, that is, to positive law. This is the element of truth in the theory that makes natural rights fundamental, as we see in the French Déclaration des Droits de l'Homme et du Citoyen and in the American Declaration of Independence.[5] But natural rights are not prior to the natural law; they are derived from the natural law. As we have seen, the precepts of the natural law first impose duties and then establish rights to what is necessary to fulfill these duties. This gives rise to a serious question for modern natural rights theory: if natural rights are not clearly seen as proceeding from precepts of the natural law, what will be their source or foundation?

If natural rights are not founded on natural duties specified by precepts of the natural law, and if they are essentially prior to positive law, then they must be founded on something regarded as prior to all law. But prior to all law we have only lawless freedom, the desire to live as we please, subject only to such restrictions as may be necessary to safeguard and foster our freedom. This translates into demands for the recognition of a system of positive rights that reflects this priority of freedom. Natural rights, thus understood, will not be rights so much as demands for rights. They will be demands that particular freedoms be recognized as rights under the positive law.

Those who first attempted to found the political order on natural rights did not necessarily think of them as prior to or separate from the natural law. Although it emphasizes natural

5. See A. P. d'Entrèves, *Natural Law: An Historical Survey*, Harper Torchbooks (New York: Harper and Row, 1965), chapter 3. In this chapter, d'Entrèves gives a brief, helpful introduction to modern natural rights theory.

rights, the Declaration of Independence begins with an appeal to the laws of nature and nature's God, and there are commonsense interpretations of the rights to "life, liberty, and the pursuit of happiness" that can certainly be justified under natural law. The French declaration does not mention the natural law, but it does assert certain natural rights—for example, to liberty, property, and security—that can easily be understood as proceeding from the natural law. But a reference to the natural law in general is not enough to establish the full system of natural rights; particular natural rights will depend on particular natural duties specified by particular natural law precepts. Without these precepts, we have no way of knowing what our natural rights are.

The danger of this modern approach to natural rights, therefore, is that the natural law will become irrelevant and be forgotten and that many natural rights—now called human rights rather than natural rights—will result from demands that particular freedoms be recognized as positive rights. We see this, for example, in abortion and homosexual marriage. For the right to abortion is promoted as a woman's freedom to choose, setting aside the question of whether or not abortion itself can be justified, and the right to homosexual marriage as a vindication of the freedom of homosexuals to marry just like heterosexuals do, again setting aside substantive questions about whether homosexual marriage is even possible. The more we separate demands for positive rights from the precepts of the natural law, the more arbitrary they become.

## Responding to Natural Rights

The natural rights that follow from the precepts of the natural law have both negative and affirmative implications. The former are rights to demand that others not harm us or arbitrarily interfere with us; the latter, rights to demand that others do something to help us. Thus, the right to life, as we considered it in chapter 6, is a right to demand that others not take our lives. But it also has affirmative implications, like the rights to a safe environment and to food and medical care that are necessary for life. Claims based on negative natural rights are always valid, but claims based on affirmative natural rights, since they make positive demands on other individuals or on the community, can be subject to conditions. Thus, if someone is unable to provide what he needs for himself, he undoubtedly has a right to be helped. But if he simply refuses to work, he cannot reasonably demand that others take care of him.

Who is responsible for responding to claims of natural right, claims that every individual is entitled to make? Some responsibility certainly falls on relatives and friends and also on persons who happen to encounter someone—even a stranger—in a moment of great need. Every man is in some measure his brother's keeper. But there are limits to what an individual can do or can reasonably be expected to do. Our response to natural rights, therefore, must also be a community response, involving families and extended families, local professional, charitable, and volunteer associations, religious communities, and public authority, always in accord with the principle of subsidiarity, as explained in chapter 10.

But how will it be possible to respond to all of these natural rights? For the list of them will be extensive. We see this, for example, in the rights enumerated by John XXIII in *Pacem in Terris*: rights to food, clothing, shelter, rest, and medical care, to respect for one's person and reputation, to the freedom to search for truth and to communicate it to others, to education, to share in the benefits of culture, to religious freedom, and many others. These follow from his description of the common good as comprising all those conditions of social living whereby individuals are enabled to achieve their perfection.[6] It might seem from this that natural rights are not rights at all, but only social ideals, perhaps utopian ideals.

6. John XXIII, *Pacem in Terris*, esp. Part I.

This difficulty arises because we think of natural rights after the manner of positive rights, which authorize claims that are particular and limited, like the right to have a sealed contract enforced or the right of an indigent person to hospital care in an emergency. But it is not always possible to respond adequately to natural rights, and to this extent they represent social ideals. But they are nevertheless real rights, since we are obligated to respond to them as much as we reasonably can, taking account of the resources available and giving preference to rights that are more fundamental or pressing. Moreover, natural rights are the dynamic principle in social development, since we are obligated to progressively transform our individual behavior and our laws, customs, and institutions so as to respond to these rights ever more adequately.

## The Welfare State

Does the obligation to respond to natural rights imply the contemporary welfare state? Not without some qualifications. First of all, there is the danger of too much state involvement and control. If the state seeks to provide for all or most of the needs and desires of the people, an enervating dependency and loss of freedom easily result. We have primary responsibility for our own happiness. Hence, we have unqualified rights to demand that others not interfere with us in our efforts to fulfill our duties and to acquire what is necessary or useful for this purpose, respecting, of course, the same rights in others. But we have only qualified rights to demand that others help us, since we have no right to expect other persons or organizations to do for us what we can do for ourselves.

By the same logic, we have no right to demand from government what we can obtain through informal arrangements and nongovernmental associations or to demand from higher levels of government what can be achieved through lower levels. These are all consequences of the principle of subsidiarity discussed in chapter 10. For if higher levels of social organization should not take over functions appropriate to lower levels or to individuals, then these latter should not demand that they do so. By following the principle of subsidiarity, we not only provide for our needs more efficiently, but also maintain a balance of power between ourselves and government, so that our freedom is not at risk.

Furthermore, the contemporary welfare state does not have an adequate understanding of happiness. It recognizes that happiness requires such things as bodily and external goods and opportunities for education and employment. Thus far it accords with the natural law, which recognizes these as natural rights. But, as we shall see, there are also natural rights founded on the very essence of human happiness, the life of virtue. Since the contemporary welfare state is not based explicitly on an understanding of happiness as the life of virtue and on the precepts of the natural law that direct us to this life, it does not fully recognize these rights.

## The Right to Life

First among the natural rights is the right to life, encompassing, as we have seen, not only the negative right not to be lethally attacked or physically injured, but also the affirmative right to be rendered the means necessary for protecting and sustaining life when one is unable to provide them for oneself. This right is the basis of public efforts to protect people from violence and other physical harms and to ensure that those responsible for the care of infants, children, and other vulnerable persons are doing their duty. It lies behind the recognition that those unable to earn a living because of disability, sickness, or unemployment are entitled to appropriate assistance. Finally, it is the basis of public efforts to ensure that food, clothing, shelter, and health care are available and affordable. Because all of these are consequences of the natural right to life, they are all themselves matters of natural right.

The most serious violation of the right to life is a lethal attack upon an innocent human being, a topic that we have already considered at length. Here I would like to emphasize that making an exception to the right to life for unborn human beings destroys the foundations of the positive legal order. For suppose it be asserted that we now have a right to life, but that we did not have this right at some earlier stage in our development. Why then do we have it now? Clearly, it is because the positive law says so. This means that we have the right to life when it has been granted to us by those who have the power to make the laws. If this were true for the right to life, it would ultimately be true also for other rights, since these depend on the right to life. By abolishing the right to life of the unborn, therefore, we undermine the whole system of positive human rights.

## The Right to Freedom

The truest freedom is the freedom of the life of virtue, a life that is preeminently free by its very nature. For freedom signifies the removal of whatever constrains our actions. But it is ignorance and vice that constrain us most fundamentally, since they prevent us from fully realizing ourselves in accord with our nature as rational beings. We are liberated from these constraints by the intellectual and moral virtues. Therefore, just as the life of virtue is the most noble and beautiful and enjoyable way of life, so also is it the most free.

This freedom is not a right, however, but rather a duty, since it coincides with the ultimate end. For rights are claims we make regarding what facilitates the achievement of the end, not the end itself. When we speak of freedom as a natural right, therefore, we are thinking of external constraints: oppression by other individuals or by government, unreasonable interference with our movements and activities, harassment and intimidation, the arbitrary closing off of opportunities for education and accomplishment, etc.

That we are meant to live in freedom is clear from our rational nature. For we understand the ends for which we act and can freely determine and choose the means to attain them. In this we differ from the animals, which act by natural instinct, imagination, and memory to attain ends that they do not understand. This is why we naturally seek to act freely, on our own initiative, without being subjected to arbitrary constraints.

Like the other natural rights, the right to freedom is based on the duty to seek the life of virtue. But as we saw earlier, natural rights are based on the life that human beings are meant to live, not on how perfectly they have achieved it. Therefore, even if an individual is not seeking to live virtuously, his freedom of action must be respected. However, restraints on persons who violate the positive law or who pose a danger to themselves or others are not violations of the right to freedom.

We should note further that if natural rights are based on the duty to live the life of virtue and therefore on the precepts of the natural law, then there cannot be any natural rights to actions opposed to these precepts. It follows that public authority can forbid such actions or limit the opportunities for them without violating the natural right to freedom of action. How far the positive law can or should go in this way depends on social conditions. The positive law does not have the power to eradicate vice completely, and an attempt to do so might lead to even worse evils. As Aquinas taught, human law is meant to lead people to virtue not suddenly, but gradually.[7]

On the principle that human law should lead people to virtue gradually, we can distinguish between progressive and regressive developments in a positive legal system. Developments that move the people toward more virtuous ways of thinking and acting are progressive, while those that tend in the opposite direction are regressive. We see this regression, for example, when there is little or no control over forces that are causing a deterioration in

---

7. *ST* I-II, q. 96, a. 2, c, ad 2.

the way people live, or, worse yet, when practices contrary to the natural law are not only tolerated, but even promoted as if they were human rights.

## The Right to Property

As we saw in chapter 7, the things of the natural world other than man, both animate and inanimate, are meant for human use. Hence, individuals, families, and communities have a natural right to take possession of these things as needed. This right differs from the rights to life and freedom in that life and freedom belong to every person immediately by nature, whereas property does not. No part of the earth or its riches is naturally ordered to the good of this or that individual, family, or community. Rather, the earth as a whole is for the good of the human race as a whole, throughout all of its generations. Its division into parts that are privately owned or controlled is the result of human choices and traditions.

Nevertheless, there is a natural right to the private ownership of property, not only of personal property, but also of productive property. This right is not among the first principles of the natural law, but is a conclusion from these principles. For, as Aquinas pointed out, productive resources are used more diligently and in a more orderly and peaceful way when they are privately owned. But the earth is meant to serve the needs of the human race as efficiently and peacefully as possible. Therefore, human beings have a natural right to the acquisition and use of productive property. However, this right must be exercised in such a way that its ultimate purpose, the good of the human race as a whole, is thereby promoted, not hindered or retarded.[8]

8. *ST* II-II, q. 66, a. 2, c; Aristotle, *Politics* II.5.1262b37–63b7. For a discussion of how the social obligations belonging to the private ownership of productive property lead to a natural law justification for legally established welfare rights, see Joseph Boyle, "Fairness in Holdings: A Natural Law Account of Property and Welfare

The private ownership of productive property is important not only for economic efficiency, but also for freedom, since it secures a certain independence to individuals, families, and businesses, making them less dependent on the state. Freedom is safeguarded especially when private ownership is widespread within the community, not concentrated primarily in large enterprises. An economy characterized by many small or moderately sized local enterprises is also more in accord with subsidiarity. Besides safeguarding freedom, private ownership stimulates enthusiasm and initiative, since it makes it possible for people to better their economic condition.[9]

Since most people today must earn their living by working for others, the right to acquire and use productive property is supplemented by the right to employment. For every individual has a natural right to provide for his needs by his labor. The natural law clearly requires that employment be suitable to the dignity of human workers; hence, there are rights to humane working conditions, to reasonable job security, to a wage sufficient to support oneself and one's family, etc. Moreover, it is important that employees have as much opportunity for individual initiative as possible, since this makes working for others more like working for oneself.

A special problem arises when many workers must earn their living at jobs that do not pay enough to support them and their families. For if the economy does not provide decent jobs, workers who cannot adequately support themselves must be helped by others or by the community. But surely it is more efficient, more respectful of human dignity, and more in accord with freedom that workers be able to satisfy their needs through their work. Hence, the fundamental importance of just wages.

Man does not exist for the economic system; the economic system exists for man—and not only for man the consumer, but

Rights," in *Natural Law and Modern Moral Philosophy*, ed. Ellen Frankel Paul, Fred D. Miller Jr., and Jeffrey Paul (New York: Cambridge University Press, 2001), 206–26.

9. Leo XIII, *Rerum Novarum*, Encyclical Letter (May 15, 1891), nos. 3–12, 35.

also for man the producer.[10] The working of an economy must therefore be ordered to the ultimate end of the political community, the happiness of its members.

Workers find satisfaction in their work especially when it is meaningful, making a genuine contribution to the community, and when it is stable, allowing them to put down roots in their communities and to raise their families without fear of unemployment and dislocation. These benefits must not be sacrificed to economic efficiency, rapid progress, and unrestrained competition. Hence, public authority has the obligation to regulate the economy so that it serves the community without compromising the rights and welfare of workers.

## The Jus Gentium

Private property is a good example of a legal institution belonging to what the Romans called the *jus gentium*, and, although this is a bit of a digression, I would like to say something about that law here. It originated from the need for a way to settle disputes between Romans and foreigners living under Roman rule, and among these foreigners themselves when they belonged to different communities. For this purpose neither the Roman civil law (the *jus civile*) nor the civil laws of the different communities under Roman rule were adequate. The Romans therefore developed a system of law based on legal principles recognized everywhere. This was the *jus gentium*. Although it did include some principles of public law, it was primarily a system of private law and should not be thought of as a law governing the relations between sovereign states, as we would think of the law of nations today.

To make this a little more concrete, here are a few examples of principles and institutions that fell under the *jus gentium*: private

10. John Paul II, *Laborum Exercens*, Encyclical Letter (September 14, 1981), nos. 6, 18.

property, marriage, slavery, justice in commercial transactions (keeping agreements, observing justice in buying and selling), the protection of property, obligations to pay for damages, the inviolability of envoys, and the rights of persons who have been banished and have lost their rights under the civil law.

Our principal concern here is to understand the relationship between the *jus gentium* and the natural law. For this purpose, we shall examine Aquinas's interpretation of two well-known statements by the Roman jurists Ulpian and Gaius.[11] According to Ulpian, the *jus naturale* is what nature has taught all animals— that is, mating and the rearing of offspring—while the *jus gentium* is what all human beings observe. Gaius clarified this further by distinguishing between the *jus civile* and the *jus gentium*. The former, he said, is the special law that each nation has established for itself; the latter is a law that natural reason has established among all peoples. From these affirmations, we may gather that the *jus gentium* is proper to us precisely as rational beings and is established by natural reason, whereas the *jus naturale*, as Ulpian understands it, concerns the natural inclinations that we share with the animals.

Aquinas interprets these texts by means of a distinction between two ways in which something can be said to be of natural law. In one way, he said, something belongs to the natural law insofar as it is considered absolutely; in another way, insofar as it is considered in the light of what follows from it. The mating of male and female and the raising of offspring are natural in the first way, because male and female are related to sexual intercourse and procreation by their very nature and, similarly, parents to the care of their offspring. Hence, what is natural in this sense can be found in animals as well as in human beings. But what is natural in the second way is found only in human beings, because only reason can consider things in relation to their consequences. This

---

11. *The Digest of Justinian* trans. ed. Alan Watson, rev. English ed. (Philadelphia: University of Pennsylvania Press, 1998), I.i.

is the sense in which private property and the other principles and institutions of the *jus gentium* are natural.[12]

As we saw in chapter 5, some precepts of the positive law are derived as conclusions from the principles of the natural law, while others are particular determinations. These latter include, for example, laws establishing a particular system of taxation or determining the punishments for various kinds of crime. The precepts of the *jus gentium* are derived from the natural law in the first way, those of the *jus civile* in the second way. Nevertheless, though derived from the natural law, the *jus gentium* is human or positive law.[13] It is a law that is embedded, so to speak, in the specific provisions of different systems of positive law and that can be abstracted from them, so as to reveal the legal principles and institutions that have been found to be useful for bringing about good order and peace in the community. Hence, it appears as a law established by natural reason, a law that human legislators are presupposing and seeking to make effective when they establish the laws of their particular communities.

If the positive law is established on the basis of utility, it might seem that it is not concerned with inviolable natural rights, like the right to life. For, as we have seen, the right to life must to respected, regardless of consequences. But it would certainly be strange if natural reason were able to overrule natural rights. In fact, it does not overrule them; rather it presupposes them. Natural reason is concerned to establish the legal principles and institutions that are genuinely useful for protecting and fostering natural rights. This is why legislators establishing positive laws must take careful account of consequences, both immediate and long-term. For not every well-intentioned public policy responding to a natural right will actually be useful, all things considered. For example, questions have been raised about the utility of government entitlements, as we saw in the first section of this chapter.

12. *ST* II-II, q. 57, a. 3, c.
13. *ST* I-II, q. 95, a. 4, c, ad 1.

Some principles and institutions of the *jus gentium* may change over time as society progresses. Thus, slavery, once an accepted way of relating workers to those who make use of their labor, is no longer tolerated, and, as we noted in chapter 7, capital punishment has been abolished or significantly restricted in most countries. The usefulness of the private ownership of productive property, however, has been strongly confirmed by contemporary experience.

A question might be raised about these changes. If the laws and institutions of the *jus gentium* are derived as conclusions from the natural law, how can they change over time? Insofar as they are useful for the peace and order of society, they do indeed derive from the natural law. But this does not mean that they are fully in accord with it. As the implications of human dignity come to be appreciated more fully, and as customs and manners become more humane, positive laws and institutions will be changed or modified. They will then reflect the natural law more perfectly. On the other hand, of course, there can be changes that reflect bad customs and false ideas. These latter changes are not introduced by natural reason, but rather by a kind of false or ideologically perverted reason, leading ultimately to unrest and disorder.

This completes our brief discussion of the *jus gentium*. While not strictly necessary for our study of natural rights, I think a consideration of this law helps to clarify institutions like the right to private property and, more generally, the relationship between natural law and systems of positive law.

## The Rights of the Family

Within the political community, there are many associations through which individuals, working cooperatively, can more easily achieve some good related to their happiness or to the happiness of the community as a whole. People have a natural right, therefore, to assemble and to form associations, and these are of great importance, because they make it possible for people to accomplish on a lower level what they might otherwise expect from the state. The state then assumes its proper role of protecting natural rights and of coordinating and supplementing the efforts of individuals and intermediate associations to achieve what is necessary for happiness.

The first and most fundamental association is the family, a natural society whose essential characteristics are determined by the natural law. For, as we have seen, man and woman are by nature adapted to the union we call marriage, and offspring are a natural result of this union. Hence, the family has certain natural rights that must be recognized and respected by public authority. Moreover, it is in the interest of the state to recognize and foster the rights of the family. For the state depends on the family to bring new human beings into the world, to see to their nourishment and education, and to provide for the needs of daily life. The state's role is to be at the service of families, supplying, through larger cooperative action, what individual families cannot accomplish on their own. For if families had been able to achieve the good life entirely on their own, there would have been no need for the state.

Because the family is founded on marriage, the first natural right pertaining to the family is the right of men and women to marry and to procreate. This right springs from the natural law obligation to bring new human beings into the world to replace those who die. Of course, it is not necessary that everyone exercise this right—only that enough people marry and procreate to ensure the future of humanity. Since the rights to marry and to procreate belong to men and women immediately by nature, prior to membership in the political community, they cannot be abrogated by human law.

Because they are responsible for the existence of their children and because the purpose of human existence is the life of virtue, parents have a natural duty and therefore a natural right to nourish and educate them. This is the work proper to the family and the chief way in which it contributes to the common good of the political community and of the human race as a whole. The family is a kind of school of virtue both for parents and for children: for parents, because they grow in love for each other and learn to practice virtue as they fulfill their marital and parental obligations; for children, because the home is the first school of virtue, and a most efficacious one, since it fosters good habits in the children on a daily basis, from the very beginning of their lives, in an environment suffused with the natural love that unites parents and children. The family thus makes an indispensable contribution to the happiness of society.

Whatever prepares children for the life of virtue falls under parental responsibility. This obviously includes the duty to provide for their physical needs and safety, because life, strength, and health, besides being intrinsically good, contribute instrumentally to the virtuous life. Furthermore, parents have the duty to educate their children. The children must be prepared to assume their duties as citizens under the constitution of their country and to contribute to its welfare through their proper vocations. They must be habituated to live virtuously, at least to the extent of being useful law-abiding citizens. This much the state must insist upon. But there is more to the life of virtue than obedience to the laws of the state, and parents have the duty—and the corresponding right—to educate their children in all the virtues, including those related to their religion.

This raises the question of state support for parents who wish to educate their children in religious schools, a question that is often discussed on the assumption that the state is primarily responsible for educating children. But this is not true. The state is responsible for seeing to it that parents are fulfilling *their* duty to educate *their* children. Schools, therefore, are first of all at the service of parents and, through parents, at the service of the state. It follows that parents, rightly concerned with the religious formation of their children, have a natural right to educate them in religious schools. The state, of course, has a right to require that religious schools not be subversive and that they provide the quality education that the community has a right to expect from them. Furthermore, since the education of children is of vital importance for the common good, the state also has the duty to assist parents who otherwise could not pay for the education of their children. It is unjust to forbid such assistance to parents who wish to send their children to religious schools.

As political society arose from families, so it depends on families. Since the strength of families depends on the strength of marriages, the state must be especially concerned with whatever weakens or destroys marriage. Among these are the evils of abortion and unnatural sexual practices, which are opposed to procreation, and divorce, which is opposed to the permanence of the marriage union. Finally, the state has the duty to promote social and economic conditions favorable to the flourishing of family life.

## The Rights of the People: Virtue, Culture, and Religion

We turn finally to the most difficult and sensitive topic: the duties of the state in relation to the ultimate end itself, the life of virtue. The general principle is clear enough. If the state exists for the sake of happiness as a common good, and if happiness consists essentially in the life of virtue, then the state must be concerned not only with what is necessary for survival—with security, for example, and with the food supply—but also with what helps the citizens achieve a virtuous life. Of course, the state cannot compel anyone to live virtuously; its power extends only to external actions, and an action is not virtuous unless it is done with the right interior motivation. But there are many ways in which a positive legal system, inspired by the natural law, can encourage and facilitate the life of virtue.

One way is through the enactment of just laws and their vigorous and even-handed enforcement. Although the threat of punishment cannot make us act justly out of a love for justice, it can and does habituate us to respect the rights of others. This leads over time to a clearer appreciation of the equal dignity of all human beings, the value that underlies all just laws. In this way, the law is an educator, and an efficacious one, since it educates not only by instructing us, but also, through its enforcement, by actually moving us to good behavior. Moreover, it creates a climate of mutual respect and trust, essential for fruitful collaboration in efforts to advance the common good.

A second way, already discussed, is through appropriate laws and policies regarding marriage and the family. For laws and policies that strengthen marriages and that promote economic conditions favorable to the flourishing of family life can help parents raise their children to be good persons and to be good citizens, conscientiously fulfilling their duties to others and to the community. Of special importance are policies that enable parents to educate their children in religious schools, since true religion, sincerely practiced, opens the way to all the virtues. By respecting the natural rights of the family, therefore, and by establishing policies favorable to family life, the state contributes significantly to the development of the life of virtue.

However, family policy, even when inspired by the natural law, is not enough. For children are formed by the culture, and if the culture is perverse, parents cannot effectively protect them against it.[14] Furthermore, it is not just children who are affected by the culture—all of us are. Ultimately futile, I think, is accepting corruption in the adult culture while trying to minimize the damage to children. Therefore, if the state is concerned with the happiness of its citizens, it must have a role with respect to culture. What should that role be?

We may describe the culture of a society briefly as the way

14. An example of this problem is pornography; see Robert P. George, "Making Children Moral: Pornography, Parents and the Public Interest," in *In Defense of Natural Law* (New York: Oxford University Press, 1999), 184–95.

the people understand themselves and the way they live.[15] It is affected by their religious convictions and practices, their education, their opportunities for work and recreation, various kinds of media, the arts, especially those that dominate popular culture, and by organizations and initiatives with various agendas, some good and useful, others less useful or even harmful. Although the state does not create culture, it does have an obligation to encourage institutions and activities that facilitate the achievement of a virtuous life and to limit the influence of such as tend against it. I would like briefly to consider two of these: religion and art.

## Religion and Art

The encouragement of religion must be clearly distinguished from the imposition of religion, for the state does not have the authority to compel its citizens to practice a particular religion or any religion at all.[16] The religious quest springs from the natural law obligation to seek the truth about God. It relates us to God, therefore, not to the state. Hence, the state must recognize the right of individuals and religious communities to practice their religion freely, provided, of course, that their teachings are not immoral or subversive, and that they promote them peacefully and with due respect for the religious convictions of others. Moreover, as we have seen, parents who wish to educate their children in religious schools must be supported in their choice no less than parents who wish to educate them in nonreligious schools.

It might be supposed that in order to avoid imposing religion on its citizens, the state must be neutral with respect to religion, denying public status to religion and nonreligion alike. But this neutrality is an illusion. For it effectively removes religion from

15. See also the section on the development of culture in Vatican Council II, *Gaudium et Spes* (December 7, 1965), nos. 53–62, esp. no. 53.

16. On this topic, see Vatican Council II, *Dignitatis Humanae* (December 7, 1965), chapter I.

the public square, replacing it, by default, with a kind of public atheism. For while the state does not deny that God exists, it treats his existence as publicly irrelevant. But if the state is to respect the natural law obligation to seek God and to follow his law, it must be open to religion and encourage the search for religious truth. It must not attempt to seal itself off from religion.[17]

How might the state encourage religion without imposing it? The first thing is to recognize that religions perform a public service, not only through their charitable activities, but also through their essential mission, bringing man to God. For the knowledge of ultimate truth is of supreme importance for all human beings. Furthermore, since those who sincerely seek God also seek to follow his law, and since divine authority is more efficacious than human authority in moving us to live as we should, religion makes an indispensable contribution to the life of virtue. The state must therefore welcome the voice of religion in discussions of public policy and must favor religious educational and charitable organizations no less than it favors nonreligious organizations engaged in similar work. Finally, since the purpose of the search for ultimate truth is the discovery of it, the state should welcome initiatives for interreligious dialogue.

If happiness consists essentially in the life of virtue, the state must also be concerned with the arts, especially with the forms of music and drama that dominate popular culture. For music can move our emotions quickly and forcefully in ways that support or impede the development of a virtuous life. Similarly, films and theatrical productions can move us to accept a certain point of view by the way they represent it—what Aquinas called the "poetic mode of persuasion."[18] They have the power to represent

17. The U.S. Supreme Court opposes this approach to the role of religion in public life; see Russell Hittinger, *The First Grace: Rediscovering the Natural Law in a Post-Christian World* (Wilmington, Del.: ISI, 2003), chapter 7.

18. In the prooemium of his *Commentary on Aristotle's "Posterior Analytics"*, Aquinas speaks of a poetic mode of argumentation. He distinguishes it from the demonstrative, dialectical, and rhetorical modes. He describes the poetic mode as

things in such a way as to make what is good seem attractive and what is evil seem unattractive or vice versa. Depending on how they are used, therefore, the dramatic arts are a great force for good or for evil. They can have an uplifting quality or a gross appeal; they can lead us toward a more human, more virtuous life or toward sensuality, a taste for violence, a false idea of freedom, cynicism, and even despair. When used perversely, the arts are especially dangerous for the young. For while mature adults can separate themselves from the popular culture, at least to some extent, the young are often completely immersed in it.

What should be the role of the state? As a general principle, we may say that just as the state must balance free enterprise with other aspects of the common good in the economic sphere, so, in the cultural sphere, it must balance freedom of artistic expression with concern for a culture that is conducive to virtue and hence to true human happiness. It can limit or marginalize the worst abuses of artistic freedom, especially those that exploit the young for ideological or commercial reasons. It might also welcome and encourage artistic initiatives that portray nobility of character and action in an attractive way. For we are naturally inclined to admire noble conduct, and when we see it portrayed positively, we can be moved to imitation. Although it cannot cause virtue, art can encourage and in some measure dispose us to desire and to seek a virtuous way of life.

Finally, the state must take account of the fact that art reflects culture even as it helps to form it, so that if there is to be a renewal of art, there must also be a renewal of culture. I do not think that culture can be renewed without religion, for it is through the search for God that a culture acquires an openness to transcendence, a respect for creation and the moral law revealed in it, and a hope for the future, not only in this life, but beyond it in eternal life. In this way, culture brings a new profundity and richness to

---

analogous to the way in which a food can be made to appear disgusting by representing it in the image of something disgusting.

art. On the other hand, a culture turned away from religion, but still seeking something to believe in, is easily infected by ideologies. Or it may degenerate into a search for arbitrary freedom and worldly prosperity, leading, ultimately, to a sense of the meaninglessness of life and to escapism. By recognizing the importance of religion and welcoming the search for religious truth, the state will indirectly encourage positive developments in the arts.

## Human Progress

This way of thinking about natural rights seems far from contemporary reality. One may object that it cannot obtain widespread acceptance or be achieved politically and is therefore an impractical ideal. For the natural law is based on a determinate idea of happiness as the life of virtue, whereas we are accustomed to think of happiness as something indeterminate and subjective and to make freedom our ideal. Nevertheless, even if it is not currently appreciated, the natural law opens for us a new perspective on human rights and duties and a new vision of human progress. Hence, it represents a valuable critique of our usual ways of thinking about the future of mankind.

If we distinguish, as is customary, between liberal and conservative approaches to political and legal questions, the natural law approach would appear to be conservative and the liberal approach progressive. By liberalism I mean here a movement away from any view of life that recognizes and submits to a divine lawgiver. For this is thought to be progress: that we become free to create our own values and to live as we please, constrained only by the equal freedom of others, and supported by material prosperity. Progress then lies especially in the public recognition and protection of new freedoms, in increased material prosperity, and in a more widespread sharing in the benefits of this prosperity. But the natural law also has a vision of progress, as a movement toward an ever more perfect fulfillment of our natural duties and an ever greater recognition and vindication of our natural rights. From this perspective, liberalism often appears as a force inhibiting genuine progress and, through a false conception of freedom, as tending toward social disintegration.

Both liberalism and natural law are dedicated to human freedom, of course, but not in the same way. For, as we have seen, freedom under natural law is oriented toward the life of virtue where it is most perfectly realized. But liberal freedom is without orientation and cannot be controlled except by external constraints imposed in the name of an equal freedom of the same kind in others. But social policy cannot simultaneously promote opposed concepts of freedom; it cannot, for example, permit euthanasia or abortion in the name of liberal freedom and simultaneously forbid it in the name of a higher freedom inspired by the natural law. Hence, liberalism will often be in conflict with the natural law.

To prevent misunderstanding, however, I want to make clear that I have here defined liberalism insofar as it is a social and political movement opposed to the natural law. I have defined the liberal ideology.[19] But I am not saying that everyone who calls himself a liberal subscribes to this ideology. People concerned with social justice, for example, may think of themselves as liberals because they want to establish government programs to help people in need. They may sometimes be statist, increasing unduly the power of the state without sufficient regard for subsidiarity, but this does not make them ideological liberals.

Hence, there is always room for dialogue and cooperation between natural law and a liberalism that emphasizes social justice. Both are concerned, for example, to provide food for the hungry, medical care for the sick, and education and opportunity for the underprivileged. These concerns are pre-ideological; they are rooted in our natural awareness of human dignity and in principles of

19. For a prescient discussion of the liberal ideology, see Leo XIII, *Libertas*, Encyclical Letter (June 20, 1888), esp. nos. 14–15.

natural law obvious to common sense. Perhaps this mutual engagement on the level of our common humanity could be a first step toward bringing the human community together and opening the way to a new dialogue between liberalism and the natural law.

# CHAPTER 12

# Natural Law and the Alternatives

As I stated in the introduction, the purpose of this book is to trace the path from human dignity to the natural law. I began with a case of murder that I believe we would all condemn without qualification. This led to the concept of human dignity, the idea that human beings exist for their own good, not for the good of some other being. This dignity must be a reality in the nature of things, because if it were only a human invention, it could not justify our unqualified condemnation of the murder. I then clarified the concept of human dignity by defining the good to which we are ordained by nature—that is, happiness, which consists essentially in a rationally appropriate life perfected by virtue. This opened the way to our study of the natural law, whose precepts guide us in living virtuously.

Since the natural law tends to be ignored or denied today, I want to begin this chapter by asking why this is so. What prevents us from recognizing and accepting what seemed evident to earlier generations? This will lead to a related question: if the natural law is denied, are there any valid human laws? And this, to a further question: is there a way of establishing the legal order without the natural law? In response to this last question, we will first consider social contract theory and utilitarianism and then look briefly at two other approaches to normative ethics, the theories of Kant and W. D Ross, which in different ways are natural law theories—neither completely satisfactory, however, as we shall see. I will conclude with some thoughts on the difference between the liberal and natural law concepts of human dignity and with a brief suggestion for further reflection, going beyond the scope of this book.

## What Prevents Us from Accepting
## the Natural Law?

Many precepts of the natural law are obvious from common experience. Most of us recognize that we ought not to harm our fellow human beings by physically injuring them, by stealing their possessions, or by deceiving or slandering them. We know also that we ought to seek the truth about God and the purpose of human existence, although we can be tempted to put such questions aside or to regard them as unanswerable. So, we do in fact accept many precepts of the natural law, but we do not tend to think of them as such.

Even the natural law precepts regarding sexual morality, though often rejected, are not difficult to understand, because the natural order is evident. Everyone can see that the sexual organs are adapted for the union of the bodies of man and woman, that this union constitutes their natural use, and that homosexual acts are therefore unnatural. It is evident also that the sexual act is naturally oriented toward procreation, and that contraception, because it is opposed to this orientation, is contrary to nature. The natural order is even more evident in the precepts concerning human life. Everyone can see, for example, that abortion is unnatural, that nature is bringing forth new life and we are destroying it. And that suicide is unnatural, for life is not our creation, but comes to us from nature, which seeks to preserve it.

The problem is not that we cannot distinguish between what is natural and what is not; the problem is that we do not want to be bound by the natural order. We think freedom means that no order should be imposed on us prior to our choices as individuals or as members of a democratic community. Even a democratic majority, we believe, should be limited as much as possible by demands for individual freedoms. As justification, we appeal to the authority of contemporary science, which does not recognize finality in nature. For if nothing in nature were for the sake of an end, we would have no natural end, and therefore no natural law to guide us to this end. We would have to create the moral order ourselves.

## Are There Any Valid Human Laws?

If there were no natural or divinely revealed law, then every law would have to be a human creation. But, as we saw in chapter 5, a law that we ourselves have created cannot of itself demand our obedience; its binding force must depend on a higher law, not created by us. Hence, if the natural law is excluded, how will human laws have the power to demand obedience? They will not seem to be laws at all, but only guidelines that we follow simply by habit or to avoid punishment or because we think they are useful for obtaining what we want for ourselves or for others.

Nevertheless, there are many human laws that are truly laws. No one in his right mind thinks that positive laws forbidding murder, theft, and perjury or requiring people to pay their debts and take care of their children are not truly laws and that we could be justified in refusing to obey them. This would seem to be generally true of positive laws. Moreover, there are positive laws that we may be obligated to obey simply out of respect for law and order, so long as they do not require us to do anything wicked.

Why must we obey these laws? Because they are in fact principles of natural law or are derived from such principles. For, as we have seen, many natural law precepts are evident from common experience and are therefore reflected in the positive law. This is why when we are defending or attacking a law, we typically resort to principles of natural law, not insofar as they are of natural law, but insofar as they are evident from common experience. This does not mean that we always apply these principles correctly. For sometimes we argue from general principles that apply in some cases and not in others, and misapplications occur when appropriate distinctions are not made.

Consider, for example, the principle that forbids discrimination. It might seem to forbid making any distinctions at all, since every distinction is a kind of discrimination. But in fact the principle does allow us to make distinctions, for we are not thought to be discriminating if we treat like cases in the same way and unlike cases differently. But what point of likeness or unlikeness is relevant to a particular application of the principle? My friends are like other people—they are human beings. Am I discriminating if I benefit my friends more than others? May I freely choose my friends? Or, to take this point a bit further, am I discriminating if I employ the people I think best for my business? Or must I employ people according to criteria established by the state? But this would seem to abolish the distinction between what is private and what is public, treating nongovernmental organizations as if they were public entities, thus violating significantly the natural right to freedom of association.

Another kind of problem arises when common sense moral principles seem to be in conflict, thus giving rise to dilemmas. Consider, again, the classic dilemma about hanging the innocent man to prevent a riot. On the one hand, it seems wrong to hang an innocent man, but, on the other hand, it seems wrong *not* to hang him when many equally innocent people will otherwise be killed in the riot. For the death of one innocent person seems preferable to the deaths of many innocent persons. As we saw in chapter 6, this dilemma cannot be easily resolved on the basis of common sense alone; a more precise knowledge of the natural law is required. What is important to notice is that both horns of this dilemma reflect principles of natural law in some measure. This is why we have the dilemma.

We find the clearest deviations from the natural law in matters that we think affect only ourselves, as in suicide, abortion, and the sexual activities of consenting adults. For if law and morality are human creations, we should be able to live as we please, subject to limitations only when the interests of others would be adversely affected. Hence, when not guided by the natural law, a positive legal system may not only tolerate suicide, abortion, and unnatural sex, but, as we have seen, even seek to establish positive rights to these practices. From this it appears that when the natural law is rejected, attempts to establish a basis for human law will be chiefly concerned with finding a viable way for people who think of themselves as radically free to live together without conflict. Let us turn now to this topic.

## What Are the Alternatives to the Natural Law?

Although it is often possible to justify proposals for new positive laws on the basis of laws already established, either directly or by close analogy, this is not always possible, and then it is necessary to go back to first principles. Otherwise, the positive law cannot be developed into a coherent system. If we do not accept the natural law, where shall we find these first principles?

To respond to this question, let us assume that there is no law prior to the laws we impose upon ourselves and that our freedom, therefore, is initially unlimited. The legal problem, then, is to find a way to limit this freedom so that we can live together. There are, I think, two plausible ways of attempting to limit an initially unlimited individual freedom within the political community, starting either from persons taken individually or from all persons taken together in an aggregate. The first way is social contract theory; the second, utilitarianism. Each reflects a principle of natural law, but without properly understanding it. Thus, social contract theory reflects individual dignity, and utilitarianism reflects the primacy of the common good.

## Social Contract Theory

Our concern here is not with a social contract theory like Locke's, which is based explicitly on a conception of the natural law, but only with theories that do not recognize a law prior to the laws that we ourselves create. In a social contract theory of this type, we must ask ourselves what limitations to our freedom we are willing to concede in return for the same concessions by others. First, what limitations are we willing to concede in order to secure our personal freedom and safety? Second, what further limitations are we willing to concede in order to enjoy the benefits of community life? For in order to live as we wish, we need many things that we cannot obtain unless we cooperate with each other. What are we going to get out of this cooperation: what possessions, what services, what opportunities, what social status, etc.? And what must we concede to the interests of others? If these demands and concessions are to become the basis of our life together, they must be such that all or most reasonable persons would agree to them. They will constitute the terms of a social contract.

The first question, the question of personal freedom and safety, is the easier of the two questions to answer. You may think what you please, say what you please, live as you please—so long as you do not harm me. There are difficulties, of course, in deciding when someone's conduct adversely affects others to the point where it should be forbidden, especially if the alleged harms are psychological or cultural rather than physical. Moreover, there will be disagreements about what kinds of law enforcement measures are necessary or appropriate for protecting people from various kinds of harm. But it should not be impossible to find compromises that reasonable people would be more or less willing to live with.

However, when it comes to the benefits that people want to obtain from social cooperation, it is difficult to see how various interests can be accommodated. Suppose that I am wealthier than you and therefore better able to live as I wish and that I am well educated and well connected and have more and better opportunities for success than you do. I would like to keep my privileged position, while you would want to improve your underprivileged one. I would probably prefer laws that strongly affirm rights to acquire and maintain wealth and that allow people to rise or fall as their talents, industry, and opportunities permit. You, on the other hand, would probably prefer laws that compensate for inequality in wealth, education, and opportunity and provide help for people who are poor, handicapped, in bad health, or lacking the talents to advance in contemporary society. If we are to live together, a compromise must be found, some middle ground between my way and yours, a compromise on which we can agree at least temporarily. The terms of the contract will shift somewhat over time, however, tending one way or the other according to the relative power of the opposed interests.

Would it help to imagine what terms we would accept if we were ignorant of our situation in life—behind a "veil of ignorance," in John Rawls's famous phrase?[1] For then it might be in our best interest to opt for a contract that emphasizes equality so that we could be sure that our life prospects would be at least reasonably satisfactory, though perhaps not ideal, wherever we might find ourselves when the veil is lifted. But would we be willing to accept the terms of this imaginary contract in real life if they were significantly contrary to our actual interests? However, Rawls did not propose his social contract as something that we would all immediately be willing to accept, but as a device for helping us understand what kind of social contract would be most fair. He was searching, in short, for an ideal of justice.

Actually, the whole force of a social contract depends on a

1. John Rawls, *A Theory of Justice* (Cambridge, Mass: Belknap Press of Harvard University Press, 1971), 11–14. Roughly speaking, Rawls's conception of justice is a clarification and development of liberal ideas of equality and freedom. Rawls did not maintain that his principles of justice were necessary truths or derivable from necessary truths. He thought that the justification of a conception of justice "is a matter of the mutual support of many considerations, of everything fitting together into one coherent view"; ibid, 21.

higher law, a law prior to any laws we create ourselves, the law that requires us to honor our agreements. But if every law is a human creation, there will be no higher law. The obligation to keep agreements will have only such value as each of us is willing to give to it. I will respect the terms of the social contract, therefore, only when they serve my interests or correspond to my particular philosophy or when I am forced to respect them. The social contract will not of itself have any power to obligate me.

## Utilitarianism

An alternative approach is utilitarianism. Like the first approach, it assumes that there is no law prior to the laws we create ourselves and that we have an unlimited freedom to satisfy our desires, whatever they may be. The problem is the same as before: how to limit this freedom so that we can live together. The utilitarian solution is not to focus on what individuals would be willing to agree to, but on what consequences would follow from any particular action, law, or social policy for all the members of the community taken together as an aggregate.

The utilitarian approach may be summarized briefly as follows. Every action will have consequences, both for the individual who acts and for others, and the consequences may be good or bad. The utilitarian tries to assess these consequences for every individual affected by a particular action. If the sum total of good consequences outweighs the sum total of bad consequences, the action has positive utility; if the opposite, it has negative utility. This result is then compared with the utility of the other actions possible in this situation, with a view to finding out which action has the greatest positive utility or, if all the options are negative, which has the least negative utility. This is the action to be chosen. In the same way, the utilitarian seeks to determine what laws and social policies will have the greatest overall utility.

What standard should we use to measure good and bad consequences? Is it pleasure and pain? But there are many kinds of pleasure, physical and spiritual, and how will we compare them? Or should we think mainly of negative consequences, with a view to minimizing the amount of suffering in the world? Or are there values other than pleasure and pain that should be taken into account? Questions like these have been discussed by utilitarians, and I do not propose to consider them here. I raise them merely to show that the application of the utilitarian principle will require some standard that is roughly measurable across the population. For example, when part of a population is educated and wealthy and part is poor, uneducated, and miserable, some redistribution of wealth to the advantage of the latter would seem to maximize utility for the community as a whole. For the transferred wealth would have great positive utility for the poor, but comparatively little negative utility for the wealthy.

Although such a redistribution would likely have immediate positive utility, what about the future? For the conscientious utilitarian must consider long-term as well as short-term consequences. Perhaps a particular redistribution policy will discourage hard work and innovation and encourage dependency, with negative economic consequences for everyone. To evaluate social and economic policies, the utilitarian must balance immediate positive consequences against possible future negative consequences. And this is not easy to do, since our predictions about the future are often mistaken.

With respect to personal conduct that seems to have little or no effect on the interests of others, utilitarian calculations will likely lead to results similar to those we would expect from social contract theory. For even the satisfaction of perverse sexual desires between consenting adults might seem to add to the sum total of personal satisfaction within the community without subtracting anything because of harm to others. Nevertheless, one might wonder about negative long-term consequences, especially if such practices become widespread within a society.

The plausibility of utilitarianism arises from its attempt

to bring about what is good or thought to be good for as many people as possible within the community. For this seems like the common good or an approximation of it, and the common good is prior to the individual good. But, as we have seen, the good of the many, even the majority, is not the same as the common good, which by its very nature is the good of all. Hence, under some circumstances, utilitarianism may allow someone to be sacrificed for the advantage of others, as in our paradigm case of hanging the innocent man to prevent a riot. For just as an individual animal in a herd is valuable not *as such* but only as a positive or negative factor in a cost/benefit analysis, so an individual human being is valuable only as a factor in calculating the overall utility of a proposed course of action.

The problems with utilitarianism can be alleviated somewhat if the utilitarian calculation is applied not to individual actions but to general rules, with individual actions being judged by the rules. This is the view proposed by the rule-utilitarians. The act-utilitarians, on the contrary, want to apply the utilitarian principle immediately to individual actions, although they admit the usefulness of what are called "rules of thumb"—that is, rules based on past experiences. The advantage of the rule-utilitarian approach is that it seems closer to common sense. Thus, most people would agree that rules or laws against killing people or stealing their possessions are useful and should be obeyed as a matter of principle, although they might perhaps be willing to admit the possibility of exceptions in extreme situations. But they would not be comfortable with the idea that individual persons might regularly decide whether or not to follow such rules based on their personal calculations.

To conclude this brief discussion of social contract theory and utilitarianism, I would like to emphasize two points. The first is that both theories are dependent on principles of the natural law for their plausibility, even when these principles are not properly understood. Thus, as I stated at the beginning of this discussion, social contract theory reflects our sense of individual dignity, while utilitarianism reflects our sense of the primacy of the common good.

The second point is that both theories are opposed more to the natural law than to each other. For what especially characterizes the natural law is that it is prior to human choice, a law that we discover, not a law that we create. But neither social contract theory (except for theories like Locke's) nor utilitarianism is based on a higher law; both are attempts to bring an initially lawless freedom under rational control. For this purpose both theories are useful, though in different ways. Thus, social contract theory is more useful for dealing with demands for individual freedoms, while utilitarianism is better for resolving conflicts between competing interests, as, for example, when a proposed monetary policy would benefit some people financially and harm others. We should not think of these theories philosophically, as claims to ultimate moral truth, but pragmatically, as attempts to order society without the natural law.

## Kant

I would like to say something about two other approaches to normative ethics: Kant's theory of the categorical imperative and W. D. Ross's theory of *prima facie* duties. The purpose is not to consider these theories in any detail, but simply to note the ways in which they are natural law theories, though imperfectly so. I shall begin with Kant, who, in one way, is far from the natural law tradition, but, in another way, not far at all.

What separates Kant radically from traditional natural law theory is his adoption of the critical principle, according to which the world is thought of primarily as an object of consciousness. This means that we do not know the world as it is in itself, but only as it appears to us. But traditional natural law theory does not begin from the critical principle, but proceeds according to our ordinary way of apprehending the natural world. This way allows us to learn directly from nature and so to discover our natural end, the law that directs us to this end, and the source of this law in the Author of nature. But this way is not open to Kant.[2]

The special character of Kant's moral philosophy, therefore, arises from his commitment to the critical principle. If we cannot know the world as it is in itself, we cannot find the moral law through a study of the natural world. The result is that we must establish it ourselves. But we cannot establish it according to the particular characteristics and preferences of human beings as they appear in our experience of the world; rather, we must proceed from the point of view of pure reason, so that we can establish laws that are objectively valid for all rational beings. Since pure reason cannot base an objectively binding law on anything from the world of appearances, Kant has nothing to go on but the idea of law itself. But it belongs to the essence of law that it be universal. Hence, the famous categorical imperative: *Act only on a maxim that you can at the same time will to become a universal law.*

At this point the natural law appears. For when explaining the categorical imperative, Kant tells us that the maxims of our actions must be able to be willed as universal laws of nature. He illustrates this with four examples. Suppose that I find life too burdensome. In this situation, self-love might move me to kill myself. But I cannot will that this should be a universal law of nature, because self-love is naturally ordered to the improvement of life, not to its destruction. Suicide, therefore, is immoral. Or suppose that I am in need of money and seek a loan, promising falsely that I will repay it. I act immorally because if my maxim were universalized, promising would no longer have any meaning. Again, while I can refuse to develop my natural talents, I cannot will that this should become a universal law of nature, since the natural purpose of a talent is to be developed for its possible uses. Finally, if I were interested only in my personal welfare, I might

2. The following notes on Immanuel Kant's two formulations of the categorical imperative are taken from his *Foundations of the Metaphysics of Morals*, trans. Lewis White Beck (Upper Saddle River, N.J.: Prentice-Hall, 1900), section 2.

not wish to help others in need. But I cannot will that this should be a universal law of nature, because this same self-interest would be frustrated by my own will if I should sometime be in need of help myself.

Kant formulated the categorical imperative also in another way, which is more intuitive, and, I think, more fruitful. Realizing that human actions must be aimed at an end, and not willing to base ethics on an end taken from the world of appearances, Kant made humanity itself the end. Hence, the formula: *Act so as to treat humanity in yourself and others as an end and not as a means only*. From a traditional natural law perspective, this formula is imperfect, because the end for man is not humanity itself but the ultimate end or good to which human beings are naturally ordained. Nevertheless, in spite of the imperfection of his formula, the fundamental meaning of Kant's imperative is clear: human beings have a value that surpasses utility—that is, they exist for their own sake, not simply to be used by others. From this principle, which expresses the value we call human dignity, Kant is able to derive traditional natural law precepts, including both absolute prohibitions, like the prohibition of suicide, and positive duties, like the obligation to develop one's natural talents.

We can illustrate Kant's application of this human dignity formula with an example of an absolute prohibition from each of the three levels of natural inclinations distinguished by Aquinas. With respect to life, we may take Kant's condemnation of suicide: if you kill yourself in order to escape a burdensome existence, you will necessarily be using yourself as a means to that end, thus debasing humanity in your person.[3] With respect to sexuality, there is his condemnation of homosexual acts.[4] He maintains that just as self-love is naturally ordered to the preservation of

---

3. Kant, *Metaphysics of Morals*, trans., ed. Mary Gregor, Part 2, *Metaphysical First Principles of the Doctrine of Virtue* (Cambridge: Cambridge University Press, 1996), On Duties to Oneself, § 6.

4. Kant, *Metaphysics of Morals*, Part 1, *Metaphysical First Principles of the Doctrine of Right*, Private Right, § 24.

the individual, so sexual love is naturally ordered to the preservation of the species, and that there is a sense in which an unnatural use of one's sexual powers debases humanity even more than suicide.[5] With respect to the natural inclinations that are proper to man as a rational being, we may take truthfulness as an example. Kant maintains that lying, even when it does not violate anyone's rights, is necessarily a violation of human dignity. For by using speech contrary to its natural purpose, we disown, as it were, our own humanity, making ourselves an object of contempt in the eyes of others and even more in our own eyes.[6]

What shall we say of Kant's moral philosophy in relation to the natural law? First of all, we should note that Kant asserts and defends traditional natural law precepts. Moreover, his concept of acting in accord with what reason prescribes as our duty has much in common with Aristotle's conception of the life of virtue as our ultimate end. There is of course a difference in terminology: Kant distinguished duty from happiness, thinking of the latter as physical and psychological well-being, the satisfaction over a lifetime of our various desires and inclinations, whereas Aristotle thought of rational activities perfected by the virtues as the very essence of happiness. Finally, Kant's emphasis on human dignity has been of great value for the defense of moral absolutes against utilitarianism.

Nevertheless, Kant's attempt to establish the moral law within the limits of the critical system and without a divine lawgiver poses a danger for the natural law morality that he was concerned to defend and preserve. For if we believe that we are not ruled by a legal authority higher than our own reason, we can easily come to believe that we are naturally free to live as we please, subject only to such limitations of our freedoms as we choose, individually or collectively, to impose upon ourselves. This is the root of the liberal ideology, fundamentally opposed to the natural law.

5. Kant, *Metaphysics of Morals*, Part 2, *Metaphysical First Principles of the Doctrine of Virtue*, On Duties to Oneself, § 7.
6. Ibid., § 9.

Kant would certainly object to this, and with good reason, but his attempt to establish the natural law within the limits of pure reason does to some extent open the way to it.

## W. D. Ross

In *The Right and the Good*, W. D. Ross distinguished between our actual duties in a particular situation and what he called "conditional" or "*prima facie*" duties.[7] Among the latter are the duties to keep promises, to speak truthfully, to make reparation for injuries to others, to repay benefits received from others, to not injure others, to promote the good of others, and to promote one's own perfection. The reason these *prima facie* duties are not necessarily our actual duties is that in a particular situation they may be in conflict. The duty to keep a promise, for example, may conflict with the duty to rescue someone in danger of death. To determine our actual duty, we must weigh these conflicting *prima facie* duties. The final decision depends on perception and is highly fallible, but it is the only guide we have to our actual duty.

Ross does not ground the validity of these *prima facie* duties on their utility, though they are useful, but on their self-evidence. Insofar as it is the fulfilling of a promise or the effecting of a just distribution of goods, an act is self-evidently right. But, as stated earlier, this does not mean that it is the right act in a particular situation. In fact, there is no *prima facie* duty that might not be outweighed in a particular situation by some other *prima facie* duty. Even the duty not to kill innocent persons might be overridden in an extreme situation by the duty to take account of the interests of society.[8]

7. W. D. Ross, *The Right and the Good* (London: Oxford University Press, 1930).

8. For Ross's statement that an action insofar as it is the fulfilling of a promise is self-evidently right but not necessarily right in a particular situation, see ibid., 29; that decisions about actual duty rest on perception, see 42; that even the duty not to kill innocent persons can have exceptions, see 61.

This simple statement of Ross's thesis ignores the richness of his development of it, but is sufficient for us to see how it relates to the natural law. His *prima facie* duties are principles of natural law whose truth we all recognize from common experience. To the question of *why* they are true, common sense may not be able to give us a complete answer, but this does not destroy our conviction that they *are* true. This is why Aristotle said that someone who wonders whether or not we should honor the gods and love our parents does not need instruction but rather punishment.[9] For only wicked people would have doubts about such obvious obligations.

As we saw earlier, however, this commonsense awareness of general principles of natural law is not sufficient for dealing with dilemmas in which moral principles seem to be in conflict. This requires a more perfect understanding of the natural law. Hence, Ross is not able to see that some actions may always be wrong, whatever the circumstances. In this respect his theory is inferior to Kant's. However, Ross's theory is superior to Kant's in that it does not presuppose the critical principle and is therefore closer to common sense.

## Two Concepts of Human Dignity

In a rather short book we have traveled a rather long way. Much more has been written and written in greater depth on all of the topics we have been considering. As I said in the introduction, this work is but a sketch or outline of the path from human dignity to the natural law. My hope is that the sketch can be filled in and the path illuminated by others who are sympathetic to this approach.

I would like to sum up the argument of this book by contrasting the concept of human dignity that leads to the natural law with the concept that underlies what I have referred to as the "lib-

9. Aristotle, *Topics*, Book I, 105a5., in *Aristotle: Posterior Analytics: Topica*, trans. E. S. Forster (Loeb Classical Library; London: William Heinemann, 1960).

eral ideology." According to this latter concept, human dignity is freedom of choice or autonomy, the freedom of every person to choose his own way, according to his own conception of what is good. Of course, a person might be mistaken about what he really wants or what he really ought to do. If you think he is mistaken, try to persuade him to change his mind. But, unless he is too young and inexperienced or too senile or mentally disturbed to understand the consequences of what he is doing, his freedom of choice is decisive. To violate his autonomy, except as necessary to protect the autonomy of others, is to violate his dignity.

This way of understanding human dignity is one-sided and incomplete, though not altogether false. For inasmuch as it is natural that rational beings should freely choose their actions, freedom of choice is worthy of respect—but not of unqualified respect. For it is also necessary that human beings guide their choices by the truth—that is, by a true understanding of human happiness. The liberal concept emphasizes but one aspect of happiness, isolating it from the very essence of happiness and raising this one aspect to the level of an absolute. This is why it is ideological. For an ideology is just this: that one element or aspect of human happiness is substituted for happiness itself, giving rise inevitably to distortions in human thought and conduct.

Because it is founded on the essence of happiness, the natural law concept of human dignity fills in what is missing in the liberal concept and brings all aspects of the human good, including freedom, into perspective. It brings meaning to our free choices, because it reveals their purpose—that is, the achievement of the life of virtue. It demonstrates the origin of our rights, distinguishing what is real from what is imaginary, what can be rationally defended from what can only be arbitrarily claimed. It does not deny the freedom by which we seek to be authentic and true to ourselves; rather, it shows what true authenticity is, a life in accord with what we really are. It opens the way, finally, to the truest freedom, the freedom from ignorance and vice, the freedom, therefore, of living in the truth.

## A Concluding Thought

In conclusion, I would like to return to a deeper question, going beyond the scope of this book. It arises from the contrast between the perfect happiness we long for and the imperfect happiness of the present life. I touched upon this at the end of chapter 3. Why must we endure the evils arising from natural disasters and from human frailty, ignorance, and wickedness? Why is there this gap in our nature between reason and the emotions, so that we see what we should do, yet follow our emotions instead? If happiness is meant for everyone, why do so many people fail to attain it? Why must even the best life come to an end, sometimes prematurely and violently?

In chapter 10, when discussing the search for truth, I suggested that answers to questions like these must be sought in divine revelation. For while the natural law can guide us in living rationally, it cannot satisfactorily explain the evils of the human condition or reveal our ultimate destiny. Only God can unveil the mystery of life, showing us why we must suffer the evils of the present life and how our natural desire for perfect happiness can be satisfied.

Our dissatisfaction with the present life can lead us to despair and to rebellion against a universe suffering from so many evils. We may even come to believe that true authenticity lies in affirming and facing the ultimate meaninglessness of human life. But this is irrational and arrogant, because it presumes that we know what we do not know. What is rational is to seek an answer to the mystery of life and its ultimate meaning and to do so with humility and perseverance. A commitment to follow the precepts of the natural law, especially the precept that requires us to search for ultimate truth, can lead us to the threshold of the answer, but the answer itself is beyond philosophy and must come to us from God. As one who believes that God has given us the answer in the Christian revelation, I hope that a study of the natural law will encourage those who are still searching not to abandon the hope of finding him.

# Bibliography

I have listed works of Aristotle and Aquinas first, and then other books and articles. Among these latter I have included some that were not cited in the notes—a sample from the many publications relevant to our topic. When I have used more than one English translation of a work of Aristotle, I list them all, including the those in the Loeb Classical Library series, which also contain the Greek text. For Aquinas, I have listed both the Latin works and the English translations used in this study.

## Works of Aristotle

Aristotle. *Metaphysics*. Translated by Hugh Tredennick. 2 vols. Loeb Classical Library. London: William Heineman, 1961 (vol. 1); 1958 (vol. 2). Originally published 1933–35.

————. *Nicomachean Ethics*. Translated by Martin Ostwald. The Library of Liberal Arts. Englewood Cliffs, N.J.: Prentice-Hall, 1962.

————. *Nicomachean Ethics*. 2nd ed. Translated by H. Rackham. Loeb Classical Library. London: William Heinemann, 1965. Originally published 1934.

————. *Nicomachean Ethics*. Translated by Terence Irwin. Indianapolis, Ind.: Hackett, 1985.

————. *Physics*. Translated by Philip H. Wicksteed and Francis Cornford. 2 vols. Loeb Classical Library. London: William Heinemann, 1957 (vol. 1); 1960 (vol. 2). Originally published 1929–34.

————. *Politics*. Translated by H. Rackham. Loeb Classical Library. London: William Heinemann, 1959. Originally published 1932.

————. *The Politics*. Translated by T. A. Sinclair. Revised and re-presented by Trevor J. Saunders. London: Penguin, 1992.

———. *Topics*. Translated by E. S. Forster. In *Aristotle: Posterior Analytics, Topica*. Loeb Classical Library. London: William Heinemann, 1960.

## Works of Thomas Aquinas

### Latin

Aquinas, Thomas. *In Aristotelis Libros "Peri Hermeneias" et "Posteriorum Analyticorum" Expositio*. Cura et studio Raymundi M. Spiazzi. Turin: Marietti, 1955.

———. *In Decem Libros Ethicorum Aristotelis ad Nicomachum Expositio*. Cura et studio P. Fr. Raymundi M. Spiazzi. Turin: Marietti, 1949.

——— *In Duodeceim Libros Metaphysicorum Aristotelis Expositio*. Editio M. R. Cathala, retractatur cura et studio P. Fr. Raymundi M. Spiazzi. Turin: Marietti, 1950.

———. *In Octo Libros De Physico Auditu sive Physicorum Aristotelis Commentaria*. Cura ac studio P. Fr. Angeli and M. Pirotta. Editio Novissima. Naples: M. D'Auria Pontificius Editor, 1953.

———. *Summa Contra Gentiles*. Editio Leonina Manualis. Turin: Marietti, 1934.

———. *Summa Theologiae*. Edited by De Rubeis, Billuart, P. Faucher et al. Cum Textu ex Recensione Leonina. 4 vols. Turin: Marietti, 1948.

### English

———. *Commentary on Aristotle's "Metaphysics."* Translated by John P. Rowan. Rev. ed. Notre Dame, Ind.: Dumb Ox, 1995. Originally published by Regnery, 1961.

———. *Commentary on Aristotle's "Nicomachean Ethics."* Translated by C. I. Litzinger. Notre Dame, Ind.: Dumb Ox, 1993. Originally published by Regnery, 1964.

———. *Commentary on Aristotle's "Physics."* Translated by Richard J. Blackwell, Richard J. Spath, and W. Edmund Thirlkel. Notre Dame, Ind.: Dumb Ox, 1999. Originally published by Yale University Press, 1963.

————. *Commentary on Aristotle's "Posterior Analytics."* Translated by Richard Berquist. Notre Dame, Ind.: Dumb Ox, 2007.

*Summa Contra Gentiles.* 5 vols. Notre Dame, Ind.: University of Notre Dame Press, 1975. Originally published as *On the Truth of the Catholic Faith: Summa Contra Gentiles.* 5 vols. Image Books. Garden City, N.Y.: Doubleday, 1955.

————. *Summa Theologica.* Translated by the Fathers of the English Dominican Province. 3 vols. New York: Benziger Brothers, 1947.

## Other Works

Augustine. *Confessions.* Translated by F. J. Sheed. Rev. ed. Indianapolis: Hackett, 1993.

Behe, Michael J. "Evidence for Design at the Foundation of Life." In *Science and Evidence for Design in the Universe*, 113–89. San Francisco: Ignatius Press, 2000.

Benedict, Ruth. *Patterns of Culture.* New York: New American Library, 1959.

Boyle, Joseph. "Natural Law and the Ethics of Traditions." In *Natural Law Theory: Contemporary Essays*, edited by Robert P. George, 3–30. Oxford: Clarendon Press, 1992.

————. "Fairness in Holdings: A Natural Law Account of Property and Welfare Rights." In *Natural Law and Modern Moral Philosophy*, edited by Ellen Frankel Paul, Fred D. Miller Jr., and Jeffrey Paul, 206–26. New York: Cambridge University Press, 2001.

Congregation for the Doctrine of the Faith. *Declaration on Procured Abortion.* November 18, 1974.

————. *Declaration on Euthanasia.* May 5, 1980.

————. *Instruction on Respect for Human Life in Its Origin and on the Dignity of Procreation—Donum Vitae.* February 22, 1987.

————. *Instruction "Dignitas personae" on Certain Biological Questions.* September 8, 2008.

Del Vecchio, Giorgio. *La Giustizia*, 6th ed. rev. Rome: Editrice Studium, 1959. English translation of an earlier version: *Justice: An Historical and Philosophical Essay.* Edited by A. H. Campbell. Translated by Lady Guthrie. New York: Philosophical Library, 1953.

———. "Su la teoria del contratto sociale." In *Contributi alla storia del pensiero giuridico e filosofico*, 217–74. Milan: Dott. A. Guiffrè, 1961.

d'Entrèves, A. P. *Natural Law: An Historical Survey*. Harper Torchbooks. New York: Harper and Row, 1965.

*The Digest of Justinian*. Translation edited by Alan Watson. Rev. English ed. Philadelphia: University of Pennsylvania Press, 1998.

Finnis, John. *Moral Absolutes: Tradition, Revision, and Truth*. Washington D.C.: The Catholic University of America Press, 1991.

———. *Natural Law and Natural Rights*. 2nd ed. New York: Oxford University Press, 2011.

Francis. *Laudato si'*. Encyclical Letter. May 24, 2015.

———. *Address of His Holiness Pope Francis to Participants in the Meeting Promoted by the Pontifical Council for Promoting the New Evangelization*. October 11, 2017.

George, Robert P. "Natural Law and International Order." In *In Defense of Natural Law*, 228–45. New York: Oxford University Press, 1999.

———. "Making Children Moral: Pornography, Parents and the Public Interest." In *In Defense of Natural Law*, 184–95. New York: Oxford University Press, 1999.

George, Robert P., and Christopher Tollefsen. *Embryo: A Defense of Human Life*. New York: Doubleday, 2008.

Glendon, Mary Ann. *Rights Talk: The Impoverishment of Public Discourse*. New York: Free Press, 1991.

Grisez, Germain. "The First Principle of Practical Reason: A Commentary on the *Summa Theologiae*, 1–2, Question 94, Article 2." *Natural Law Forum* 10 (1965): 168–201.

Grisez, Germain, Joseph Boyle, and John Finnis. "Practical Principles, Moral Truth, and Ultimate Ends." *American Journal of Jurisprudence* 32, no. 1 (1987): 99–151.

Grisez, Germain, Joseph Boyle, John Finnis, and William May. "Every Marital Act Ought to Be Open to a New Life: Toward a Clearer Understanding." *Thomist* 52, no. 3 (1988): 365–426.

Grotius, Hugo. *The Law of War and Peace*. Translated by Francis W. Kelsey, with the collaboration of Arthur E. R. Boak et al. In *De jure belli ac pacis libri tres/Hugo Grotius*, vol. 2, *Prolegomena*. Oxford: Clarendon Press, 1925.

Harvey, John F. *The Truth about Homosexuality*. San Francisco: Ignatius Press, 1996.

Hittinger, Russell. *The First Grace: Rediscovering the Natural Law in a Post-Christian World*. Wilmington, Del.: ISI, 2003.

Holy See Press Office. *New Revision of Number 2267 of the Catechism of the Catholic Church on the Death Penalty*. Summary of Bulletin. February 8, 2018.

Hume, David. *A Treatise of Human Nature*. 2nd ed. Edited by L. A. Selby-Bigge. Text revised by P. H. Nidditch. Oxford: Clarendon Press, 1978.

Jensen, Steven J. *Living the Good Life: A Beginner's Thomistic Ethics*. Washington, D.C.: The Catholic University of America Press, 2013.

———. *Knowing the Natural Law: From Precepts and Inclinations to Deriving Oughts*. Washington, D.C.: The Catholic University of America Press, 2015.

John XXIII. *Mater et Magistra*. Encyclical Letter. May 15, 1961.

———. *Pacem in Terris*. Encyclical Letter. April 11, 1963.

John Paul II. *Laborum Exercens*. Encyclical Letter. September 14, 1981.

———. *Familiaris Consortio*. Apostolic Exhortation. December 15, 1981.

———. *Veritatis Splendor*. Encyclical Letter. August 6, 1993.

———. *Evangelium Vitae*. Encyclical Letter. March 25, 1995.

Kant, Immanuel. *Foundations of the Metaphysics of Morals*. Translated by Lewis White Beck. Upper Saddle River, N.J.: Prentice-Hall, 1900.

———. *The Metaphysics of Morals*. Translated and edited by Mary Gregor. Cambridge: Cambridge University Press, 1996. This work has two parts: *Metaphysical First Principles of the Doctrine of Right* and *Metaphysical First Principles of the Doctrine of Virtue*.

Leo XIII. *Libertas*. Encyclical Letter. June 20, 1888.

———. *Rerum Novarum*. Encyclical Letter. May 15, 1891.

Locke, John. *Second Treatise of Government*. Edited by C. B. Macpherson. Indianapolis: Hackett, 1980.

Lorenz, Konrad. *The Foundations of Ethology*. New York: Springer-Verlag New York, 1981.

MacIntyre, Alasdair. *After Virtue: A Study in Moral Theory*. 3rd ed. Notre Dame, Ind.: University of Notre Dame Press, 2007.

Maritain, Jacques. *The Rights of Man and Natural Law*. New York: Charles Scribner's Sons, 1943.

———. *Man and the State*. Chicago: University of Chicago Press, 1951.

May, William E. "Contemporary Perspectives on Thomistic Natural Law." In *St. Thomas Aquinas and the Natural Law Tradition: Contemporary Perspectives*, edited by John Goyette, Mark S. Latkovic, and Richard S. Myers, 25–39. Washington D.C.: The Catholic University of America Press, 2004.

———. *Catholic Bioethics and the Gift of Human Life*. 2nd ed. Huntington, Ind.: Our Sunday Visitor, 2008.

———. *Marriage: The Rock on Which the Family Is Built*. 2nd ed. San Francisco: Ignatius Press, 2009.

McInerny, Ralph. "The Principles of Natural Law." *American Journal of Jurisprudence* 25 (1980): 1–16.

———. *Aquinas on Human Action: A Theory of Practice*. Washington D.C.: The Catholic University of America Press, 1992.

———. *Ethica Thomistica: The Moral Philosophy of Thomas Aquinas*. Rev. ed. Washington, D.C.: The Catholic University of America Press, 1997.

———. "Thomistic Natural Law and Aristotelian Philosophy." In *St. Thomas Aquinas and the Natural Law Tradition: Contemporary Perspectives*, edited by John Goyette, Mark S. Latkovic, and Richard S. Myers, 25–39. Washington D.C.: The Catholic University of America Press, 2004.

Monod, Jacques. *Chance and Necessity*. New York: Alfred A.Knopf, 1971.

Nielsen, Kai. "An Examination of the Thomistic Theory of Natural Law." *Natural Law Forum* 4 (1959): 63–71.

———. "The Myth of Natural Law." In *Law and Philosophy: A Symposium*, edited by Sydney Hook, 122–43. New York: New York University Press, 1964.

Olsen, Glenn W. "Natural Law: The First Grace." *Communio* 35 (Fall 2008): 354–73.

Paul VI. *Humanae Vitae*. Encyclical Letter. July 25, 1968.

Rawls, John. *A Theory of Justice*. Cambridge, Mass.: Belknap Press of Harvard University Press, 1971.

Ross, W. D. *The Right and the Good*. London: Oxford University Press, 1930.

Schall, James V. "Entitlements: Unintended Paradoxes of the Generous State." In *Reason, Revelation and Human Affairs: Selected Writings of James V Schall*, edited by Marc D. Guerra, 23–34. Lanham, Md.: Lexington, 2001.

Smith, Janet E. *Humanae Vitae: A Generation Later*. Washington D.C.: The Catholic University of America Press, 1991.

Sokolowski, Robert. "What Is Natural Law? Human Purposes and Natural Ends." *Thomist* 68, no. 4 (2004): 507–29.

Tollefsen, Christopher. "The New Natural Law Theory." *Lyceum* 10, no. 1 (2009): 1–17.

Vatican Council II. *Dignitatis Humanae*. December 7, 1965.

———. *Gaudium et Spes*. December 7, 1965.

# Index

*From Human Dignity to Natural Law: An Introduction* was designed in Chaparral with Quadraat Sans display type and composed by Kachergis Book Design of Pittsboro, North Carolina. It was printed on 60-pound House Natural Smooth and bound by Sheridan Books of Chelsea, Michigan.